# Managing Rural Finances in India

## About the Editor

**Dr Gursharan Singh Kainth** started his career as Lecturer at Post-Graduate Department of Economics, Government College Gurdaspur and later at Khalsa College; Amritsar specializes in Quantitative and Development Economics. He has the distinction of serving the prestigious Punjab Agricultural University Ludhiana for more than two decades (1981-2000) and remained Director-Principal of Saint Soldier Management and Technical Institute Jalandhar. Currently, he is heading GAD Institute of Development Studies, Amritsar. A recipient of Cultural Doctorate of Philosophy of Economics from the World University, Arizona, USA is an active member of various professional bodies, namely, Indian Society of Agricultural Economics, Indian Society of Agricultural Marketing, Indian Institute of Public Administration, Agricultural Economics Research Association (India). He participated in various International/ national/ regional seminars, conferences etc. and presented papers. He remained member of the Academic Council of Punjab Technical University, Jalandhar. An unwearied researcher has about 200 research papers published in various international and national journals of repute and ten research monographs to his kitty. Besides, he has authored/co-authored/edited 15 books which have been well received and highly acclaimed during his three decades of professional career. He was honoured by various awards, namely, *Guru Draunacharya Samman*, *Vijay Rattan Award* and so on.

# Managing Rural Finances in India

*Edited by*

**Dr. Gursharan Singh Kainth**

CONCEPT PUBLISHING COMPANY PVT. LTD.,
NEW DELHI-110059

**ISBN-13:978-81-8069-657-2** **ISBN-10:81-8069-657-X**

First Published 2010

*Published and Printed by*

**Concept Publishing Company Pvt. Ltd.**
**Regd. Office:**
A/15-16, Commercial Block, Mohan Garden
New Delhi-110059 (India)
*Phones* : 25351460, 25351794, *Fax* : 091-11-25357109
*Email* : publishing@conceptpub.com,
*Website*: www.conceptpub.com

**Editorial Office:**
H-13, Bali Nagar, New Delhi-110 015, India.

Cataloging in Publication Data--*Courtesy:* D.K. Agencies (P) Ltd. <docinfo@dkagencies.com>

**Managing rural finances in India** / edited by Gursharan Singh Kainth.
p. cm.
Contributed articles.
Includes bibliographical references.
Includes index.
ISBN 13: 9788180696572 ISBN 10: 818069657X

1. Rural credit--India. 2. Agricultural credit--India. 3. Microfinance--India. 4. Rural development--India--Finance. I. Kainth, G. S. (Gursharan Singh), 1952-

DDC 332.710954 22

डा. किरीट एस. पारीख
Dr. Kirit S. Parikh

सदस्य
योजना आयोग
योजना भवन
नई दिल्ली–११० ००१
MEMBER
PLANNING COMMISSION
YOJANA BHAWAN
NEW DELHI-110 001

# Foreword

Since independence successive governments have emphasized the link between access to finance and poverty. India has a relatively deep financial system and a wide network of rural banks. But despite improvements in the delivery of financial services over the past three decades, India's financial markets and institutions have not served the poor people satisfactorily. The vast majority of India's poor households, who are concentrated in rural areas, do not have access to formal finance. To identify what it would take to improve access to finance for India's rural poor, it is necessary to examine the current level and pattern of access to finance for India's rural households, analyze what lies behind the lack of adequate financial access for the rural poor, and evaluate various approaches for delivering financial services to the rural poor.

The collection of articles in this book examines the reasons and factors affecting both banks, and their clients. First is the problem of uncertainty about the repayment capacity of poor rural borrowers, and their irregular/volatile income streams and expenditure patterns, which, in the absence of credit information, drive up default risk. Second, the transactions costs of rural lending in India are high, mainly due to small size of loans, high frequency of transactions, large geographical spread, and heterogeneity of borrowers and widespread illiteracy.

Government policies of debt right off have made things worse from the banks' perspective, creating a "financial climate" not conducive to lending in general and rural banking in particular. New approaches and products to improve rural access, namely, the 'Self-Help Groups (SHGs) Bank Linkage' model, the growth of which has been truly remarkable; specialized micro-finance institutions: and, partnerships between private Banks, micro-financiers, and service providers, and the Kisan Credit Card are reviewed in this book.

Furthermore, a potential means of reducing default risk in rural finance, that has recently caught the attention of the Government, is the establishment of a "warehouse receipts system" to cover the agricultural risk management of products for farmers. The policy agenda to improve access to finance by the rural poor looked at include the following: introduction of flexible products; composite financial services; simplified procedures to access finance; and, improved staffing policies and doorstep banking, including an enabling policy and legal and regulatory environment for micro-finance. The bright spot on the horizon is that the private sector is now looking at the rural areas as a potentially important market and is increasing its investments accordingly, thereby opening up new opportunities for Indian farmers. Encouraging policies that promote competition will also ensure that farmers receive better prices.

This compilation by Dr. Kainth will help inform administrators and political leaders how to effectively provide finance to the poor. The book will be a source of reference not only for planners, policy makers but also for students of rural finance.

Kirit Parikh

**Dr. K.G. Karmakar**
Managing Director

**NATIONAL BANK FOR AGRICULTURE AND RURAL DEVELOPMENT**
Plot No. C-24, G-Block
Bandra-Kurla Complex
Post Box No. 8121
Post Box No. 8121
Bandra (East), Mumbai-400 051
Tel: 022-2653 0131/26530132(O)
Fax No.: 022-2653 0002
E-mail: md@nabard.org

# Preface

---

The present volume with contributions from eminent economists and bankers could not have come at a better time. The rural financial market has been undergoing a sea change since the introduction of liberalization. The resurgence of money-lenders, the fatigue of cooperative credit institutions, the advent of micro-finance with its multi-faceted activities, the paramount importance of marketing of crops in a globalize environment have added knots and twists to the structure and processes of the rural financial market. The present volume focuses on many of these aspects of the rural credit market.

Quite a number of papers deal with institutional credit both in regional and national perspectives and seek to show how institutional credit makes a difference in bringing about economic development. These perspectives have not lost sight of the distributive aspects of institutional credit, dwelling on the indebtedness patterns of labour households, women folk, tenants, etc.

Some of the papers have presented in-depth analyses of recent innovations in rural credit including micro-finance and have sought to illustrate how the micro-finance industry and institutions in the country could be developed in future. While micro-finance has certainly added certain innovative strengths to rural credit, the revival of cooperative credit institutions has been receiving attention at present, through the implementation of the recommendations by the Vaidyanathan Committee. The papers on cooperative credit institutions will certainly be helpful to all concerned with the cooperative credit movement in India.

A salutary feature of the present volume, thanks to the Editor, is that it has given an important focus on marketing aspects that it rightfully deserves. After all, it has to be recognized that credit alone cannot bring in development unless accompanied by the provision of forward and backward linkages especially those related to the remunerative disposal of final products in the integrated global commodity markets. Much of the prosperity of farmers and the agricultural sector as a whole depends upon how they are enabled to take advantage of these arrays of opportunities.

I am confident that the learned contributions in the volume will benefit the researchers, students, bankers and policy-makers immensely.

National Bank for Agriculture
and Rural Development, Mumbai

**Dr. K.G. Karmakar,**
Managing Director.

# Contents

# Editor's Note

Indian agriculture is at the crossroads. Inspite of substantial acceleration of Indian economy, growth of agriculture has a distinct slow down during the past two decades. The slow down is accompanied by a significant reduction in the share of agriculture in national product, but without much reduction in the share of workers depending on it for their livelihood. GDP from agriculture and allied sectors grew by 2.1 per cent during the Ninth Plan and only 2.3 per cent during the Tenth Plan. The two faces of the emerging distress are the manifestation of agrarian crisis that threatens the livelihoods of farmers, particularly those of the small and marginal ones; and the agricultural development crisis of reduction in its overall growth rate accompanied by declining profitability. The support systems to farming have weakened, public investments in agriculture have declined and institutions have become unresponsive. In the absence of any breakthrough in cost reducing technologies, the rising input prices have made cultivation un-remunerative. The result is the manifestation of agrarian crisis, often, in the extreme form of distress that results in suicides by some farmers. It is declining earnings that results in the inability to repay debt that trigger farmers' decision to commit suicide. Hence, indebtedness of farmers becomes a central issue to be addressed. It is in this context that the present volume seeks to examine the indebtedness of farmers in its totality with a view to designing and implementing effective policies, programmes and instruments of intervention.

Improving access to finance in rural areas is one of the biggest developmental challenges facing India today. More than one fourth of the population who live in poverty, the overwhelming majority eke out subsistence in rural villages. They are cut off from formal sources of credit and dependent on the services of pitiless loan sharks. India has one of the densest networks of rural banking institutions, but the people who run them regard their postings as a punishment and look forward to returning to the cities. In addition, the whole structure is not geared mandarins at Finance Ministries and Central Bank have tended to see rural finance as a necessary evil rather than an integral part of the financial system essential for fuelling the growth of the economy. It has been a stop-start approach: every now and then there is an upsurge of concern for the flow of credit to rural areas, the mandarins wake up and a new financial service delivery channel or piecemeal measure of reform is added. Consistent and harmonious systems generate financial and economic inclusion; incremental flavouring merely generates a soggy mess. It is just because the designated financial services regulator is presently unfamiliar with rural conditions.

The present reader consisting of 14 well researched papers contributed by eminent scholars from various universities and research institutes ventures to probe into this area and cover broad spectrum of rural finance. It's hoped that this valuable compilation will be of immense use for all those who are interested and concerned with rural-oriented economic development.

My sincere and profuse appreciation is due to Dr. Kirit Parikh, an eminent economist and now Member, Planning Commission, Government of India for his keen interest in going through the draft of the book inspite of extremely busy schedule at Yojana Bhawan and not only contributing a very thought provoking foreword but also giving very useful suggestions. Thanks are also due to Dr. K.G. Karmakar, Managing Director National Bank for Agriculture and Rural Development, Mumbai for contributing an excellent Preface to the book. Also, immensely beneficial were the discussions with Dr. Rajinder Singh Bawa, Dr. Pritam Singh Raikhy and Dr. Manmohan Singh Gill. A number of improvements are due to the candidness with which they made suggestions.

Being a collective effort, the credit goes to the worthy contributors who have contributed to this compilation. I owe a heavy debt to all of them who very smilingly took the responsibility to prepare/revise their papers well in time. Also my huge debt is to Ms. Rashpal Kaur and Ms. Sandeep Kaur for editorial assistance and to Ms. Poonam Bala for secretarial assistance. Mr. Ashok Kumar Mittal, my energetic publisher also deserves special thanks for his keen interest in its publication and bringing it out well in time.

**Dr. Gursharan Singh Kainth,**
Director, GAD Institute of Development Studies,
Amritsar 143 008.

# List of Contributors

**Dr. Anita Arya** is a faculty member of Sardar Patel Institute of Economic and Social Research, Thaltej Road, Ahmedabad and editor of '***Anvesak***'. Her areas of research interests include agriculture and rural development, infrastructure, etc. She has a book and number of publications in reputed journals to her credit.

**Mr. Brahm Prakash** after post-graduation in Economics in 1984, entered in service in July 1986 at Directorate of Pulses Research (Indian Council of Agricultural Research), Kanpur and still serving the same Directorate which has been upgraded to Indian Institute of Pulses Research, Kanpur as Senior Technical Officer. A Fellow of Indian Society of Pulses Research, Kanpur, is a life member of various professional organizations. He has got published 10 book chapters, 12 technical bulletins, 126 research articles and 62 scientific/popular articles.

**Mr. Hemantkumar P. Bulsara** having more than 8 years of experience is currently serving as a Lecturer (Economics & Management) at S V National Institute of Technology, Surat. He has done FDPM from Indian Institute of Management, Ahmedabad and pursuing his Ph.D. in Management from NIT Surat.

**Dr. Manmohan Singh Gill** is Professor of Sociology at Guru Nanak Dev University, Amritsar. Having a teaching experience of 24 years is associated with many academic bodies of the university. His areas of specialization are Rural Sociology and Urban Ecology. A recipient of Vijay Rattan award for his outstanding work in the field of environment education for the year 2005 has completed research projects on Untouchability and Dynamics of caste-land relations and three books to his credit. He is on the advisory panel of All India Foundation for Peace and Disaster Management, New Delhi.

**Dr. Kundalik Jadhav** graduated from College of Agriculture, Pune, post graduation in Agricultural Economics from Dr. B.S.K.K.V, Dapoli and Ph.D. degree in Agricultural Economics by Mahatma Phule Krishi Vidyapeeth, Rahuri (MS). Presently he is working as Junior Research Assistant in Agricultural Economics, Mahatma Phule Krishi Vidyapeeth, Rahuri having to his credit 45 research papers, two books and four Radio and T.V. Talks.

**Dr Gursharan Singh Kainth** started his career as Lecturer at Post-Graduate Department of Economics, Government College Gurdaspur and later at Khalsa College; Amritsar specializes in Quantitative and Development Economics. He has the distinction of serving the prestigious Punjab Agricultural University Ludhiana for more than two decades (1981-2000) and remained Director-Principal of Saint Soldier Management and Technical Institute Jalandhar. Currently, he is heading GAD Institute of Development Studies, Amritsar. A recipient of Cultural Doctorate of Philosophy of Economics from the World University, Arizona, USA is an active member of various professional bodies, namely, Indian Society of Agricultural Economics, Indian Society of Agricultural Marketing, Indian Institute of Public Administration, Agricultural Economics Research Association (India). He participated in various International/national/regional seminars, conferences etc. and presented papers. He remained member of the Academic Council of Punjab Technical University, Jalandhar. An unwearied researcher has about 200 research papers published in various international and national journals of repute and ten research monographs to his kitty. Besides, he has authored/co-authored /edited 15 books which have been well received and highly acclaimed during his three decades of professional career. He was honoured by various awards, namely, *Guru Draunacharya Samman*, *Vijay Rattan Award* and so on.

**Dr. A. Malaisamy** got Ph.D fellowship from International Food Policy Research Institute in 2004. His Ph.D research work was quoted in ***Human Development Report*** of World Bank in 2006 as one of best finding and his research paper was awarded by Oxford University as best research in 2008. He joined the Department of Agricultural Economics, Tamil Nadu Agricultural University, Coimbatore as Assistant Professor. Having 9 years research and teaching experience in Agricultural Economics, currently he is working as Agricultural Economist in International Livestock Research Institute, New Delhi.

**Dr. Vaidehi Pandurengan** having more than 15 years of experience is Professor (Management) at Easwari Engineering College, Chennai. She has done FDPM from Indian Institute of Management, Ahmedabad.

**Mr. Rathindra Nath Pramanik** is a Sr. Lecturer in Economics, Palli Charcha Kendra Department of Social Studies and Rural Development, Visva-Bharati, Santiniketan, West Bengal. His research interest covers Agricultural Economics and Development of Women. He has edited a book and numerous papers published in different journals.

**Dr. V. M. Rao** is Head, Centre for Research and Publications, Vaikunth Mehta National Institute of Cooperative Management, Pune and completed consultancy projects worth over Rs. 60 lakhs, the highest by any individual faculty at the Institute. He has published 13 books, over 80 articles in journals of repute, and contributed papers to national and international seminars. His areas of interest include agribusiness management, rural cooperatives, gender integration and economics of animal husbandry.

**Dr. Swami Prakash Srivastava** is with the Department of Economics, Faculty of Social Sciences at Dayal Bagh Educational Institute (Deemed University) Agra. During his two decades of teaching and research since 1998, Dr. Srivastava has contributed many articles and research papers in the diverse field of Rural Economics, International Trade and Industrial Economics to various professional and academic journal of repute. he attended about 20 national and 5 international seminar/conferences and presented papers.

**Dr. H. Shivappa** has published a few research articles in leading national journals. He has successfully completed two major research projects funded by the University Grants Commission, New Delhi. He has presented several papers in national conferences and has guided a number of M. Phil students. Having more than 30 years of teaching experience, currently he is working as Professor of Commerce and Management, A.R.G. College of Arts & Commerce (Affiliated to Kuvempu University), Davangere, Karnataka.

**Dr. Ram Pravesh Singh** (b 1948), began his career as Assistant Professor in Department of Agricultural Economics at Rajendra Agricultural University (Pusa), Samastipur, Bihar in 1975 and later transferred to Ranchi Agricultural College, Birsa Agricultural University, Kanke Ranchi, Jharkhand. Presently he is working as University Professor and Chairman, Department of Agricultural Economics, Birsa Agricultural University, Kanke Ranchi, Jharkhand. He has about 130 research papers published in various research national journals and authored three books/periodicals/manuals and also contributed three chapters in books. Besides he has acted as Principal Investigators and C.C.P.I. of ICAR funded World Bank funded NATP projects. He is an active life member of various professional societies and also participated in various national and regional seminars and conferences etc.

**Prof. Prabal K. Sen** had served the Institute of Rural Management Anand as Bank of Borada Chair Professor before joining XLRI, Jamshedpur as Professor in Economics Area and Chairperson of the Institute's Entrepreneur Development Centre (EDC) in March 2007. He had earlier taught at the Post-Graduate Department of Economics at Burdwan University, West Bengal and served a public sector bank for more than two decades, where he had occupied senior management positions across areas related to economic research and rural credit. Prof. Sen has provided consultancy, among others, to the Ministry of Rural Development, Government of India and SIDBI Foundation for Micro Credit. He is associated in advisory capacity with a number of academic and professional bodies across the country and participated in various regional, national and International levels conferences.

# List of Tables

# List of Figures

1

# Institutional Credit for Agriculture in India: Status, Constraints and Future Agenda

GURSHARAN SINGH KAINTH

*"Indian agriculture is currently passing through a period of severe crisis. The current agrarian distress has two dimensions—agricultural crisis and agrarian crisis. The root cause of the agricultural crisis lies in the neglect of agriculture in designing development programme and in the allocation of development and plan resources. The existing seed fertilizer technology has reached a plateau and no longer cost efficient due to reduced public investment in agricultural research and development. An inclusive four per cent agricultural growth is considered an absolute necessity for mitigating farmers distress. To boost agricultural growth, India needs massive investments in both the public as well as private investment. Structural transformation taking place in the Indian economy has worked against the agricultural sector. The main story of extensions of rural credit has been the ascending of commercial banks along with RRBs with a corresponding fall in the share of cooperatives. This reflected in the increasing concern in recent years over the effectiveness, governance and financial health of rural cooperatives. There is a strong need to revitalize rural cooperatives and put on a sound business footing."*

India's long-term economic prospect depends mainly on agriculture sector, which contribute quarter of Gross Domestic Product (GDP) and provide livelihoods to two-thirds of population. In pre-independent India, the majority of population was impoverished and live in sub-human condition. Despite the existence of excellent river systems, agriculture industry in India is proverbially called "*A Gamble on the Monsoon*" and hence has been an inherently risky activity. Moreover, we have also had onerous rural tax system under different empires. Indigenous system of credit had to develop as a consequence of seasonal need. Development of rural credit system has therefore been intrinsically very difficult and an issue of continuing official concern for over a century. The practice of intending institutional credit to agriculture can be traced back to British Council Government as early as the 1870's when farmer was provided such credit by the government during drought year. *The Land Improvement Loans Act* of 1883 was the first consolidated law intended to provide advancement for agriculture. Thinking to do with credit cooperation began in the latter part of the nineteenth century. Finally, the *Cooperative Land Mortgage Bank* was created for providing long-term loans to agriculturist for redemption of debts. This was followed by the enactment of *Cooperative Credit Societies Act* of 1904 to meet the short-term credit needs of the farmers. In fact the major thrust in the area of agricultural credit during the pre-independence era was more on the prevention of exploitation of the farmers by the money lenders, rather than the promotion of capital formation in agriculture.

Long before the organization of *Reserve Bank of India*, great faith was laid in India in the potentialities of the cooperative organizations to serve the rural credit needs of the country. A new Act was passed in 1912 giving legal recognition to credit societies and the like. *Mac Lagan Committee on Cooperation India* (1915) advocated the establishment of provincial cooperative banks. As a result Cooperative Banks were got established in almost all the provinces by 1930, thus giving rise to the 3-tier cooperative credit structure. *Royal Commission of Agriculture* further examines the programme of rural credit in 1926-27. *Malcolm Darling* submitted another report on Cooperative Credit in India in 1953 to the then Government of India just before the founding of Reserve Bank of India.

Agricultural sector would require an organized flow of funds to break the inertia came to focus only when *All India Rural Credit*

*Survey Committee* (ARCSC) of 1954 headed by Mr. Gorawala came to the conclusion that existing structure of primary credit societies was not sufficient to meet the credit requirements of the Indian peasantry, especially those of small and marginal farmers. Survey reported that agricultural credit fell short of the right quantity, was not of the right type, did not serve the right purpose and often failed to reach the right people. The committee also observed that the performance of cooperatives was deficient in many ways. But at the same time, it had a vital role to channeling credit to farmers. ARCSC summed up that *Cooperation had failed but cooperation must succeed.* ARCSC also urged a well defined role for commercial banks in delivering credit for agriculture in specialized area such as marketing, processing, storage and warehousing. It recommended the establishment of State Bank of India and through it, extension of commercial banking facilities in the rural and semi-urban areas. Thus, concerned with the inadequate extension of agricultural credit had a significant role in the creation of Reserve Bank of India and transformation of Imperial Bank of India to State Bank of India.

Since the inception of Economic Planning in 1950, Government has identified the credit need for the rural people and framed policies conclusive for the flow of institutional credit for farm sector. The inadequacy of rural credit continued to engage the attention of the Reserve Bank of India and the Government throughout the 1950s and 1960s. The *Agricultural Refinance Corporation* (ARC) was set up by the Reserve Bank of India in 1963 to provide funds by way of refinance, but credit cooperatives still did not functions too well. Consequently, the *All India Rural Credit Review Committee* (Chairman: Shri B. Venkatappiah) was set up in July 1966 to, *inter alia,* review the supply of rural credit in the context of Fourth Five Year Plan in general and the requirements of the intensive programme of agricultural production in different parts of the country, in particular and to make recommendations for improving the flow of agricultural credit. After a comprehensive review, the committee recommended that the commercial banks should play a complementary role along with cooperatives, in extending rural credit. The social control and the subsequent nationalization of major commercial banks in 1969 (and subsequently in 1980) acted as a catalyst in providing momentum to the efforts of leveraging the commercial banking system for extending agricultural credit. The outreach of banks was enlarged considerably within a relatively short period of time. The concept of priority sector was introduced in 1969 to underscore the imperative of financing certain neglected sectors like agriculture. The channelling of credit to the priority sector was sought to be achieved through the stipulation that a certain proportion of the total net bank credit to be deployed in these sectors by specific target dates. Decentralized credit planning through the *Lead Bank Scheme* was also introduced under which, each district was placed with one of the commercial bank (called the *District Lead Bank)* to spearhead the credit allocation for, *inter alia,* agricultural lending. In order to emphasize the developmental and promotional role assigned to ARC in addition to refinancing, the corporation was renamed as *Agricultural Refinance and Development Corporation* (ARDC) by an amendment to the Act in 1975. Moreover 1950s and 1960s had been characterized by a big industrial push with inadequate attention being given to agriculture. It was the 1965-1967 droughts that brought matters to a head and focused concentrated attention to agriculture. *Green Revolution* than followed in the late 1960s and 1970s necessitating adequate availability of credit that could enable the purchase of inputs such as fertilizer, high yielding varieties of seeds, pumps sets for irrigation and the like. Despite all these efforts, the flow of credit to agriculture sector failed to exhibit any appreciable improvement due mainly to the fact that the commercial banks were not tuned to the needs and requirements of the small and marginal farmers, while the cooperatives, on the other hands lacked resources to meet the expected demand. The solution that was found involved the establishment of a separate banking structure, capable of combining the local feel and familiarity of rural problems characteristic of cooperatives and the professionalism and large resource base of commercial Banks. Following the recommendations of Narasimham Working Group (1975) *Regional Rural Banks* (RRBs) were set up. Thus by the end of 1977, there emerged three separate institutions for providing rural credit, which is often, described as the "multi-agency approach". Following the recommendations of the *Committee to Review Arrangements for Institutional Credit for Agriculture and Rural Development,* the National Bank for Agriculture and Rural Development (NABARD) was set up in 1982 for providing credit for promotion of, among other things, agriculture. NABARD took over the entire undertake of ARNC and the refinancing functions of RBI with respective to RRBs and State Cooperatives. NABARD is the open institution, which has been entrusted with the pivotal role in the sphere of policy planning and providing refinance facilities to RFIs. Since its inception, NABARD has played a major player facilitating institutional development and encouraging promotional efforts in the area of rural credit. NABARD also administered *Rural Infrastructure Development Fund* (RIDF) set up in 1995-96; the corpus of which is contributed by scheduled commercial banks to the extent of short fall in agricultural lending under priority sector large etc. Introduction of *Kisan Credit Card* (KCC) has also aided the process in the recent years. NABARD has also been playing a catalytic role in *micro finance credit* through conduct of SHGs/JLGs. At present scheduled commercial banks (excluding RBIs) constitute 40 per cent of net bank credit and within the credit goes to agricultural sector. To ensure that the focus gets diluted, lending under indirect category should not exceed 4.5 per cent of net bank credit. While institutional setup was strengthened for flow of credit to rural sector, banks were advised to step up direct finance to agriculture including allied sectors. This was done with an objective to reach 16 per cent of their total outstanding credit by March 1987; 17 per cent by March 1989 and 18 per cent by March 1990. After the introduction of FSR, RBI directed then banks to finance not exceeding 4.5 per cent of total credit.

Notwithstanding the impressive geographical speared, functional reach and consequent decline in the influence of informal sources of credit, rural financial institutions were characterized by several weakness, viz., decline in productivity and efficiency, erosion of repayments ethics and profitability. On the eve of 1991 Economic Reforms, rural credit delivery system was again found to be in a poor shape. *Report of the Committee of Financial Sector Reform in India* of 1991 headed by Mr. S Narasimham, popularly known as *Bisham Pitamaha,* provided blue print for carrying out over all financial sector reforms during 1990s. Furthermore, weakness in the performance of rural financial institutions since 1991 resulted in setting up of various committee/working groups/taskforces to look into their operations.

1. High level *Committee on Agricultural Credit Though Commercial Banks* headed by Mr. R.V. Gupta, 1998.
2. Task force to *Study the Function of Cooperative Credit System and Suggests Measures for its Strengthening* headed by Mr. Jagdish Kapoor, 1999.

3. Report of the *Expert Committee on Rural Credit* headed by Dr. V.S. Vyas, 2001.
4. Working Group to suggest Amendments in the *Regional Rural Bank Act – 1976* headed by Mr. M.V.S. Chalapathi, 2002.
5. Advisory Committee on *Flow of Credit to Agriculture and Related Activities from Banking System* headed by Prof. V.S. Vyas, 2001.
6. Taskforce to examine the Reform required in the *Cooperative Banking System including the Appropriate Regulatory Regime* headed by Prof. Vaidyanathan, 2004.
7. *Expert Group on Investment Credit in Agriculture*, headed by Dr. Y.S.P. Thorat, June 2005.
8. *Expert Group on Credit Deposit Ratio,* headed by Dr. Y.P.S. Thorat, 2005.
9. *Expert Group on Agricultural Indebtedness* headed by R. Radhakrishna, July 2007.
10. *Committee of Financial Inclusion* headed by C. Rangarajan, 2006.
11. *Expert Group on Agricultural Distress* headed by S.S. Johl.
12. *Sub-Group on Institutional Credit for 11th Five Year Plan.*

Kapoor taskforce (1999) suggested adoption of a Model Cooperative Act; setting up of a Cooperative Rehabilitation and Development Fund at NABARD and Mutual Assistance Fund at State level. Vyas (2001) committee recommended restoration of health of primaries by scrapping the cadre system, selective delayering of cooperative credit structure and integration of short and long-term structures. Chalapathi Rao (2002) working group had, in addition to suggesting diversification of business of RRBs, recommended introduction of capital adequacy norms for RRBs in a phased manner, along with the RRBs specific amount of equity based on the risk weighted assets ratio.

Out of 99 recommendations of Vyas Committee (2004), 33 were accepted and implemented. These related to procedural modification and rationalization of systems and procedures; tie ups with related farm machinery by banks, use of a flexible revolving credit limits to small borrowers of production or investment loans for meeting temporary shortfalls in family cash flow; cooperating Joint Liability Groups (JLGs) and Self-Help Groups (SHGs) approaches in addressing issues relative to financing oral lessees; addressing delays/ refusal in opening saving bank accounts of SHGs; improving staffing in rural areas to promote retail lending to agriculture, use of individual volunteers, farmer's club or NGOs/SHGs as direct selling experts, building synergy between good working primaries and commercial banks, use of IT in rural branches, working out appropriate incentives structure for prompt repayment, making the interest rate on small loans reasonable and improving the efficiency of credit delivery to small borrowers and association with contact farming

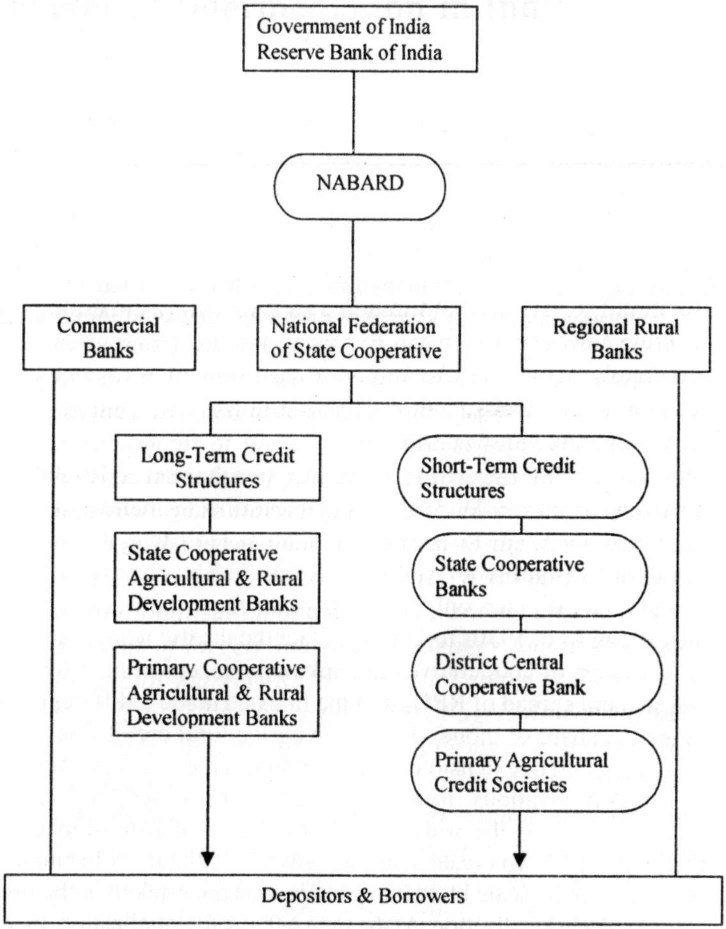


**Fig. 1.1:** Structure of Agricultural Credit System in India

These committees/working groups/taskforces made far reaching recommendations having a bearing and delivery of agricultural credit financial sector reforms and form an integral part of overall economic structural reform initiated in 1991. The following orgenogram (Fig. 1.1) depicts the network of agricultural credit system in India. Inadequacy of agricultural credit has had more than a century old tortuous history. Agricultural credit system has been a product of both evolution and intervention and symbolizes the systems response to the stimuli from continuing dissatisfaction with its delivery. Supply lending approach to the institutional development for agricultural credit has been followed in India.

## Sources

Agricultural credit apparently started to grow after banks nationalization and it has been growing continuously since then with all the concerns and skepticism expressed, the difficult and continuous changes in institutional credit have in deed borne fruit. Over the years, there has been significant increase in the access of rural cultivators to institutional credit and simultaneously, the role of informal agencies including money-lenders as source of credit has declined. According to *All India Debt and Investment Survey* the relative shares of various institutional agencies jumped from 7.3 per cent in 1951-52 to 31.7 per cent in 1971, which further increased to 63.2 per cent in 1981 and reached 75 per cent in 1995-96.

The age old problem of rural credit has been the excessive reliance of borrowers on money-lenders and other informal agencies that have entailed usurious interest rates and exploitation. How long it has taken to break this shackle of slavery? Remarkably change of any significance took place only after 50 years from the beginning of serious attention in 1930s to 1980s. In fact the drastic action ranging from formation of cooperatives to bank nationalization in 1969 and the subsequent spread of RRBs and the like had made a difference in reducing the share of money-lenders in agricultural credit finally.

Indian record of extension of rural credit is quite a success story of institutional innovations. Remarkable feature of agricultural credit extension in India is the wide spread or network of Rural Financial Institutions (RFIs). To create a strong network of financial institution in rural areas, large scale branch expansion was undertaken in the first phase of bank nationalization. At the time of bank nationalization, there were only 1833 Scheduled Commercial Banks (SCBs) which jumped to 32406 by March 2003. Likewise, the network of cooperatives catering mainly to agriculture expanded from 95871 in ending June 1980 to 1, 10,000 at present. Although the share of cooperative credit is now much lower than that of commercial banks, the reach of cooperative credit societies is much wider. Cooperative credit societies have more than twice the number of rural outlets and four times more accounts than those of scheduled commercial banks and RRBs taken together. The share of rural branches of SCBs in total increased sharply from 22 per cent in June 1969 to 47 per cent in March 2003. Policy of forcing banks to open more branches in the rural areas using the 1:3 rule, under which banks get a license to open one branch in a location that already has a branch of another bank only if they open branches in three other unbanked locations, was instrumental in rural network of banks expansion. But this rule was abandoned and there was near stagnation in the expansion of bank branches in the rural areas. The banks were allowed to convert their non-viable rural branches into satellite offices and to close zonal bank branches. RRBs were allowed to relocate their loss-making branches to new places even outside rural areas. As a result rural branches have steadily come down from 32981 (51.2 per cent of the total) in March 1966 to 31967 (45.7 per cent of the total) by March 2005. What is more during this period a sharp decline has taken place in the absolute number of agricultural loan accounts? Their number declined from 277.4 lakhs in March 1992 to 198.4 lakhs in March 2001, but started rising thereafter. Similar trend was noticed in the share of agriculture in total outstanding bank credit. Furthermore, large share of agricultural credit is going to farm sizes of more than five acres. The average amount of loans outstanding per account has grown much more rapidly in case of farm sizes of more than five acres and above as compare to small and marginal farm sizes.

## Flow of Institutional Credit

Institutional credit for agricultue in India was viewed from the grip of loan sharks-money-lenders. It was hardly considered as an instrument of production enhancement. Traditionally, the role of credit is to give a push to the development process. It is a catalytic-lubricant, which keeps the wheels of development moving. How agricultural credit contributes to agricultural development is a complex issue as credit is a means to an end. But when it results into investments, it leads to a growth in output. Rural credit environment is a very typical with number of inherent peculiar problems such as low spatial density of clients leading to higher transaction costs, mix of economic activities with consequent higher level of risk, low level of human capital, bad debts, week credit portfolios, poor repayments practices and so on. On the other hand, higher demand for credit is envisaged as a result of market orientation of agricultural sector for both the inputs as well as outputs. Apparently, it is feared that supply demand gap for agricultural credit from formal institutional institutions would widen unless the right kind of intervention are not being made

Since the inception of central economic planning in 1950, the government has identified the credit needs of the rural people and framed policies conducive for flow of institutional credit for farm sector. While institutional set up was strengthened for flow of credit to rural sector, on the other hand banks were advised to step up direct finance to agricultural sector (including allied sectors). This was done with an objective to reach 16 per cent of their total outstanding credit by March 1987, 17 per cent by March 1989 and 18 per cent by March 1990. After the introduction of financial sector reforms in the nineties, the Reserve Bank of India directed these banks to lend 18 per cent of the net bank credit to agriculture (including indirect finance not exceeding 4.5 per cent of the total credit).

There has been substantial improvement in the flow of institutional credit to agriculture during the past three decades. Agricultural credit started to grow only after bank nationalization and has been growing continuously since then. Table 1.1 along with Fig.1.2 depicts the flow of institutional credit to agriculture over the last five decades. During the period 2002-07, GLC flow to the agriculture and allied activities witnessed a growth of 37 per cent, with the increase of 32 per cent in the crop loan and 46 per cent in terms of loan disbursements. The GLC flow during 2005-06 reveals that both crop loans (38%) and term loans (53%) witnessed high growth over the previous year. Sub-sectoral credit flow during 2005-06 revealed that it had more than doubled in most of the sectors except fisheries where it has declined by 22 per cent.

During the Tenth Plan period (2002-07), Credit flow for agriculture and allied activities aggregated Rs. 6,65,632 crores and has increased at a CAGR of 31 per cent. To achieve the target for 2006-07, 83.50 lakhs new farmers were brought under the institutional fold; 74.70 lakhs KCCs were issued; 631 agri-clinics were financed and debt relief of Rs. 4823.37 crores and Rs. 673.90 crores to farmers in distress and in arrears respectively were extended. The banks also provided Rs. 460.06 crores to small and marginal farmers under One Time Settlements (OTS). Commercial banks, Co-operative banks and RRBs extended loans to the extent of Rs. 39.69 crores, Rs. 12.39 crores and Rs. 21.34 crores to 13202, 9432 and 516 farmers respectively to redeem their past debts from informal sources.

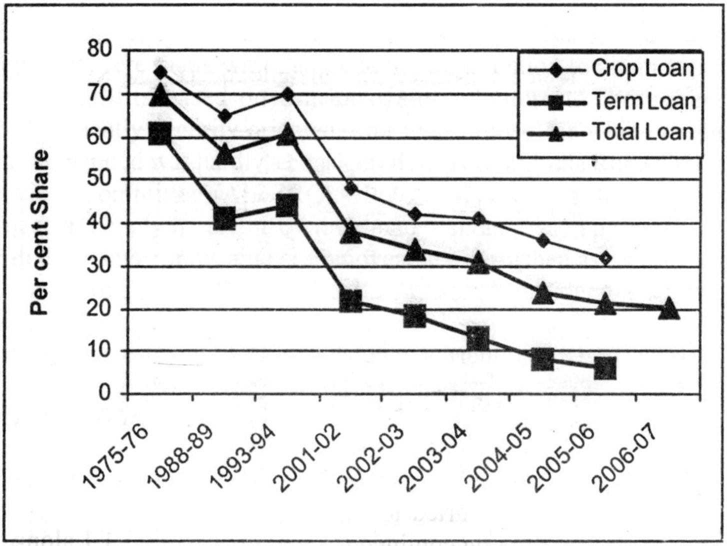


**Fig. 1.2:** Share of Co-operative Loan in Total Agricultural Credit.

The overall performance of Indian Banking System is 15 per cent as against the norms of 18 per cent of Net Banking Credit (NBC). Banks were allowed to waive margin/security requirements for agriculture loans up to Rs. 50 thousand and in case of agri-business/ agri-clinics for loans up to Rs. 5 lakhs. Since tenant farmers are not adequately served, banks are advised to open a separate window for SHGs/JLGs of tenant farmers.

Banks were further advised to increase the number of borrower by another 50 millions to their portfolio and also to make efforts to increase this disbursement to small and marginal farmers to 40 per cent of these direct advances under *Special Assistance Credit Plan (SACP)* by March 2007. Government had decided to bring down the interest rate on short-term credit to 7 per cent from 9 per cent or more on loans less than Rs. 3 lakhs. NABARD will provide refinance to the lending institutions at economical rates for this purpose. Another really significant measure and relief is that farmers who had taken crop loans from banks would get an amount equal to two percentage points of this liability (principal amount ceiling Rs. 3 lakh) deposited in their bank account before 31st of March 2006. Government had provided Rs. 1700 crores for this purpose.

**Table 1.1:** Trends in flow of Agricultural Credit (1999-2000 Series)

| *Year* | *Short-Term Credit, (Rs. Crore)* | *Term Credit, (Rs. Crore)* | *Total Credit Flow (Short and Long Term), (Rs. Crore)* | *Short-Term Credit as per cent of Value of Inputs* | *Term Credit as per cent of Private Sector GCF* | *Total Credit Flow as per cent of Agricultural GDP* |
|---|---|---|---|---|---|---|
| 1980-81 | 2047 | 1389 | 3436 | 13.4 | 56.3 | 7.3 |
| 1985-86 | 4529 | 2629 | 7158 | 19.3 | 73.9 | 9.0 |
| 1990-91 | 5979 | 4209 | 10188 | 15.2 | 34.4 | 6.8 |
| 1996-97 | 16998 | 9413 | 26411 | 22.8 | 55.7 | 7.7 |
| 1999-00 | 28965 | 17303 | 46268 | 25.5 | 41.7 | 10.4 |
| 2000-01 | 33314 | 19513 | 52827 | 28.9 | 51.0 | 11.7 |
| 2001-02 | 40509 | 21536 | 62045 | 32.7 | 43.1 | 12.7 |
| 2002-03 | 45586 | 23974 | 69560 | 35.3 | 45.8 | 14.7 |
| 2003-04 | 54977 | 32004 | 86981 | 38.3 | 64.5 | 16.3 |
| 2004-05 | 71847 | 53462 | 125309 | 51.1 | 89.6 | 23.4 |
| 2005-06 | 105282 | 75204 | 180486 | — | — | 30.3 |
| 2006-07 | | | 203296 | | | |

*Note*: GCF denotes Gross Capital Formation. GDP denotes Gross Domestic Product.

*Source*: For Credit Data as in Table 1.2 and Central Statistical Organisation, *National Account Statistics*, various Years.

The agency-wise share of credit flow to agriculture (Table 1.2 along with Fig. 1.3) shows that the Commercial Banks accounted for the major share (61 per cent) followed by Co-operative Banks (28 per cent) and Regional Rural Banks (11 per cent). However there is a declining trend in the share of co-operative banks in the flow of institutional credit over the years, which is indicative of the need for restructuring and reforming these banks.

**Table 1.2:** Source-wise Credit Flow to Agriculture: 1975-76 to 2005-06

*(Rs. in Crore)*

| *Agency* | *1975-76* | *1983-84* | *1993-94* | *2001-02* | *2002-03* | *2003-04* | *2004-05* | *2005-06* |
|---|---|---|---|---|---|---|---|---|
| *A. Short-Term* | *1177* | *3335* | *11271* | *40509* | *45586* | *54977* | *74064* | *105350* |
| Cooperatives | 881 | 2158 | 7839 | 18787 | 19668 | 22640 | 27157 | 34930 |
| Regional Rural Banks | 2 | 120 | 732 | 3777 | 4775 | 6088 | 10010 | 12712 |
| Scheduled Commercial Banks | 213 | 872 | 2700 | 17904 | 21104 | 26192 | 36793 | 57640 |
| Other Agencies | — | — | 0 | 41 | 39 | 57 | 104 | 68 |
| *B. Medium & Long-Term* | *498* | *1909* | *5223* | *21536* | *23974* | *32004* | *51245* | *75136* |
| Cooperatives | 305 | 780 | 2278 | 4737 | 3968 | 4235 | 4074 | 4474 |
| Regional Rural Banks | 2 | 143 | 245 | 1077 | 1295 | 1493 | 2394 | 2511 |
| Scheduled Commercial Banks | 192 | 986 | 2700 | 15683 | 18670 | 26249 | 44688 | 67837 |
| Other Agencies | — | — | 0 | 39 | 41 | 27 | 89 | 314 |
| *C. Total Credit* | *1675* | *5244* | *16494* | *62045* | *69560* | *86981* | *125309* | *180486* |
| Cooperatives | 1186 | 2938 | 10117 | 23524 | 23636 | 26,875 | 31231 | 39404 |
| Regional Rural Banks | 2 | 263 | 977 | 4854 | 6070 | 7581 | 12404 | 15223 |
| Scheduled Commercial Banks | 405 | 1885 | 5400 | 33587 | 39774 | 52441 | 81481 | 125477 |
| Other Agencies | 82 | 185 | 0 | 80 | 80 | 84 | 193 | 382 |

*Source*: For Commercial Banks from Reserve Bank of India (RBI); for Cooperatives and Regional Rural Banks from National Bank for Agriculture and Rural Development (NABARD).

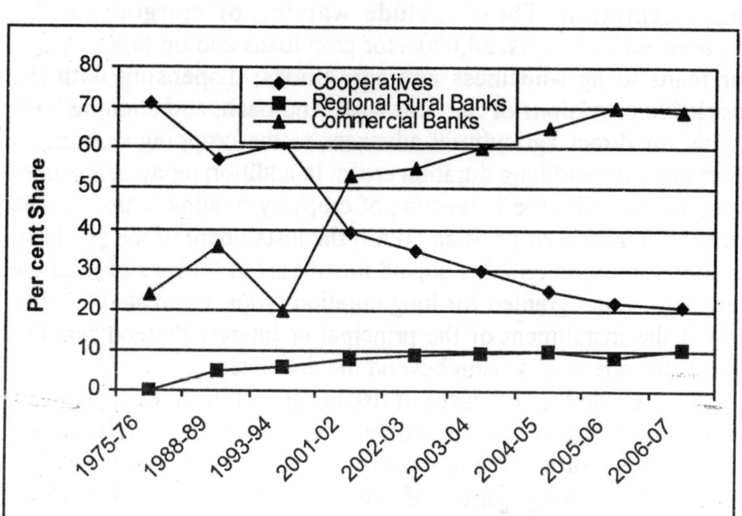


**Fig. 1.3:** Share of Different Agencies in Total Credit

Realizing the need to enhance credit flow to agriculture, the Government, in consultation with the Reserve Bank of India (RBI), NABARD and commercial banks, announced on June 18, 2004, a credit package for the agricultural sector, which envisaged doubling of agricultural credit over three years. Interestingly, the ambitious target of doubling the institutional credit as per farm credit package (June 18, 2004) in three years to farmers is being achieved. But the position is not, however, clear on certain qualitative aspects such as the class of beneficiaries, credit delivery mechanism, actual interest rates charged and so on. But the available evidences suggest that the volume of credit flowing to small and marginal farmers in general is less than proportionate to their area. Furthermore what the small and marginal farmers actually need is the adequate availability of institutional credit, as they have to borrow from informal sources at interest rates exceeding 60 per cent in certain cases. The issue of credit delivery, therefore, needs a serious attention of the policy makers.

Reserve Bank of India had also set up an Advisory Committee on the flow of credit to agriculture and related activities under the Chairmanship of Prof. V.S. Vyas, which submitted its report to the Government on June 30, 2004. Several recommendation of the committee have been accepted and communicated to the banks for implementation. These include waiving of margin/security requirements up to Rs. 50,000/- for crop loans and up to Rs. 5 lakh for loans to agri-business and agri-clinics; dispensing with the restrictive provisions of Services Area Approach; and aligning NPA norms for direct agricultural advances to the cropping seasons of short duration and long duration crops. In addition repayments dates were aligned with the harvesting of crops by treating loans granted for short duration crops as an NPA if the installment of the principal or interest thereon remains unpaid for two crops seasons beyond the due dates. Loan granted for long duration crops are treated as NPA only if the installment of the principal or interest thereon remains unpaid for one crop season beyond the due dates.

To examine the core issue of risk in agriculture and how that is a key determinant of all the problems encountered in agricultural lending, it is worth while to examine the record of Non-Performing Assets (NPAs) in agriculture of commercial banks. Is the hesitation of banks to lend for agriculture really caused by the experience of a much higher level of NPAs? No doubt, the proportion of NPAs is indeed higher for agriculture than they are for the non-priority sector. However, they are not as high as those of Small Scale Industries (SSIs) and for other priority sectors. In fact for private sector banks, agricultural NPAs are as low as 5 per cent of total outstanding advances to agriculture and are lower than the non-priority sector. In fact, it is likely that if public sector enterprises are excluded from the data for the non-priority sector, the performance of NPAs in agriculture may not be much higher than for lending to the non-priority sector-private sector credit exposure as a whole. This implies that agricultural lending may be more risky than non-priority sectors, but the difference is not so large enough to warrant excessive caution in bank lending for agricultural purposes.

Agricultural growth is crucial for alleviating rural poverty. Access to institutional credit to more farmers and appropriate quantity and quality of agricultural credits are crucial for realizing the full potential of agriculture as a profitable activity. Recognizing the crucial role of credit, the Tenth Five Year Plan (2002-07) envisages a substantial jump in credit flows to agriculture to Rs. 7, 36,750 crores in the plan period as compared to the credit flow of Rs. 2,29,956 crores achieved in the Ninth Five Year Plan period. Credit flow to agricultural sector from all formal sources was much below the levels envisaged in the Tenth Plan. Concerned over the slower growth of agricultural credit, the Government announced a comprehensive policy on June 18, 2004. The policy envisages a 30 per cent increase in credit to agricultural sector in 2004-05 over an estimated credit flow of Rs. 80,000 crores in 2003-04. The implementation of the policy has been entrusted to PSBs, private sector banks, Regional Rural Bank (RRBs) and cooperative banks. The policy has indicated that each rural and semi-urban branch of commercial banks, on an average, will take up at least two to three new investment projects in the area of plantations and horticulture, fisheries, organic farming, agro-processing, livestock, micro-irrigation, sprinkler irrigation, watershed management, village pond development and other agricultural activities. NABARD has been asked to advise District Level Technical Committees to review the scales of finance to meet the realistic credit needs of farmers, especially for capital intensive agricultural operations.

The Budget for 2004-05, presented in the Parliament on July 08, 2004 proposed doubling of credit to agriculture in three years and announced further measures to achieve the target growth in agricultural credit. These measures include holding the sponsor bank of each RRB squarely responsible for the performance of RRB under its control and an incentive scheme under which RRBs adapting new governance standards and abiding by prudential regulations will qualify for receiving funds from the Government for their restructuring. The Budget proposed setting up of a Task Force to examine the reforms required in the co-operative banking system including the appropriate regulatory regime. Task Force has since submitted its draft report. The draft report has been put on the websites of the RBI and Ministry of Finance on January 11, 2005 for inviting comments. The report is likely to be finalized shortly after taking into account the feedback received. Farm Credit Package announced in June 2004 stipulated among other things doubling of flow of institutional credit for agriculture in the ensuing three years. The credit flow however got doubled during the first two years as against stipulated time period of three years. Short-term loans will continue to be disbursed at 7 per cent per annum with an initial provision of Rs. 1,600 crores for interest subvention in 2008-09.

As indicated in its mid-term review of November, 2003, the RBI constituted an Advisory Committee on flow of Credit to Agriculture and Related Activities from the Banking System (Chairman: Prof. V.S Vyas). The Advisory Committee submitted its interim report in April, 2004 and the final report in June, 2004. Based on the recommendations contained in the interim report of the Vyas Committee, the RBI, in its annual policy statement for 2004-05, announced a number of measures to improve credit delivery to agriculture. These included, treating loans to the storage units designed to store agricultural products, irrespective of location, as indirect credit to agriculture, treating investment by banks in securitized assets representing direct (Indirect) lending to agriculture as direct (Indirect) lending to agriculture and waiver of margin/security requirement for agricultural loans upto Rs. 50, 000 and in case of agri business and agri clinics for loans up to Rs. 5 lakh. In addition, RBI also aligned repayment dates with harvesting of crops by treating loans granted for short duration crops as an NPA, if the installment of the principal or interest thereon remains unpaid for two crop seasons beyond the due date. Loans granted for long duration crops are treated as an NPA, only if the installment of the principal or interest thereon remains unpaid for one crop seasons beyond the due date. As recommended by the Vyas Committee, RBI announced that micro-finance institutions would not be permitted to accept public deposits, unless they comply with the extent regulatory framework. The recommendation relating to Service Area Approach (SAA) was accepted and an announcement to this effect was made in the RBI's mid-term review of annual policy statement for 2004-05.

During 2005-06, most of the PSBs, Co-operative banks and RRBs have reduced the rate of interest on farm loans up to Rs. 50,000 to 9.0 per cent and, in some cases, to 8.5 per cent. This has enabled the farmers to derive the benefit of falling interest rates and to improve their margins on farming and allied operations. Also, as measure to minimize the incidence of under-financing, the scale of finance for crop loans and unit costs of farmer investments have been further revised and made more realistic. Further more, to mitigate the risk of agriculture arising out of drought conditions, banks either postponed the recovery of loans or converted short-term credit into medium-term credit with appropriate reschedule in repayment in the concerned areas. The norms of financing in the *Rabi* season have been liberalized taking into account the likely shortfall in *Kharif* output on account of deficient rainfall.

Nonetheless, recent years have again been characterized by a concern over the following share of agricultural credit as a proportion of total credit. This is indeed true, but is this the correct metric to look at the progress of agricultural credit? What would be more relevant is to evaluate agricultural credit as a proportion of agricultural GDP; or short-term credit as a proportion of the value of inputs or long-term credit as a proportion of private investment. As might be expected the share of the agricultural value added has been falling as a share of total GDP (Table 1.3). Hence credit to agriculture may also be expected to fall as a proportion to total credit, assuming relative stability in the share of purchased inputs as a proportion of value added. Interestingly, the share of agricultural credit as a proportion of agricultural GDP has been rising continuously since 1950's and even as a proportion of total GDP until 1980's. There was indeed a fall in mid-1990's but has again risen now. It is true; however, that agricultural credit has indeed fallen as a proportion of total credit. Credit flow as a percentage of agricultural GDP and term credit as a percentage of capital formation in agriculture have gone up steadily. Short-term credit as a percentage of farm inputs and total institutional credit as a percentage of GDP have also increased. The bank credit to agricultural GDP ratio gets considerably inflated due to the slowing down of growth in agriculture. As increase in short-term credit as a proportion of the value of farm inputs could be attributed to the diversification that is taking place in agriculture. The ratio of term credit to private sector gross capital formation in agriculture has more than doubled in the recent past.

**Table 1.3:** Share of Agriculture in GDP and Employment

| Year | Share of Agriculture in GDP at 1999-2000 Prices (%) | Share of Agriculture in Employment—UPSS (%) | Ratio of Worker Productivity in Agriculture to non-agriculture | Ratio of Worker Productivity in Non-agriculture to Agriculture |
|---|---|---|---|---|
| 1972-73 | 41.0 | 73.9 | 0.287 | 3.49 |
| 1993-94 | 30.0 | 63.9 | 0.285 | 3.51 |
| 1999-00 | 25.0 | 60.2 | 0.252 | 3.97 |
| 2004-05 | 20.2 | 56.5 | 0.199 | 4.94 |
| 2005-06 | 19.7 | — | — | — |
| 2006-07 | 20.5 | — | — | — |

*Note*: GDP denotes Gross Domestic Product and UPSS denote Usual Principal and Subsidiary Status.

*Source*: Central Statistical Organisation (CSO), *National Accounts Statistics*, various years and National Sample Survey Organisation (NSSO), *Employment and Unemployment Situation in India*, various rounds.

The existing agricultural credit system is geared to the needs of foodgrain production: with the share of foodgrains production falling as a per cent of total agricultural production. It is all the more creditable that agricultural credit has not fallen as a proportion of agricultural GDP. With the share of agriculture in GDP falling continuously from 36 per cent in 1981 to 29 per cent in 1991 and to 19 per cent in 2007, it is expected that the share of agricultural credit would also fall as a proportion of total credit, unless the trend is corrected by increasing commercialization of agriculture.

Historically, cooperative societies have played a vital role in the provision of institutional credit to agricultural sector. With the entry of commercial banks in the rural areas, the share of cooperative credit in total agricultural credit had gone down. It fell from 70.8 per cent in 1975-76 to only 21.8 per cent in 2006-07. The share of cooperative in short-term credit in the form of crop loans declined from 74.9 to 33.2 per cent; its share in long-term credit declined steeply from 61.2

to 6.0 per cent. Concurrently, commercial banks became the dominant source of credit to the agricultural sector.

The expansion of commercial banks credit to agriculture has been impressive, particularly after bank nationalization. The share of agricultural credit in total commercial bank lending rose from 10 per cent in mid-1970s to a peak of about 18 per cent (the official target set for the public sector) at the end of the 1980s. Thereafter, it steadily declined to a low of around 11 per cent during the period 2004 to 2006. Even than, commercial banks accounted for 69.5 per cent of total institutional credit to agriculture in 2006-07 up from 24.2 per cent disbursed in 1975-96. When the banks fail to fulfil the 18 per cent target they have the option of investing the shortfall in Rural Infrastructure Development Fund. For some times, many commercial banks have availed this soft option. The option has been made less attractive because of the low rates of interest on RIDF deposits. In actual operations, however, the entire shortfall does not flow into RIDF.

The main story in the expansion of rural credit in 1980's and 1990's has been the ascendancy of commercial banks along with RRBs with a corresponding fall in the share of cooperatives as is evident from Table 1.3 and depicted graphically in Fig. 1.3. This is reflected in the increasing concern in recent years over the effectiveness, governance and financial health of rural cooperative banks. Since just under half of rural credit continuous to be entered by them, there is a strong need to revitalize cooperatives and put cooperative on a second business footing.

Structural transformation taking place in the Indian economy has worked against the agricultural sector. Dependence of small and marginal farmers on primaries for institutional access to finance is much more than the big landlords who can depend on their own resources as well on commercial banks. No doubt out-reach of primaries extends to almost every corner, the fact remains that there disbursement is much higher than their total deposits and share capital including that of Government. Furthermore Kerala is the only state accounting more than 50 per cent of the total mobilization, which reflects rather poor credit mobilization by the primaries in the rest of India. They have failed miserably in their basic task of resource mobilization and disbursement of credit.

The objective of the primaries when they set up was primarily mobilization of local resources and disbarment of credit. In fact, if

**Table 1.4:** Gross Capital Formation (GCF) in Agriculture *(1999-2000 Series)*

| *Year* | *Total GCF (Rs. Crore)* | *Public GCF (Rs. Crore)* | *Private GCF (Rs. Crore)* | *Share of Public (%)* | *Share of Private (%)* | *GCF in Agr*. as per cent of Total GDP*** | *GCF in Agr. as per cent of Agr. GDP* | *GCF in Agr. as per cent of Aggregate GCF* |
|---|---|---|---|---|---|---|---|---|
| 1980-81 | 4342 | 1876 | 2466 | 43.2 | 56.8 | 3.0 | 9.2 | 16.1 |
| 1990-91 | 15839 | 3586 | 12253 | 22.6 | 77.4 | 2.8 | 10.5 | 11.5 |
| 1995-96 | 17392 | 5952 | 11440 | 34.2 | 65.8 | 1.7 | 6.9 | 6.3 |
| 1999-00 | 43473 | 7716 | 35757 | 17.7 | 82.3 | 2.2 | 8.9 | 8.6 |
| 2000-01 | 38735 | 7155 | 31580 | 18.5 | 81.5 | 1.9 | 7.9 | 7.7 |
| 2001-02 | 47043 | 8746 | 38297 | 18.6 | 81.4 | 2.2 | 9.1 | 9.0 |
| 2002-03 | 46823 | 7962 | 38861 | 17.0 | 83.0 | 2.1 | 9.6 | 7.5 |
| 2003-04 | 45132 | 9376 | 35756 | 20.8 | 79.2 | 1.9 | 8.5 | 5.8 |
| 2004-05 | 48576 | 10267 | 38309 | 21.1 | 78.0 | 1.9 | 9.1 | 4.9 |
| 2005-06 | 54539 | 13219 | 41320 | 24.2 | 75.8 | 1.9 | 9.6 | 4.5 |
| 2006-07 | 60762 | 15191 | 45571 | 24.9 | 75.1 | 1.9 | 9.8 | 4.7 |

*Note:* Gross Domestic Product.

*Source:* Casual Statistical Organisation *National Account*, Various years

refinance from higher structure were not available, the cooperative societies would soon have to close shop. Availability of easy finance from NABARD is the major factor preventing the growth and development potential of primaries. Borrowings of the primary agricultural cooperative societies from SCB/NABARD account for 89 per cent of the total borrowings whereas State Cooperative Banks borrowing from NABARD are to the extent of 79 per cent. The primary transaction cost advantage which the primary society was supposed to enjoy on account of the fact that its operations were spatially confined and restricted to a group of people who were the primary stakeholders has now been lost as the PACS must borrows from DCCB which in turn must borrow from SCB which is refinanced by NABARD. Furthermore, National Federation of State Cooperative Banks plays only a very nominal role in the business transaction—at best it is an advocacy group—implying higher transaction costs. Moreover, all the three tiers namely, State-District-Societies are operating in the same catchments and competing rather than collaborating for business. Furthermore, transfer of funds from NABARD to the primaries through the channel of State Cooperative Banks and District Central Cooperative Banks (DCCBs) is not only costly but also time consuming and worse leaves the borrowers totally dependent on external sources of funds.

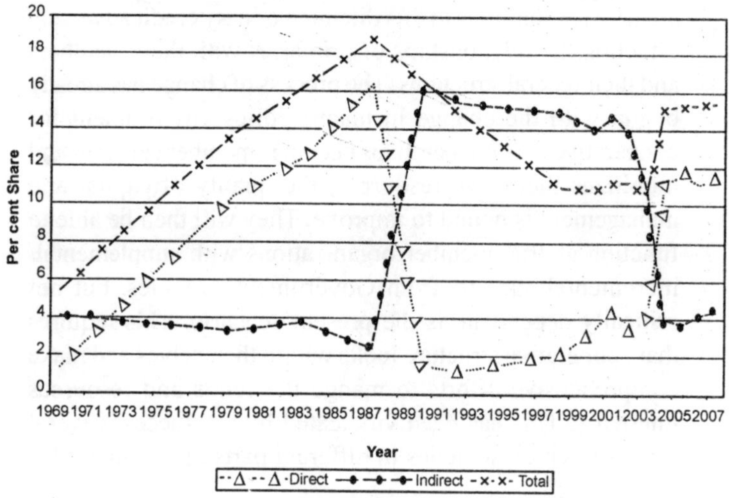


**Fig. 1.4:** Share of Agricultural Credit to Total Bank Credit

Inspite of leading role-played by NABARD in meeting agricultural credit, the future of cooperatives leave a question mark, especially because the relationship between the primaries and its federal structure has not evolved organically and the dependence of primaries on NABARD is getting more pronounced. Message is very clear:

> "*Without NABARD's support the entire structure of cooperatives would collapse!*"

Primaries are not mobilizing and distributing resources internally. There is a distinct move away from member centrality. Though there is no effect on cooperative scenario in the short-run, but in long-run it may have an adverse effect on primaries. Moreover both the structure of cooperative, that is, short-term as well as long-term, should be emerged into one entity so as to provide good governance and healthy competition in the banking sector. The biggest challenge to the cooperative sector in the area of agricultural credit is one of sustainability and relevance. In the absence of any transaction cost advantages to the primaries, the village level branch of a Commercial Bank or RRBs may find it easier to access funds from its own headquarters then the PACS. There are no easy solutions to this dilemma of easy credit adversely affecting the relationships of primaries with their members and their federal structures. The process of change has already begun with the change in macro policy environment for cooperatives. As cooperatives becomes member centered and mobilizes their own resources, the quality of capital and management is bound to improve. They will then be able to function as true member organizations with supplemental/ incremental support from Government agencies, but not critically dependent as the present scenario. This requires that cooperative structure looks within themselves and make comprehensive efforts to mange the funds and resources internally. This has been vindicated by the success several thrift and credit societies in different parts of the globe.”

**Debt Waiver and Debt Relief**

Acceleration of growth of agricultural sector will not only push the overall GDP growth upwards, but make the growth more inclusive. To provide impetus to this sector, Finance Minister introduces a plethora of schemes for the staggering farm community hoping for largesse in his agro-political economy based budget.

Indebtedness is one of the major factors for farmer's suicides and agrarian crisis. To give boost to the agricultural sector, the scheme of *Debt Waiver and Debt Relief* for farmers has been announced. All agricultural loans disbursed by scheduled commercial banks, regional rural banks and cooperative credit institutions up to March 31, 2007 and overdue as on December 31, 2007 will be covered under the scheme. The total vale of overdue loans being waived is estimated at Rs. 50,000 crores. For marginal and small farmers (holding up to 2 hectare), there will be a complete waiver of all loans that were over- due on December 31, 2007 and remained unpaid upto February 29, 2008. In respect of other farmers, there will be a *One Time Settlement* (OTS) scheme estimated at Rs. 10, 000 crores for all loans that were overdue on December 31, 2007 and remained unpaid up to

February 29, 2008. Under OTS, a rebate of 25 per cent will be given against payment of balance of 75 per cent. Agricultural loans which were rescheduled by banks in 2004 and 2006 through special package will also be eligible under this debt wavier and debt relief package. The implementation of this scheme will be completed by June 30, 2008 and farmers will be eligible for fresh loan upon being granted debt wavier or signing of an agreement for debt relief under the OTS.

The relief package has taken into account recommendations of the *Expert Group on Agriculture Indebtedness* chaired by Prof. R. Radhakrishna setup by the Ministry of Finance in August 2006 and submitted its report last year. The group's recommendations include rescheduling farm loans to all affected families, disbursement of fresh loans and waiver of interest liability by up to two years for both short and longterm loans with the burden be shared by the Central and States Governments. But the strong advocate of abolishing freebies has moved on the same path.

None of the committees' setup by the government on agricultural reforms and farmers welfare has ever recommended a complete waiver of loans. Rather they have always recommended relief on interest rates. Such a scheme will spoil the credit culture as those who have already paid their loans will take more loans and not repay them leading to high (NPA) non-performing assets of lending institutions. A loan waiver is a total disaster. Such waiver has never worked in the past, nor will this. It sets a wrong precedent and nation is going to pay a very heavy price for this misdeed. In fact had the government spent this waiver amount on constructing warehouses, irrigation canales, rural roads, power and other rural infrastructure farmers would have benefited much more? Providing remission of 25 per cent of the total loan even to big farmers seems to be taken in self interest of most of the brother MP's earning huge agriculture income. Providing huge benefit is a crime in the eyes of general public. One will never know how many of our affluent sections, including politicians own sizeable parcels of land. There area many business people or otherwise rich guys who have bought cheap waste land across the country and registered themselves as *Kisan* (farmers). They not only take loan but cheat the Government to pay their income tax with an excuse that they have lost whole of the harvest while they did not cultivate an inch or to say they don't even know where there land (so called farms) is. What about those farmers who have already paid or paying regularly? Will these small farmers get some kind of refund for their sincerity and hard work? Moreover, what about the farmers who have committed suicide? Budget should have some sops to such households.

There is still another problem. What about one-half of the farmers who are in debt to informal sources? Nearly 25 per cent farmers borrow from money-lenders *(arhtiyas)* who charges anywhere between 25 to 40 per cent interest per annum and even more. Most of the private money-lenders are local politicians and their relatives. They might have even lost their lands through foreclosure. Another 15 per cent borrow from traders and are forced to sell their produce to them at lower rates while paying the same rate of interest. Another 10 per cent borrow from relatives. C. Rangarajan *Committee on Farm Loans* reported that only one-fourth of total farm households are indebted to formal sources—of which one third also borrows from informal sources. The question arises: Why does the small farmer go to the private money-lenders rather than the public sector bank? It is because Indian banks had failed to serve the rural poor since nationalization of banks. Moreover, the local money-lenders know how to attract the farmers with individual attention. They will adapt the interest rate and terms of lending to make their loans attractive. Public sector, in contrast follows the philosophy of what may be called Kick Your Customers. There is urgent need to address the endemic corruption and inability of the public sector banks to serve the rural poor.

Government should have reduced interest rates on farm loans to 4 per cent and form a *National Debt Relief Commission*. Such a package will favour closure of rural banks. It is also not clear that waiver is available to all tiller or just the owner of agricultural land. Majority of farmers does not own land yet till land taken on contract. There is a strong need to increase the paying capacity of the farmers, otherwise waiver and relief package will further strengthen the poverty trap of the farmers. The real problem is that the per unit cost of production has increased even at constant prices. Efforts are required in this direction.

**Future Agenda**

Agenda for future, therefore, consist of:

- There is a strong need to revitalize rural cooperative and put on a sound business footing. Structural transformation taking place in the Indian economy has worked against the agricultural sector. Looking at the credit flow towards agriculture and allied sector, there is a positive hope of reverse migration taking place in the country. The villagers in the country will become prosperous and urbanities will like to go back to the villages for peaceful living.

- There is need for legal and institutional changes relating to governance, regulation, and functioning for rural cooperative structure and RRBs, who have to be critical instruments for rural credit in future. Both the structure of cooperative, namely, short-run and long run lending institutions must be merged into one entity to provide good governance and healthy competition in the baking sector. Furthermore, all the three tiers of cooperative, that is, state, district and primaries must function in collaboration with each other rather than competing. There is need to foster credit culture to make enhanced rural credit a lasting phenomenon. Rural credit system must be compatible with the goals of higher growth and better equity.
- The majority of rural households are with limited land resources coupled with small economic activity accompanied with poor technology. Lending by the formal financial institutions to the poor has been unsatisfactory. But their demand for credit has been rising due to growing family size, increased consumption requirements, social obligations and so on. But the institutional agencies not only lack of required mechanism to access their needs but also often look their demand for credit on their ground that their needs are for non-productive purposes. Besides, perceived high risks, transaction costs and absence of collateral security kept the poor away from the hold of formal financial institutions. To reach the poor, institutional innovations are needed. Banking infrastructure needs to re-orient its finance service for rural poor. Currently, Government has several developmental and anti-poverty programmes for the rural poor. To ensure that these programme benefit the poor farmers, farmers' organizations should have a role in their design, implementation and monitoring. This will also serve as a

platform for asserting their rights and for their economic improvement. The state should play a pro-active role in promoting such organizations.

- There is a need for comprehensive public policy on risk management in agriculture, not only as a means of relief for distressed farmers but as an ingredient for more efficient commercialization of agriculture. India would need new market institutions for risk mitigation. A future market is a step in the right direction, which needs to be strengthened. The key issue is minimizing the market risks for farmers for creating a scale of marketing the produce of the small farmers.
- There is overhang problem of non-performing loans and erosions of deposits in both cooperatives and RRBs. One time fiscal support is justifiable, urgent and essential, which has to be transparent. Current acceleration in credit delivery can be sustained in medium term provided rural cooperatives structure and RRBs are revived or reorganized and put in proper place.
- An independent and broad base research project may be undertaken to lessen the administrative loads and costs such as reduction in the documentations required in sanctioning the credit to farmers. Information technology can play a significant role in rural credit delivery system. Therefore, nature of technology suitable at various levels may be identified.
- Government should promulgate a Prevention of Atrocities on farmers and Farm Labourers Act for addressing usurious money-lending and land grabbing. Such an Act must stipulate that all lands grabbed by money-lenders in the last 10 to 15 years should be reverted back to the owners and there should be securitizing of money-lender's assets. Courts must be instructed to fast track such cases instituted under the Act. RBI should securities loan of legal money-lenders to farmers and take the assets pledged with money-lenders as their own security. For landless workers, banks should take over the loans on their books against the cash flow due to these people under NREGP.
- The declining growth rate in agriculture is something most serious. The 1990's have also seen a gradual decline in the

growth rates of many crops. The seed fertilizer technology seems to have exhausted and is no longer cost efficient. To boost agricultural growth rates, India needs massive investment in both the pubic as well as private investments. The public investment over the years has declined or stagnated. On the other hand, subsidies to agricultural sector have been blooming. There is a need to reverse the ratio (4:1) of investment to subsidies as marginal return in terms of agricultural growth and poverty alleviation are much higher through investment than subsidies.

Indian agricultural sector now must be managed like any other economic activity. Unless we bring all the best tools that are within our reach, that Information Technology (IT), Management Principles, Science and Technology etc. which could generate adequate incremental income. Corporate view rural markets with a huge potential for growth, the Government and policy-makers should consider giving agricultural lending a boost in order to create a huge market for other industries. The true picture of Rural India is the mix of scattered Islands of prosperity on one extreme and cases of starvation, deaths and suicides of farmers on another extreme. Looking at credit flow towards agriculture and allied activities, there is a positive hope of reverse migration taking place in the country. We can hope the villages in the country will become prosperous and urbanities will like to go back to the villages for peaceful living. The challenge before us, therefore, is not a small one. No great cause is achieved without even greater efforts. This is a great cause—one that can ennoble each of us just as freedom movement ennobled those who served it. It is a cause that can be achieved only if each of us plays a part, and it is a cause, that must be achieved because the future of our nation depends on it.

## REFERENCES

Capoor, Jagdish (1999), "Structural Reforms in Agriculture and Rural Development", *Reserve Bank of India Bulletin,* Vol. 53, No. 10, October.

Dandekar, V.M. (1993),"Limits of Credit, Non Credit Limits", *Economic and Political Weekly,* Vol. 38, No. 39, September.

Darling, M.L. (1925), *The Peasants in Prosperity and Debt,* Oxford University Press, Delhi.

Desai, Bhupat M. and N.V. Namboodri (1993), *Rural Financial Institutions: Promotions and Performance,* Oxford, New Delhi

Deasi, D.K. (1988), "Institutional Requirements for Agricultural Production: 2000 AD", *Indian Journal of Agricultural Economics,* Vol. 43, No. 3, July-September.

Gadgil, M.V. (1986), "Agricultural Credit in India: A Review of Performance and Policies", *Indian Journal of Agricultural Economics,* Vol. 3, No. 3, July-September.

Gadgil, M.V.(1992), "Future of Institutional Agricultural Credit in India: Likely Impact of Narsimham and Khusro Committee Reports", *Indian Journal of Agricultural Economics,* Vol. 47, No. 2, April-June

Government of India; *Economic Survey* (various Issues), Ministry of Finance, New Delhi

_______ (1991), *Report of the Committee on the Financial System,* (Chairman Mr. M. Narasimham) Ministry of Finance, New Delhi.

_______ (1998), *Report of the Committee on the Banking Sector Reforms,* (Chairman: Mr. M. Narasimham), Ministry of Finance, Government of India, New Delhi.

_______ (2002), *Report of the Working Group to Suggest Amendments in the Regional Rural Banks Act, 1976,* (Chairman: Mr. M.V.S. Chalapathi Rao), Ministry of Finance, Government of India, New Delhi.

_______ (2007), *Report of the Expert Group on Agricultural Indebtedness,* (Chairman Prof. R Radhakrishna), Ministry of Finance, Government of India, New Delhi.

Gulati, Ashok and Seema Bathla (2002), *Institutional Credit to Indian Agriculture: Defaults and Policy Options,* Occasional Paper 23, National Bank for Agriculture and Rural Development, Mumbai.

Indian Banks Association (2002) *Report on the Working Group on Agricultural Credit.*

Kainth, Gursharan Singh (1979) "Emerging *Pastern* of Cooperative Credit in Punjab", *The Indian Journal of Economics,* Vol. 59, No. 235, April.

Kainth, Gursharan Singh (1979), "Estimation of Demand for Credit in Punjab", *Indian Cooperative Review,* Vol. 16, No. 3, April

Kainth, Gursharan Singh (1998) "Agricultural Cooperative Credit in India", *The Cooperator*, Vol. XXXV, No. 8, February.

Kainth, Gursharan Singh (2005), "Rural Finance in India—Interface with Micro-Finance", paper presented at the 65th Annual Conference of Indian Society of Agricultural Economics organized by Department of Economics, Punjab Agricultural University, Ludhiana, November 24-26.

Kainth, Gursharan Singh (2006). "Institutional Credit for Agriculture—Issues and Future Agenda", *Key-note paper* presented at the NABARD and Planning Commission jointly sponsored National Seminar on *Rural Finance in India* organized by St. Soldier Management and Technical Institute, Jalandhar, March 30-31.

Kainth, Gursharan Singh (2006), "Innovation in Rural Financial System", paper presented at the Planning Commission and NABARD jointly sponsored National Seminar on *Rural Finance in India* organized by St. Soldier Management and Technical Institute, Jalandhar, March 30-31. Also published in *Kurukshetra,* Vol. 56, No. 6, April 2007.

Kainth, Gursharan Singh (2007), "Rural Finance in India", *Yojana,* February, 2007.

Kainth, Gursharan Singh (2008), "Budget 2008-09: New Era of Renaissance", *Kurukshetra,* Vol. 56, No. 6, April 2008.

Kainth, Gursharan Singh (2008),"Future Trading in Indian Agriculture", *Portfolio Organizer,* August.

Kainth, Gursharan Singh (2008), "Indian Food Price Crisis: Where lies the fault", *The Analyst*, July.

Kumar, Ranjana (2005), "Constraints Facing Indian Agriculture: Need for Policy Intervention", *Indian Journal of Agricultural Economics,* Vol. 60, No. 1, January-March.

Mohan, Rakesh (2004), "Agricultural Credit in India: Status, Issues and Future Agenda, Presidential Address delivered at the 17th National Conference of Agricultural Marketing, Indian Society of Agricultural Marketing Hyderabad on Feb 5, 2004 and Published in *Indian Journal of Agricultural Marketing,* Vol. 18, No. 1 January—April 2004.

Mohanty, Suchitra and T. Haque (2003), Regional Disparities in the Flow of Institutional Credit in India", *Journal of Rural Development*, Vol. 22, No. 1, January-March.

Mujumdar, N.A. (2001), *The New Architecture of the Rural Credit System,* Department of Economics, University of Mumbai, Mumbai, August.

NABARD Various issues of *Annual Reports.*

NABARD (1999), *Report of the Task Force on Supportive Policy and Regulatory Framework for Micro-finance,* National Bank for Agricultural and Rural Development, Mumbai, October.

NABARD (2001), *Report of the Expert Committee on Rural Credit,* National Bank for Agricultural and Rural Development, July, (Chairman: Dr. V.S. Vyas).

Puhazhendi, V. and B. Jayaraman,(1999), "Rural Credit Delivery: Performance and Challenges Before Banks", *Economic and Political Weekly*, Vol. 34, No. 3, January 16.

Rangarajan, C. (1996), "Rural India: The Role of Credit", *Reserve Bank of India Bulletin,* May.

Rao, C.H.H., (1994), "Policy Issues Relating to Irrigation and Rural Credit in India", in G.S. Bhalla ed., *Economic Liberalization and Indian Agriculture,* Institute for Studies in Industrial Development, New Delhi.

Rao, C.H.H., (2003), "Reform Agenda for Agriculture", *Economic and Political Weekly,* Vol. 38, No. 7, February 15.

RBI (1970) *History*, Reserve Bank of India, Mumbai.

______*Annual Reports* (Various issues).

_____(2000) *Functions and Working.*

_____*Handbook of Statistics on Indian Economy,* (Various Issues).

_____ *Report on Currency and Finance* (Various Issues).

_____*Report on Trend and Progress of Banking in India* (Various Issues).

_____*RBI Monthly Bulletin* (Various Issues).

_____ *All India Rural Debt and Investment Survey,* (Various Issues).

_____(1985) Report on the *Committee to Review the Working of Monetary System in India,* (Chairman: Prof. Sukhamoy Chakravarty).

_____(1991), Report of the *Committee on the Financial System,* (Chairman: M. Narsimham).

_____(1999) Report of *Task Force on Revival/Restructuring for Cooperative Banks (*Chairman: Sh. Jagdish Kapoor).

_____(1998), Report of the *High Level Committee on Agricultural Credit Through Commercial Banks* (Chairman: Sh. R.V. Gupta).

_____(2004), Report of the *Advisory Committee on Flow of Credit to Agricultural and Related Activities from Banking System* (Chairman: Prof. Vijay Shankar Vyas) June.

_____(2004), Report of the *Advisory Committee on the Flow of Credit to Agriculture,* (Chairman: Dr V.S. Vyas) May.

_____(1954), Report of the *All India Rural Credit Survey Committee: 1951-52 (*Chairman: A.D. Gorwala).

_____(1969), Report of the *All India Rural Credit Review Committee* (Chairman: B. Venkatappiah).

_____(1989), *Review of the All- India Agricultural Credit System in India: Report of the Agricultural Credit Review Committee* (Chairman: A.M. Khusro).

_____(2000), Report of the *Task Force to Study the Cooperative Credit System and to Suggest Measures for its Strengthening,*(Chairman: Jagdish Kapoor) August.

_____ ( ), Report of the *Committee on Cooperation in India: 1915* (Mac lagan Committee.

_____(2005), Report of the *Expert Group on Investment Credit* (Chairman: Y.S.P. Thorat).

_____(2004), Report of *Task Force on Revival of Cooperative Credit Institution,* (Chairman: Prof. A. Vaidyanathan).

_____(2006), *Financial Inclusion by Extension of Banking Services—Use of Business Facilitators and Correspondents,* Mumbai.

Namboodiri, N.V. (2003), Rapporteur's Report on "Agricultural Credit and Indebtedness", *Indian Journal of Agricultural Economics,* Vol. 60, No. 3, July-September.

Reddy, Y.V. (2004), "Rural Credit: Status and Agenda", *Reserve Bank of India Bulletin*, December

Shah, Mihir, Rangu Rao and P.S. Vijay Shankar (2007), "Rural Credit in 20th

Century India: Overview of History and Perspective", *Economic and Political Weekly*, Vol. 42, No. 15, April 14.

Sharma, Anil (2005), *The Kisan Credit Card Scheme: Impact, Weakness and Further Reforms*, National Council of Applied and Economic Research, New Delhi.

Sidhu, R.S. and Sucha Singh Gill (2006), Agricultural Credit and Indebtedness in India: Some Issues", *Indian Journal of Agricultural Economics*, Vol. 61, No. 1, January-March.

Subramanian, K. and T.K. Velaudham (1997), *Banking Reform in India: Managing Change*, Tata McGraw Hill, New Delhi.

Singh, Surjit and Vidya Sagar, (2004), *Agricultural Credit in India: Status of the Indian Farmers*, Ministry of Agriculture, Government of India and Academic Foundation, New Delhi.

Tewari, S. K. (2007) Rapporteur's Report on Trends in Rural Finance, *Indian Journal of Agricultural Economics*, Vol. 62, No. 3, July-September.

Thorat, Y.S.P. (2006), "Rural Credit in India: Issues and Concerns", Presidential Address delivered at the 65th Annual Conference of Indian Society of Agricultural Economics held at Punjab Agricultural University, Ludhiana on November 24, 2005 and published in *Indian Journal of Agricultural Economics*, Vol. 61, No. 1, January—March.

# 2

# Rural Credit in India–Status, Issues and Future Agenda

SWAMI PRAKASH SRIVASTAVA

*Rural finance is important in an agrarian economy like India where 70 per cent of the population depends upon agriculture for its livelihood. Finance being the lifeblood of every commercial venture, availability of adequate funds at reasonable terms is a must to ensure speedy economic development. The demand for rural credit in India is anticipated to grow rapidly considering the envisaged high growth in the agricultural sector, greater market orientation, and the emerging importance of subsidiary activities. Meeting this growing demand is a challenging task. A large potential exists in both demand and supply of rural credit. However the existence of potential is not a sufficient conditions unless it is translated into actual demand and improving the present credit delivery system. In other words the convergence of credit availability, credit delivery system and the credit absorbing capacity of the farming households must be achieved. But the rural financial institutions since the start of the 1990s were characteristics by several weaknesses. The policy pursued today is to pump in credit to the indebted poor households without adequately addressing the problems of the not indebted ones. This paper tries to explore the issues of growth of institutional agricultural credit in India, its distribution in different regions and accessibility of credit to rural poor especially small and marginal farmers and economic viability of the operations of agricultural credit disbursement in terms of recovery performance and margins. The degree of indebtedness and factors causing indebtedness and suicides was also studied in Punjab, Andhra Pradesh, Maharashtra, Tamil Nadu and other States.*

## Introduction

Finance is an essential requirement for almost every activity. Both producers and consumers in rural as well as urban areas need finance for their day to day requirement and for all productive activities. In rural areas of India, credit requirements are more pressing. Rural population is composed of agricultural producers, tenant cultivators, village artisans, landless labour, etc. All these categories are in need of credit. Among the agricultural producers, the earning of small and marginal farmers and tenant cultivators are not sufficient to meet even the minimum requirement of life. In their ease, the prospects of 'plough back' are very weak. Therefore, they need credit not only for productive purpose but also for day to day minimum consumption purposes. The industrial producers too need credit but agricultural producers have certain peculiar problems and therefore, financing of agricultural sector is associated with certain special problems.

The administered allocation of credit to priority sectors at concessional interest rate is an important policy dimension of directed credit programme. The rational for this policy was that, without Government intervention through directed credit programme, banks would not finance those activities with high social return or those categories of credit worthy people who are marginalized in the credit market. (Stiglits, 1994). The directed credit policies in India have been used to promote agriculture and small scale industry. Agriculture has been targeted because it is a risky activity and households are credit rationed by the formal banking sector (Swaminathan 1991; Kochar 1997). It has always been maintained that the availability of concessional credit would help the farmer to adopt new technology, encourage investment in machinery and irrigation and augment the use of quality inputs to increase agricultural productivity. These, commercial and cooperative banks were directed to expand their rural branch networks and intensify their lending to agriculture.

The institutional structure of rural banking as it is today in India, consists of four sets of institutions, viz, the commercial banks both nationalized and others, a three tier federal cooperative banking with the state cooperative bank at the state level, district cooperative central banks at the district level and the primary agricultural credit societies at the village level (in some of the smaller states, the structure is two tier with the SCB at the state level and the PACs at the village level), the State Cooperative Agriculture and Rural Development Banks (SCARBDs) with primary cooperative agriculture and rural development banks affiliated to them or supported by a network of branches at the taluka/block level and finally the regional rural banks (RRBs). This multi-agency approach was introduced after the nationalization of the banks and has come to stay. The cooperative banks give short and medium term loans and the SCARBDs and the PCARDBs extend medium and long-term loans, while RRBs focus primarily on the small and marginal farmers, agricultural labourers and rural artisans. The commercial banks in addition to general banking functions are bound by the guidelines issued by the RBI to lend 40 per cent of the aggregate credit to the priority sector. These banks are expected to have 18 per cent of their net outstanding bank credit to the agricultural sector of which 75 per cent has to be for direct agriculture.

Inspite of the various measures to rejuvenate farm credit, the flow of credit to agricultural sector remained quantitatively and qualitatively poor. The institutional sources of credit meet 51 per cent of the credit requirement of the farm sector (Rao, 2003). The non-institutional sources were mainly approached by the farmers due to lack of security assets with them, frequent needs, inadequate supply of institutional credit, undue delays, sophisticated procedure and malpractices adopted by institutional lending agencies (Singh, 1971; Singh H, 1971; Sharma, 1978; Nathatkar *et al.*, 2002; Rao, 2003).

This paper tries to explore the issues of growth of institutional agricultural credit in India, its distribution in different regions and accessibility of credit to rural poor especially small and marginal farmers and economic viability of the operations of agricultural credit disbursement in terms of recovery performance and margins. The paper is divided into eleven sections. The second section is devoted to Review of Literature, The third section presents the Historical

Overview of Rural Credit, and the fourth section deliberates on Demand and Supply of Rural Credit. The fifth section presents the Micro Finance and Kisan Credit Card. The sixth section discusses about the role of rural credit by Commercial Banks. The seventh section presents the role of RRBs in rural credit. The eighth section devoted to Co-operative Credit. Section ninth presents the Prime Minister Rojgar Yojana and Rural Credit. The tenth section devoted to problem of Rural Credit and the eleventh section present the suggestions and finally a summary and the conclusions are presented in the last section.

## Review of Literature

The effectiveness of directed credit programmes in stimulating investments, raising growth and reducing poverty was often debated (Naastepad, 2001). It was argued that directed credit programme was inferior to a market-based allocations of resources in achieving growth and redistributive objectives (World Bank 1989, Odedokun 1996; Yaron et al 1998). Hence, notwithstanding the empirical support for the positive growth effects of directed credit in both agriculture and small scale industry, the recent financial reforms in India sought to phase out the directed credit programme (Shajahan 1999; Naastepad 2001). Several studies have been carried out focusing on the rural credit including indebtedness of rural as well as farmers' households in India (for detail see, Shivamaggi, 1986; Gadgil, 1986; Desai, 1987; Desai 1988; Mujumdar 1988; Singh and Sager 2004). Some studies have analyzed the interlink-age of land, labour and credit (Bardhan and Rudra, 1978; Bardhan 1980; Sarap, 1991; Binswanger and Rosenzweig, 1986) while other have analysed the intensity of indebatedness among the rural households (Gothaskar, 1988; Tandon, 1986; Narayanmurthy, 2001). Quite a few studies have been carried out on the indebtedness of rural and urban households using the data available from the decadal *All India Debt and Investment Surveys*.

## Historical Overview of Agricultural Credit

Agriculture in India has always been heavily dependent on the monsoons and has hence been an inherently risky activity. At different times we have also had onerous rural tax systems under different empires, most recently under the British. Indigenous systems of credit had to develop as a consequence of seasonal needs and fluctuations in order to facilitate smoothing of the consumption pattern of farmers over the year. With intermittent failures of the monsoons and other customary vicissitudes of farming, rural indebtedness has been a serious and continuous characteristics of Indian agriculture. Because of the high risk inherent in traditional farming activity rather than the exception, and concomitant exploitations and misery often resulted. Development of rural credit systems has therefore been found to be intrinsically very difficult and as we will see, an issue of continuing official concern for over a century.

These problems began to engage the attention of even the British colonial government as early as the 1870s; the practice of extending institutional credit to agriculture can be traced back to that period when farmers were provided with such credit by the government during drought years. Thinking about co-operative credit, co-operation began in the latter part of the 19th century. Finally, the Co-operative Societies Act was passed in 1904 and Co-operatives were seen as the premier institutions for disbursing agricultural credit. "For some decades, that is, since long before the organization of the Reserve Bank, great faith has been placed in India in the potentialities of the Co-operative organization to serve the credit needs of the country, especially of the rural sector".

India may perhaps be one of the very few countries in the world which is during the last three decades introduced several policies in the sphere of agriculture and rural development through assigning the pivotal role to the banking systems. In this process, the very structure and texture of Indian banking has been metamorphically changed which one can not imagine. Following changes that Government had initiated. Realizing the fact that Co-operative credit structure can not deliver the expected amount of credit, not only country's largest bank "the State Bank of India" (earlier Imperial Bank of India) was asked to lend to agriculture in 1956 but also 14 private commercial banks were nationalized for this purpose in 1969 and other eight in 1981. To meet unsatisfied credit demand from rural areas, 196 regional rural banks have been established from 1975 onwards.

To augment long-term lendable resources for investment in agriculture, the Agriculture Refinance Corporation (ARC) was set up in 1964, which was converted into the Agricultural Refinance and Development Corporation (ARDC) for providing technical expertise to banks and entrepreneurs willing to invest in agriculture. Since July

1982, ARDCs scope of activities has been expanded to cover entire gamut of activities related to agriculture, Tiny/village industries, non-farm sector and rural development renamed as the NABARD as Apex Bank for the country for this purpose.

## Demand and Supply of Rural Credit

The demand for rural credit in India is anticipated to grow rapidly considering the envisaged high growth in the agricultural sector, greater market orientation, and the emerging importance of subsidiary activities. Meeting this growing demand is a challenging task. A large potential exists in both demand and supply of rural credit. However the existence of potential is not a sufficient conditions unless it is translated into actual demand and improving the present credit delivery system. In other words the convergence of credit availability, credit delivery system and the credit absorbing capacity of the farming households must be achieved. But the rural financial institutions since the start of the 1990s were characteristics by several weaknesses. The policy pursued today is to pump in credit to the indebted poor households without adequately addressing the problems of the not indebted ones.

It was observed that the investment credit has been losing its share in the total credit portfolio since the early 1990s. Cooperative institutions have showed relatively low growth in credit dispensions to the agricultural sector as compared with the Commercial Banks and Regional Rural Banks. This has resulted in the decline in the share of cooperatives in total credit flow. Besides there was decline in the number of small farm households covered by the formal credit institutions, Regional imbalance in the flow of credit has also been rising alarmingly. The outreach of formal agricultural credit institutions seems to be inadequate to the poor, small and marginal farmers as well as in the agriculturally less developed regions.

## Micro finance

The ineffectiveness of the vast network of banks and other financial institutions, the failure of poverty alleviation programmes, and that of primary cooperatives and Regional Rural Banks, specially established to meet the needs of the rural sector and the poor, led to the entrance of Non-Government Organizations (NGOs) into micro finance. A good definition of micro-finance as provided by Robinson is, 'micro-finance refers to small scale financial services for both credits and deposits—that are provided to people who farm or fish or herd; operate small or micro-enterprises where goods are produced, recycled, repaired or traded; provide services; work for wages or commissions; from renting out small amounts of lands, vehicles, draft animals, or machinery and tools; and to other individuals and local groups in developing countries, in both urban and rural areas'. The banks are well on their way to achieving the target set down by NABARD to finance a third of India's rural poor through Self-Help Groups (SHGs) by 2007. A cumulative Rs. 4,000 crore has been disbursed to these groups of mostly poor, rural women with an average amount of Rs. 36,000 per groups. This is a non-trivial amount considering the loans are unsecured and the groups with an average of 15 members, totally informal. SHGs take loans from Banks/ Voluntary agencies/Self-Help promoting institutions to meet the needs of the farm women. The SHG itself with the help of NGO makes assessment of individual credit needs of its members and submits to the bank for sanction of collective loans in its name. The NGO helps the SHG in procuring raw materials and also marketing of produce. The entire loan amount disbursed to the SHG is represented by NABARD to the financing Bank. Emphasis therefore shifted from the rapid disbursement of subsidized loans to target populations, towards the building of local sustainable institution to serve the poor.

The efficacy and potential of the Co-operative movement in addressing the problems of rural India stand proved. Since rural development essentially encompasses a multi-disciplinary approach, there must be an inbuilt mechanism to evolve people's representations in the conceptualization, planning and management of any rural development programme, water conservation and minor irrigation. Self-help is the best help. Self-help groups are examples of the new "social economy" emerging in India. Collectively they represent a large network of grassroots entrepreneurs to generate incomes in rural areas. Today there are more than 25 lakhs SHGs with nearly 75 lakhs "*swarojgaris*". We must encourage them, for they can transform rural India by unleashing the entrepreneurial energies of ordinary Indians.

The proposed amendment to the National Bank for Agriculture and Rural Development Act, 1981 that seeks to provide a formal framework for the micro-finance sector does not take a gender or empowerment perspective, but rather, a supply dominated view of micro-finance. With the objectives of extending the outreach of micro-finance, the bill seeks to enables trusts and charitable societies to take deposits from individuals and SHGs, subject to their authorization by NABARD as Micro Finance Organizations. However, these organizations are not "banking" institutions, nor Non-Banking Financial Companies (NBFCs), because they neither have the required capital nor the ability to ensure compliance with RBI's norms. They have been allowed a lower level of capitalization of Rs. 5 lakhs according to the Amendment. The Amendment fails to recognize the fact that public sector banks have extended outreach to women's SHGs tremendously over the past few years. (Ghosh, 2005), making the SHG-bank linkage programme of India the largest in the world, having provided loans to over one million SHGs so far.

**Table 2.1:** SHGs provided with Bank Loans

| *Banks* | *Cumulative Nos. of SHGs provided with Bank Loans upto March 2001* | *Cumulative Nos. of SHGs provided with Bank Loans upto March 2004* |
|---|---|---|
| Public Sector Banks | 118855 | 516697 |
| Private Sector Banks | 5391 | 21725 |
| Regional Rural Banks | 84775 | 405998 |
| Co-operative Banks | 12773 | 134671 |
| Total | 2217494 | 1079091 |

*Source*: NABARD cited in Ghosh (2005).

## Kisan Credit Card Scheme (KCCs)

The introduction of KCC Scheme in the year 1998-99 has been one among the recent innovation in loan products. The purpose of the KCC scheme is to facilitate short-term credit to farmers. At the all-India-level, the cumulative number of Kisan Credit Cards (KCCs) issued by all the implementing agencies as on March 31, 2004, stood at 413.79 lakhs (Government of India, 2003-04), and the corresponding figure for Punjab was 13.88 lakhs. The KCC aims at extending adequate and timely support from banking system to the farmers, to meet the crop production and ancillary activities. The credit limit (loan) is sanctioned in proportion to the size of own land but some flexibility is also provided for the farmer cultivating leased–in land in addition to the owned holding. Further the borrowing limit is fixed on the basis of proposed cropping pattern. Most of the banks are adhering to the Scales of Finance

(SOF) decided by the State Level Bankers Committee (SLBC) but some banks have fixed their own SOF, which are in all cases higher than those, recommended by SLBC. The nature of credit extended under KCCs is revolving cash credit, i.e. it provides for any number of withdrawals and repayments within the limit. This feature would provide flexibility and reduce the interest burden upon the KCCs beneficiary. Security and margins norms would be in conformity with the guidelines issued by the RBI and NABARD from time to time. With effect from 2001-02 it was made obligatory for the implementing agencies to operate the KCC with an in-built component of life insurance for KCCs beneficiary. The KCCs as envisaged has substituted all other existing, institutional modes of short-term credit delivery.

The KCCs scheme is being implemented in all the State and Union Territories through all Commercial Banks, RRBs, State Co-operative Banks, Central Co-operative Banks and Primary Co-operative Banks. KCCs schemes has made swift progress since its inception with the banking sectors issuing more than 642.49 lakhs cards with cumulative credit of Rs. 1,11,459 crores sanctioned up to December 31, 2006. The implementation has been taken up by all the PSBs, Co-operative Banks and RRBs throughout the country. The Co-operative Sector Banks account for 50 per cent of KCCs issued and 63 per cent of the amount sanctioned. Highest number of KCCs was issued by co-operative banks (31.9 lakhs), followed by commercial banks (243.71 lakhs) and RRBs (79.18 lakhs). Among all the states of Indian Union, Punjab lead the chart with highest KCCs penetration ratio of 118.17 per cent against All-India averages of 32.44 per cent. Haryana follows Punjab at 85.75 per cent and Andhra Pradesh at 62.23 per cent. More than 100 penetration ratio in case of Punjab implies that some operational holdings have more than one KCCs.

Growing popularity of KCCs scheme reflects its effectiveness in ensuring hassle-free and timely operations as well as availability of credit with minimum transactions costs and documentations. In order to safeguard the interest of KCCs holders coverage under Personal Accident Insurance Scheme (PAIS). NABARD has allowed discretion to the banks to opt for any of the insurance company of their choice at competitive rates/terms. Further banks has been advised to ensure that KCCs continue to be renewed in a hassle-free manner and to direct their efforts towards ensuring quality in operations and more importantly crop loans are routed only through KCCs.

National Council of Applied Economic Research (NCAER) at the instance of RBI conducted a survey for assessing the impact of

KCCs scheme. National Impact Assessment Survey shows that KCCs had augmented flows of credit to agricultural sector, about 6 per cent decrease in the cost of borrowing for farmers after they were given KCCs, cost of the borrowing for KCCs, holders from formal sector is about 3 per cent lower than those of non-KCCs holders, significant decline in the number of borrowers depending exclusively on non-formal sources for their short-term credit needs, reduction in cost of borrowing from informal source by about 3 per cent, significant saving in-time spent in obtaining short-term agricultural loans and finally decline in cost delivering due to simplified procedure. The survey also had identified certain areas requiring policy initiative to make the scheme more effective. These relates to restrictions imposed on the issuance of KCCs by Banks, restrictions on the use of KCCs only at the card issuing branches, non-availability of incentives for timely repayments, low-credit limits and low awareness regarding the provisions of personal accident insurance scheme. RBI has advised the Indian Bankers Association to examine these suggestions and come up with remedial measures. Keeping in view the directive of Government of India for doubling the flow of credit to agriculture, NABARD advised the Co-operative and Regional Rural Banks to identify and bring into their fold such farmers including defaulters, oral lessees, tenant farmers, share croppers who may have been outside the fold of scheme for any reason as also new farmers. KCCs need to be promoted as a single window for comprehensive rural credit delivery. In the recent past, NABARD has enlarged the scope of KCCs by including even long-term loans for agriculture and allied activities under its purview. In addition to this, KCCs schemes have been extended to long-term borrowers of the Cooperative credit structure too.

## Commercial Banks and Rural Credit

Rural India has vast potential to increase the banking activities. Only 30 per cent of the rural households have so far availed banking facilities. Remaining 70 per cent of the families do not know what is banking. At least 50 per cent of them can be given finances for self employment schemes, housing and other non-farm activities. The role of Commercial Banks in agriculture and rural finance was negligible till very recently. It was paradoxical that the agricultural sector, which support a vast majority and which contributes nearly 30 per cent to India's national income is not receiving adequate credits support from the organized money markets in India. As per the All India Rural Debt and Investment Survey of 1989, the institutional share in the total borrowings by the cultivators is 62 per cent. Of this, the share of Co-operatives is around 31 per cent and the rest about 30 per cent is by Commercial Banks, RRBs and Government. During the Economic Reform Phase, credit lending by Commercial Banks to priority sectors including agriculture, declined from 39 to 32 per cent. The credit from Commercial Banks to agriculture declined from 15.3 per cent in 1991 to 12.5 per cent in 1997.

At present, Scheduled Commercial Banks (excluding RRBs) are expected to ensure that priority sector advances constitute 40 per cent of net bank credit and within the overall lending target of 40 per cent, 8 per cent of net bank credit goes to the agricultural sector. To ensure that the focus of banks on direct agricultural advances does not get diluted, lending under indirect finance should not exceed one-fourth of the agricultural sub-target of 18 per cent. i.e. 4.5 per cent of net bank credit.

The lack of proportion between lending in rural areas and the other sectors is very clear. Out of the total borrowers of 5.42 crore, 45 per cent are in rural India but they account for only 13.4 per cent of outstanding loans. As against this, 15 per cent of the loanees from metros got 54 per cent of the overall lending. 98.5 per cent of the rural borrowers operate small borrowed accounts with credit limit below Rs. 1 lakh. As on March 2003, the total agricultural advances by public and private sector banks were only 15.34 per cent and 10.78 per cent respectively, against, the target of 18 per cent. Credit/Deposit Ratio in rural areas by all banks were very low: 42.7 per cent banks (Public Sector Banks (PSBs) and 33.32 per cent for private sector banks. The total number of branches in the rural areas fell from 35,329 to 32,381 during the economic reforms period up to June 2003. Of these branches, 96.5 per cent are public sector banks and the rest 3.5 per cent belong to old private sector banks. Now private banks and foreign banks have nothing to do with rural banking.

These rural branches managed to tap deposits to the tune of Rs. 177,000 crore (13.8 per cent of the total deposits) but credit disbursement in these areas was only Rs. 75,000 crore (9.9 per cent only), indicating transfer of rural funds to urban areas at the cost of the credit starved priority sector. Instead of deploying the low cost rural funds to the rural development. It is siphoned off to big business in urban and metro areas. Incidentally, the credit deposit ratio in the rural sector is only 42.5 per cent compared to 83 per cent in metros.

Rural banking system in India being the most unparallel in the world has been providing product and investment credit in agricultural sector. Besides, public sector banks also provides credit facilities for a wide range of activities concerning to socio-economic development of rural population. Loan facilities for purposes such as consumption, housing, personal, consumer-durables and the like are considered. For meeting credit needs of agriculture sector, a target of 18 per cent of Net Bank Credit (NBC) in case of 22 public sector banks and SBI with its seven Associates–Banks has been stipulated. For catering to the credit needs of weaker sections of the society, 10 per cent target of NBC has also been prescribed. In order to ensure continuous supply of credit to this sector, Cash Reserve Ratio (CRR) has now been brought down to 9 per cent of Demand and Time liability of public sector banks. Banks also provide huge sum of credit every year to a very large number of poor belonging to weaker sections of the society under government sponsored programmes of poverty alleviation and generation of self-employment.

**Table 2.2:** Outstanding Agricultural Advances by Commercial Banks

| | *Public Sector Banks* | | *Private Sector Banks* | |
|---|---|---|---|---|
| *Year* | *Amount Outstanding (Rs. in Crore)* | *Per cent of Net Bank Credit* | *Amount Outstanding (Rs. in Crore)* | *Per cent of Net Bank Credit* |
| 1998-99 | 37,632 | 14.2 | 3,467 | 9.1 |
| 1999-00 | 45,269 | 14.3 | 4,023 | 8.3 |
| 2000-01 | 53,577 | 15.7 | 5,634 | 9.6 |
| 2001-02 | 58,142 | 14.8 | 6,581 | 8.5 |
| 2002-03 | 70,501 | 14.5 | 9,924 | 10.9 |
| 2003-04 | 86,187 | 15.4 | 17,652 | 12.3 |
| 2004-05 | 1,12,475 | 15.7 | 21,473 | 12.1 |

*Note*: 18 per cent of net bank credit should be provided for Agricultural Sector.
*Source*: *RBI Annual Report* 2004, p. 137 and 2005, p. 118.

It is a sorry state of affairs that banks have not designed products, which really meet the needs of rural population. From time to time, Government has introduced rural development schemes which have become products for bankers. Now, banks will have to constantly survey and search for new products which suit to different strata of rural population area-wise and time span-wise. Their constant rapport with Agricultural Universities, NGOs, rural population, rural traders, teachers, different size of land-holders will help fully understand the types of new products rural clients' need which banks could design, provide, test and modify suitably.

**Regional Rural Banks in Rural Credit (RRBs)**

Among the various institutional agencies engaged in rural finance, Regional Rural Bank (RRBs) play a significant role in financing the target group in the rural sector. They are specially designed financial institutions working under the guidance of NABARD and the parent commercial banks, spread in rural areas with a close network of branches serving a particular district or region. In view of the grave neglect of the rural sector banking by the commercial banks, it is imperative to identify alternative sources of credit to the rural population. It is a matter of great urgency to reduce the urban rural credit gap, which is presently 86:14. Provision of adequate credit is inevitable for the development of agriculture and other priority sectors as well as to generate rural employment. The regional rural banks are the best suited under the present conditions to champion the cause of rural finance.

Banks can be regarded as one of the most important contribute of 20th century because it is the institutions which first mobilize savings and then chanelises each paisa is made possible. Bank is equally important for all classes of people, rural or urban or poor, modern or traditional. Since our country is a land of the poor, the recommendations of Narhimahan Group, (1975), for setting up of Grameen Bank as small man's bank is really a right approach for development of the whole country. Since its inception in 1975, the Grameen Banks are continuously playing a pivotal role in development of rural areas. They not only provide financial help to needy people, but also develop banking culture in these areas.

RRBs are established under the Rural Banks Act, 1976 as part of the efforts of Government to devise alternate agencies to provide institutional credit to rural people. With a view to examining various aspects of the functioning of RRBs and making recommendations so as to enables these banks to function effectively in the wake of the financial sector reforms, the Government set up a committee to suggest amendments in the RRB Act, 1976 under the chairmanship of MVS

Chalapathy Rao, Managing Director, NABARD, in July 2001. In its report submitted in June, 2002, the committee recommended:

1. Change in capital structure and ownership pattern,
2. Enlarged role of sponsors banks,
3. Computer-based management system,
4. Introduction of asset-liability and risk management system,
5. Additional supervisory authority, and
6. Introduction of capital adequacy norms in a phased manner.

At the end of March 2004, there were 196 RRBs deployed 26 states in India, having 14, 446 branches out of which 11,989 branches are situated in rural areas, covering 518 districts. It has been explicitly stated in RRBs Act that such banks shall, in particular, extend financial assistance to small and marginal farmers and agricultural labourers whether individually or in group and to cooperative societies, Agricultural Marketing Societies or for other purposes connected therewith. It may be seen from Table 2.3 that in 1994, 46.7 per cent of total advances granted to farm sector. In 2005, 50.8 per cent of total advances granted to farm sector. An analysis of last ten years of agricultural credit by RRBs indicates that they provided an average of 47 per cent of total advances to agricultural sector. This means RRBs are the banks for agriculture.

**Table 2.3:** Outstanding Agricultural Credit by RRBs (Rs. Crore)

| *Year* | *Agricultural Advances* | *Percentage to Total* |
|---|---|---|
| 1994 | 2,560 | 46.7 |
| 1995 | 3,009 | 47.8 |
| 1994 | 3,467 | 46.1 |
| 1994 | 4,044 | 46.3 |
| 1994 | 4,683 | 47.5 |
| 1994 | 5,460 | 48.1 |
| 2000 | 6,227 | 47.5 |
| 2001 | 7,217 | 45.7 |
| 2002 | 8,405 | 45.2 |
| 2003 | 10,261 | 46.3 |
| 2004 | 11,722 | 44.9 |
| 2005 | 16,710 | 50.8 |

*Note*: 18 per cent of net bank credit should be provided for Agricultural Sector.

*Source*: RBI Report on *Trend and Progress of Banking in India*, Various Issues from 1994 to 2005.

RRBs were major instrument of finance inclusion as they provided credit to farmers, artisans and rural traders. Out of nearly 600 districts across the country, the RRBs set up are present in 525 districts. As on March 31, 2006, the total number of RRB branches across the country stood at 14,494 with deposit and advances growth rates of 12 per cent and 21 per cent respectively. The growth opportunities were infinite in view of the increased demand for rural credit. However, there were still 40 RRBs with negative net worth. With the process of consolidation and amalgamation launched in 2005 the number of RRBs stood reduced from 196 to 133 as on March 31, 2006, and further 102 till date. According to official data on RRBs for the last three years, their total business increased from Rs. 82,463.94 crore in 2003-04 to Rs. 1,11,041.40 crore in 2005-06. The disbursal of farm loans also doubled from Rs. 7,174.97 crore in 2003-04 to Rs.15,298.88 crore in 2005-06.

RRBs have emerged as the third arm for developing rural credit. RRBs would undertake an aggressive branch expansion programme and in 2007-08 open at least one branch in the 80 uncovered districts of the country. Regional Rural Bank (RRBs) with negative net worth may get recapitalization support from the centre soon. Union Finance Minister P. Chidambaram has proposed such capital support in a phased manner. This will help some 31 RRBs across the country whose operations are being constrained as they operate with negative net worth. According to data available with the NABARD, these banks will collectively need a capital support of Rs. 1,700 crore. While this move would help these banks in particular, the Finance Minister has also outlined a few measures for strengthening RRBs as a cluster. If this proposal gets approved, the RRBs will be allowed to access NRE and FCNR deposits from people working outside the country. These banks will also allow using the securitization and reconstruction of financial assets and Enforcement of Securities Interest (Sarfaesi) Act for recovering Non Performing Assets (NPAs). At present, there are 96 RRBs operating in the country and they collectively have a gross NPA of Rs. 2,890.47 crore, which is 7.28 per cent of gross advances as on March 31, 2006. The gross NPA, however, declined from 8.53 per cent in 2004-05. "The RRBs need to play a critical role in the financial inclusion drive. In this regard, the proposals to strengthen the set up of RRBs by expanding and deepening their role are positive steps. The rural mass in general will be benefited if RRBs expand their branch network and access NRE and FCNR deposits. At the same time, scores of migrant labourers working outside the country will be able to remit monies through RRBs.

This, to accompany the process of State-wide amalgamation of RRBs in many areas than has reduced their number from 196 to just 102 by end of Oct. 2006. The logic of this latter process is to enable the RRBs to function in a competitive environment by taking advantage of economies of scale and reducing transaction costs. Unfortunately, this strategy is based on a series of myths-infect, inclusion requires us to get beyond these myths, far from being amalgamated in order to make them efficient. RRBs need action to make them functional in relation to their original objectives. This needs two simple drastic measures.

First, decontrol of interest rates in small value loans so that banks, rural or commercial can lend to weaker sections at rates that cover their costs. Since commercial banks would be unable to compete with the lower salaries, and local knowledge of rural bank staff. This would provide the latter with a substantial advantage in this, their natural market segment.

Second, and equally important, the message for the weaker sections, of the loan Mela culture of the 1980's was that a RRBs loan was *Sarkari Paisa* (government money), and therefore, not necessary *not* returnable. Times have changed but an equivocal approach to soft loans remains. The way to change this, and to improve RRBs efficiency at the same time, is to render the image palpably untrue; privatize the RRBs and no one will be able to characterize RRBs money as not returnable.

Finally, the effect of amalgamation even if, the significantly greater efficiency was to be achieved the RRBs objective of financial inclusion would not be. It is well established that making small loans is widely uneconomical in the present restricted interest rates regime and at the PLRs prevailing in the commercial banking sector. The more efficient and competitive amalgamated RRBs would chase the same customs profile as the commercial banks and the financially excluded "Weaker Section" would continue to weaken.

## Co-operatives–Recipe for Revival

The Co-operatives were the only agencies providing institutional credit to rural sector till the commercial banks emerged on the scene in a big way. The Co-operative credit structure in India has two main wings—

the long-term credit structure and short-term credit structure. Long term credit is provided generally by a two-tier structure comprising the State Co-operative Agricultural and Rural Development Banks and Primary Co-operative Agricultural and Rural Development Banks. Short term credit, on the other hand, is provided by a three-tier structure of State Co-operative Banks, District Central Co-operative Banks and Primary Agricultural Credit Societies. During the year 2002-03, the share of Co-operative Banks was 55 per cent as short- term credit and in respect of medium and long-term loans; the share of Co-operative Bank was 28 per cent. Table 2.4 exhibits rural credit granted by Co-operative Bank from the years 1997-98 to 2002-03. It is clear from the table that average 42 per cent of the agricultural credit is provided by the cooperatives. The volume of disbursement by the cooperative banks shows a steady upward trend. During 2003-04, the total flow of agricultural credit has reported to be Rs. 80,000 crore.

**Table 2.4:** Agricultural Credit by Co-operative Banks

| *Years* | *Agricultural Credit (in Crore)* | *Percentage to total Agricultural Credit* |
|---|---|---|
| 1997-98 | 14,085 | 44 |
| 1998-99 | 15,957 | 43 |
| 1999-00 | 18,363 | 40 |
| 2000-01 | 20,784 | 39 |
| 2001-02 | 27,080 | 42 |
| 2002-03 | 35,111 | 43 |

*Note*: 1ɛ per cent of net bank credit should be provided for Agricultural Sector.

*Source*: Valsamma Antony, "Co-Operative Banks in Grip of NPAs", *Southern Economist*, Feb. 15, 2005.

Various committees that examined the problems of agricultural credit, while recognizing the role of commercial banks, without exception concluded that in the Indian conditions there was no alternative to the Co-operatives at the village level for the provision of agricultural credit. The rural credit survey committee (1954) has made the historical statement the "cooperatives have failed, but the cooperation must succeed". Concerned at this state of affairs, the Government constituted a special task force to suggest and "implementable action programme" for the revival of cooperatives. While its diagnosis of the weaknesses and the remedies were not very different from earlier committees, it broke new ground in several important respects.

The Common Minimum Programme of the UPA Government promised several measures to redress the perceived neglect of agriculture. Important among them was a large expansion in rural credit. The Cooperatives Credit structure was expected to play a significant role in this undertaking. However, the structure was too weak and debilitated a state to do so. Nearly half of the primary agricultural cooperatives society and a third of the District Central Cooperative Banks are incurring losses; recovery rates are very low; accumulated losses are huge and the incidence of "non-performing assets" high. The share of cooperatives in total ground level credit flow has declined from 62 per cent in the early 1990s to barely a third in 2003-04. The level of fresh lending has tapered off and has shown little or no growth since 2000.

There are 29 State Cooperative Banks, 367 district central cooperative banks and over 90,000 primary agricultural societies at the village level. The long-term cooperative credit system has 19 State Cooperative agriculture and rural development banks which operate through 755 primary cooperative agriculture and rural development banks in the federal system and 1,937 branches in the unitary system. During 2002-03, the cooperative provided aggregate loans of Rs. 23,638 crore for agriculture and allied purposes. The cooperatives have played an important role in development of agriculture in India. They have over 10 crore members of whom nearly four crores are borrowing members. The commercial banks with their very impressive network of branches have less then two crore agriculture borrowers. The agriculture and rural development banks (SCARDBs and PCARDBs) have played an important role in farm investments. In financing wells and other irrigation sources, mechanization, land development, horticulture development, etc. The bulk of the small and medium sized animal husbandry investments outside the government sponsored IRDP were also financed by these banks. The Cooperative credit system during its over a 100 year existence has created an indispensable financial infrastructure in the rural areas and is seen as the prime socio-economic movement of the country. The over 90,000 PACs are not only the most important 'scheme' lifeline of institutional credit for small and marginal farmers, they also supply agriculture inputs like fertilizers and are the main delivery agency for the Public Distribution System (PDS) in the rural areas.

The financial weakness of the Cooperative credit structure is no recent phenomenon. These and the underlying deficiencies in the way they are organized, managed and supervised have been widely noted and commented on by several committees in the past. They have argued the case for financial restructuring with Government funding and also pointed to the need to make them democratic, function without Governmental and political interference, and accountable for prudent management of their resources, but these did not lead to any action for lack of agreement on the sharing of costs of financial restructuring between the centre and the states. Moreover, politician across the entire spectrum of parties-are reluctant to give up control over cooperatives which have been used everywhere as instruments of patronage and political mobilization. On the contrary, governments have actively contributed to politicizing the movement and eroding what little credit discipline there was in sanctioning and recovery of loans.

### Prime Minister Rojgar Yojana

Loans under the Prime Minister's Rojgar Yojana are on the rise. Since most part of the disbursal are back loaded, the last quarter of last fiscal must have seen a major spurt in release of money. Under the scheme, no third party guarantee/collateral is required for projects up to Rs. 1 lakh. Advances under the scheme are treated as advances under priority sector.

**Table 2.5:** Prime Minister Rojgar Yojana

| Years | *Loan Sanctioned* | | *Loans Disbursed* | |
|---|---|---|---|---|
| | *Number* | *Amount (in Rs. lakhs)* | *Number* | *Amount (in Rs. lakhs)* |
| 2002-03 | 2,28,031 | 1,49,699 | 1,90,521 | 119,847 |
| 2003-04 | 264,012 | 1,67,890 | 219,444 | 1,36,755 |
| 2004-05 | 298,033 | 192,325 | 248,264 | 154,279 |
| 2005-06 | 312,008 | 200,679 | 2,62,281 | 161,936 |
| 2006-07 (up to Dec. 2006) | 95,531 | 61,061 | 51,383 | 32,111 |

Data as reported by Scheduled Commercial Banks.

### Problems of Rural Finance

There is no doubt deceleration in agricultural growth. However, it is risky to argue that this deceleration was because of a limited availability of agricultural credit alone. The reported data on agricultural credit need to be analyzed with care. The outstanding credit is cumulative disbursement plus overdues minus repayment. In the pre-reform period, the outstanding level did not reflect real status of lending. That's why; the banks had huge problems in the beginning of the reform period in maintaining the ratio of 18 per cent as a good amount of NPA was knocked out of the outstanding level. Agricultural growth, in fact, has been halted because of non-conducive market conditions and lack of public sector investment. The flow of credit to the agricultural sector declined because.

1. The formal sector had not reached out to small and marginal farmers significantly who needs credit much more, even in the pre-reform period;
2. The credit need of other farmers declined because there was not much market incentive to make more investment;
3. A new consciousness of transaction cost had surfaced and the credit risk arising out of uncertain and unfriendly market conditions and expectations of a loan waiver increased;
4. India is a vast country based on agriculture. Here more than two-third of people depend upon agriculture for their earnings. But the financial needs of rural farmers can not be matched with the finance provided by the Financial Institutions;
5. The repayment habit of farmers is very poor. It severely affects the financial performance of such institution;
6. Political intervention in the lending programmes creates serious problems to identify the right beneficiaries;
7. The farmers in India generally are not utilizing the financial assistance provided to them in commensurate manner;
8. At last, the lack of awareness among the rural people leads to so many problems in rural credits.

**Suggestions**

1. India has about 5 lakhs villages. As the scheduled banks have already diverted their attention to urban and metro cities resulting in closure of many rural branches, the only alternatives is RRBs, barring the cooperatives. It is essential

that all these villages, Panachayats, blocks and taluka must come under these banks. A close network of the branches situated on a regional basis would plug undue competition, complacency and duplication of efforts and promote competence. Hence, it is essential to multiply the number of branches to cover the entire rural area of our country.

2. The C-D ratio must be maintained at around 75 per cent. The priority sector advances target should be fulfilled at any cost. Almost all the advances must go to the rural sector. No question of the rural funds siphoned off to other sectors.
3. Strict guidelines are to be issued as regards the deployment of funds. It is rural sector reforms that should be borne in mind.
4. The RRBs should have the status of the market leader of rural finance. The number of other players must be restricted. Almost all the requirements of the rural population must be met through the RRBs themselves, except long-term needs, capital investment, housing etc. Other agencies such as SIDBI, SFCs and NABARD can contribute in specific areas or arranging for refinance facility, The RBI could help by arranging additional flow of funds.
5. The concept of agricultural banking and credit should be replaced by rural banking and credit for total integrated rural development and not farm sector or for that matter any other sector in isolation. Rural household can be extended credit facilities for any purpose except for anti-national and purposes prohibited by the Government. Similarly, banking facilities should cover all financial services as in urban centers.
6. All rural branches of commercial banks and regional rural banks must bring within the banking fold all small and marginal farmers, landless labourers, tenant farmers, oral lessees and share croppers in each of their service area villages through provision of credit and mobilizing saving.
7. All rural branches of Commercial Banks and RRBs including Primary Agricultural Credit Societies must be assigned the role of micro-financ e institutions and their performance monitored to ensure that 193 million people below poverty

line (as against 23.96 million persons covered by 35,294 branches of 560 banks in last 13 years) are brought within the banks' credit linkage programme in five years and through financial and non-financial support from Banks, Panchayati Raj Institutions (PRIs), Governments, NGOs, Industrial, commercial, business houses each one of them transforms from "survival stages to entrepreneurial stage" creating wealth and sharing wealth in rural areas.

8. Around 50 per cent credits linked SHGs are concentrated in Andhra Pradesh, Tamil Nadu and Karnataka. Banks, State Governments and Panchayati Raj Institutions in all other states must form, promote, nurture and credit link SHGs of almost all below poverty line households in next three years by drawing suitable action plans.
9. Panchayati Raj Institutions (PRIs) role, responsibilities and functions should be clearly and unambiguously defined through legislation in order to make them accountable to accelerate the process of agricultural and rural development.

## Conclusion

Despite high density of the retail outlets of formal credit institution, the presence of informal agencies for rural credits continued to exist although their share has been declining over the years. Informal agencies largely extend credit for consumption and social ceremonies and their interest and other terms of conditions are onerous. Yet they coexists with the formal financial institutions mainly due to their proximity, feel–at-ease, timely and quick services, all time access, purpose free credit, flexibility in loan repayments and low transaction costs. To reach the poor, institutional innovations are needed that enable services to be expanded while substantially reducing transactions costs for both the financial institutions and the clients.

India's economy is based on rural sector because more than two-third of the population is dependent upon agriculture. Finance being the lifeline of every commercial venture, availability of adequate funds at reasonable terms is mandatory to ensure repaid economic development. In India, the institutional finance to agriculture, which contributes 22.1 per cent of GDP's, is inadequate. The financial institutions now are concentrating on profits rater than service. Even today, the farmers largely depend upon the local indigenous money-lenders for their financial assistance. They exploit the farmers by means of charging high rate of interest and take their agriculture output at low price.

Although the Commercial Banks provide vast amounts of loans to agricultural activities, it constitutes only 14 per cent of total bank credit. Private sector commercial banks only provide nearly 10 per cent of their credit to agriculture, which is below the limit prescribed by the RBI. Therefore, the RBI should austerely instruct the banks to provide at least 18 per cent to agricultural activities. At the same time, there is need to look into the position of financial institutions in rural credit. Financial strength of the financial institutions largely depends on proper recycling of funds. Good recovery position leads to better performance in lending. Therefore, on the one hand, the government should organize drive for recovery operations, and on the other hand, the Government and Non-Government Organizations should take steps to organize awareness programmes in the rural households so that they can make use of the credit to the maximum extent for generating income and regular repayment.

A review of the performance of agricultural credit in India reveals that though the overall flow of institutional credit has increased over the years, there are several gaps in the system like inadequate provision of credit to small and marginal farmers, paucity of medium and long term lending and limited deposit mobilization and heavy dependence on borrowed funds by major agricultural credit purveyors. These have major implications for agricultural development as also the well-being of the farming community. Efforts are therefore required to address and rectify these issues.

It is felt that the localized institutions, i.e. the co-operatives, need special support to overcome their handicaps due to design defects and limitations on operations caused by their supervision or regulators of limited vision and understanding. If the support is not forthcoming, the farmers and the artisans in many areas would suffer a lot due to the failures of these localized institutions. In some of the states like Maharashtra, Orissa, Bihar and Assam the longterm cooperative credit structure has nearly collapsed with the result that a large number of the farmers in these states are being deprived of longterm investment credit opportunity which are important for improving the economic well-being of the farmers as well as improving the productivity of agriculture in that region. While it is important that these institutions set their house in order without any further delay, the Government has also to step in quickly and help these cooperative banks with liberal financial assistance to enable them to lend in their area. Experience shows that the mighty and favoured commercial banks have rarely stepped in and increased their lending in the area of operations of the cooperatives banks, SCARDBs or PCARDBs, which have been weakened mainly due to factors beyond their control. If the desired and deserving support to cooperative banks does not come quickly, the small/marginal farmers, the artisans and other weaker sections in these areas would continue suffering and at some stage or the other, lose respect and goodwill for the authorities.

The multi agency approach adopted in our country is also a reflection of the need for different players in the field of agricultural credit. The refrain of all committees and working groups, which have looked into the performance of the cooperative credit system either directly as part of their enquiry for the specific purpose or indirectly enquiring into other related matters has been that the cooperative have not done as well as they should have but there is no question of getting away from the system in the long run. The performance of the commercial bank has shown same kind of weakness in rural lending that afflicted the cooperative system. It may not be wrong to believe that the weakness of the cooperatives in fact are not the weakness of the cooperative system itself, but are those associated with the clientele which they have been serving. The weakness in fact arises from the peculiarities/deficiencies relating to the structure of agriculture production itself. Since cooperative mainly deal with agricultural loans and bulk of their loans go to small and marginal farmers, they have little scope for geographical or sectoral diversification, leading to greater risk profile and consequential weak financial position.

It has come out strongly in favour of revival and revitalization of the cooperative credit system at public cost on the ground that other financial institutions are neither capable of nor interested in providing adequate credit at reasonable cost to millions of assetless and asset poor people in rural areas. The only hope for these classes lies in genuinely democratic and self-governing cooperatives based on the principle of mutual help and thrift. Therefore, while justifying large public funding for financial restructuring both eligibility for assistance and its release to state governments and through them to the individual cooperatives should be conditional on their agreeing to a set of specific legal and institutional reforms and their implementation in a phased manner.

## REFERENCES

1. *Economic and Political Weekly*, March 16, 2006 pp. 1014-1015.
2. *Economic and Political Weekly*, October 21, 2006 pp. 4396.
3. *The Hindu*, January 26th, 2007, pp. 18.
4. *The Hindu,* December 27th 2006, pp. 17.
5. *Kurukshetra,* September, 2000, pp. 3.
6. Facts for You, February 2005, pp. 35.
7. *Economic and Political Weekly*, February 25, 2006, pp. 668.
8. *The Economic Times*, March Ist, 2007, pp. 11.
9. *The Economic Times,* March 2nd, 2007, pp. 6.
10. *The Economic Times*, March 5th, 2007, pp. 8.
11. Venkata Reddy, K. *Agriculture and Rural Development—A Gandhian Perspective*, 2001, pp. 189.
12. NIRD, *Rural Development Statistics*, 1996, pp. 115.
13. *The Hindu*, Jan 26th, 2007, pp. 7.
14. *The Economic Times*, March 17th, 2007, pp. 10.
15. *Kurukshetra, March* 2007, pp. 25.
16. Third Concept, July 2006, pp. 26.
17. RBI Annual Report 2003-04, supplement to RBI bulletin, September 2004, pp. 14 and 137.
18. Valsamma Antony, "Co-operative Banks in Grip of NPA's", *Southern Economist*, Feb. 15, 2005, pp. 21.
19. RBI Report on Trend and Progress of Banking in India, supplement to RBI Bulletin, various issues from 1994 to 2004.
20. *Economic and Political Weekly*, March 24, 2007, pp.1007.
21. *The Hindu*, April 8th, 2007, pp. 13.
22. *The Economic Times*, April 7th 2007, pp. 14.

# 3

# Agricultural Credit in India: Problems and Prospects

BRAHM PRAKASH

---

*The share of public investment in total investment in agriculture has been declining since 1980-81. The relative shares of institutional agencies in total cash debt of rural cultivators increased from 31.7 to 66.3 per cent during 1971-1991. Total direct investment in agricultural credit which was Rs. 7.44 crore during 1970-71 increased to Rs. 41,385 crore during 2001-02. The share of non-institutional sources has declined sharply since independence. The amount of credit has recorded an upward swing across all the size categories. During 1997-98 and 2005-06, the share of cooperative banks to total ground level credit has declined considerably from 44.0 to 23.6 per cent while share of commercial banks has increased significantly from 49.5 to 67.4 per cent during the corresponding period, while share of RRBs has slightly increased from 6.4 to 8.9 per cent. The total ground level credit flow for agriculture and allied activities which was Rs. 31,956 crore during 1997-98 increased to Rs. 15,7,480 crore during 2005-06. Significant increase in credit flow was observed in case of minor irrigation, land development and hi-tech agriculture, while moderate increase was observed in respect of farm mechanization, fisheries and plantation and horticulture sector. The Southern states stood out with a substantially higher share of agricultural credit followed by Northern and Central Regions. Per capita credit was also highest in the Southern states followed by Northern and Western States. It was extremely low in case of Eastern and North Eastern Regions. Dependence on DCCBs, high level of overdue, restricted access of small farmers, clear regional disparities and poor management are major constraints of cooperative banking system while poor quality of lending, inadequate staff in rural branches, establishing a large number of rural branches without adequate business potential, unsatisfactory recovery position and regional imbalances in the credit disbursed the banks are major bottlenecks of commercial banks. Multi-agency control, restricted area of operation, unplanned growth, inefficient staff, high incidence of overdue hampers growth of RRBs. The paper suggests that these problems should be addressed immediately for revamping of the agricultural credit.*

## Introduction

Agricultural credit is one of the essential requirements for the growth of agricultural production and productivity. Majority of the farmers in India fall in the category of small and marginal farmers. Unless they have an adequate access to credit at reasonable terms and conditions and at the right time, they can not adopt modern agricultural technology which requires sufficient financial resources. Paucity of capital flow compels the farmers for seeking loans from money-lenders and landlords at exorbitant rates of interest and after that, debt trap reduces them to penury. Considering the importance of agricultural credit, an attempt has been made to study the sources of agricultural credit in India; to review their progress, to identify constraints and to suggest measures for their better prospects. This study is based on the secondary data collected from different sources.

## Sources of Agricultural Finance

Sources of agricultural finance can be divided into two categories (i) non-institutional sources *viz.*, money-lenders, relatives, traders, commission agents and landlords, and (ii) institutional sources comprising of Cooperatives, Regional Rural Banks and Scheduled Commercial banks. The state governments also provide "*Taccavi*" loans to farmers besides providing financial assistance to State Cooperative Banks and the Land Development Banks. In the field of cooperation, the Primary Agricultural Credit Societies provide mainly short and medium term loans and Land Development Banks provide long term loan to agriculture. The commercial banks including Regional Rural Banks provide both short and medium term loan for agriculture and allied activities. The National Bank for Agriculture and Rural Development is the apex institution at national level for agricultural credit and provides refinance assistance to all the agencies. The Reserve Bank of India plays a vital role in this endeavour as a Central Bank of the country by giving necessary directives to NABARD.

## Institutional Credit Structure

Rural and semi-urban branches of commercial banks and Regional Rural Banks (RRBs), Primary Agricultural Credit Societies (PACSs), District Central Cooperatives Banks (DCCBs), State Cooperative Banks (SCBs) along with branches of State Land Development Banks (SLDBs) are the major sources of credit in the agricultural sector. On 31 March 1999, there were 45434 rural and semi-urban branches of commercial banks and 14454 branches of Regional Rural Banks (RRBs), 91720 Primary Agricultural Credit Societies (PACSs), 364 District Central Cooperatives Banks (DCCBs), 28 State Cooperative Banks (SCBs) which were providing credit to agricultural sector. About 2337 branches of 19 State Land Development Banks (SLDBs) were providing long-term credit in the agricultural sector.

## Performances of Institutional Sources of Credit

### *Increasing Share of Production Credit as Compared to Investment Credit*

Capital formation in agriculture helps in improving the stock of equipments, tools and productivity of natural resources, which in turn enables farmers to use their resources more productively. Creation of capital goods, thus, is necessary for raising the productivity of existing resources and realizing long-term growth potential. In the era of globalization, when agriculture is expected to satisfy not only the domestic demand but also to encash on its comparative advantages and contribute substantially to foreign exchange earnings by way of exports, modernization of production technology and management practices are significant. Hence, the need for increasing investment in agriculture is being felt as never before.

Investment in agriculture is made by public as well as by private sectors. Public sector investment in agriculture is made by Central and State Governments and investment through Departmental Commercial Undertakings (for crops and animal husbandry, soil and water conservation *etc.*), Non Departmental Commercial Undertakings like Irrigation and Water Resource Development Corporation, Tubewell Corporations, Poultry Boards, Forestry Boards, Tea Corporations and Fisheries Corporations owned by Central and State Governments (for animal husbandry and minor irrigation). While Private sector investment is made by private corporate and unorganized entities like sugar/milk cooperatives and household sector for irrigation, land development and land reclamation *etc.*

The annual compound growth rate of gross capital formation in agriculture had declined by (-)0.3 per cent during 1980's and had registered a marginal growth of 2.5 per cent during 1990's. The share of gross capital formation in agriculture in total GDP, which hovered around 2 per cent during the period 1999-2004 had declined to 1.7 per cent during 2004-05 (Table 3.1). The gross capital formation in agriculture (at 1999-2000 prices) fluctuated between Rs. 38,176 crore and Rs. 47,833 crore during 2000-2001 and 2003-04. The share of public investment in total investment in agriculture has been declining since 1980-81 and fluctuated between 17.1 and 18.4 per cent during the period 1999-2003, the fall in its share was particularly steep during the 1990's. While the share of investment in the manufacturing and tertiary sector ranged between 33-40 and 55 to 60 per cent, respectively. The share of public sector in agriculture has not only declined but it has declined in absolute terms as well, despite an increase in the gross capital formation in the economy. This decline in public investment can be attributed to diversion of resources from investment to current expenditure in the form of increased output and input subsidiaries.

According to the All India Debt and Investment Survey 1991-92, the relative shares of institutional agencies in total cash debt of rural cultivators increased from 31.7 per cent in 1971 to 63.2 per cent in 1981 and subsequently to 66.3 per cent in 1991. But the financial sector liberalization has led to a reduction of credit available to the agricultural sector (Table 3.2).

**Table 3.1:** Gross Capital Formation (GCF) in Agriculture.

| *Year* | *Public Sector* | *Private Sector* | *Total* | *Ratio of GCF in Agriculture to (%)* | |
|---|---|---|---|---|---|
| | | | | *Agri. GDP* | *Total GDP* |
| 1999-00 | 7754 | 35719 | 43473 | 9.6 | 2.2 |
| 2000-01 | 7018 | 31158 | 38176 | 8.4 | 1.9 |
| 2001-02 | 8529 | 38215 | 46744 | 9.7 | 2.2 |
| 2002-03 | 7849 | 38018 | 45867 | 10.2 | 2.1 |
| 2003-04 | 12809 | 35024 | 47833 | 9.7 | 2.0 |
| 2004-05* | 12591 | 30532 | 43123 | 8.7 | 1.7 |

**Quick Estimates*

*Source*: NABARD Annual Report (2005-06). pp. 26

**Table 3.2:** Share of Agriculture in Gross Bank Credit.

| *Years* | *1972* | *1980* | *1985* | *1990* | *1994* | *1996* | *2001* |
|---|---|---|---|---|---|---|---|
| Share (%) | 8.0 | 8.9 | 16.0 | 16.2 | 13.5 | 11.7 | 11.1 |

Total direct investment agricultural credit which was Rs. 7.44 crore during 1970-71 increased to Rs. 34.38 crore, Rs. 98.29 crore and Rs. 41,385 crore during 1980-81, 1990-91 and 2001-02, respectively. The data on relative share of borrowing of cultivator households from different sources revealed that share of non-institutional sources which was 92.7 per cent during 1951 declined to 81.3 per cent in 1961, to 68.3 per cent in 1971, 36.8 per cent in 1981 and 30.6 per cent in 1991.

## Share of Commercial Banks and Cooperatives in Growth of Production Credit/Investment Credit

Data on flow of institutional credit to agricultural sector during 1997-98 to 2005-06 depicted in Table 3.3 revealed that amount of credit has recorded an upward swing across all the size-wise categories with the increase being highest in the case of small-holders. During 1997-98 and 2005-06, the share of cooperative banks to total ground level credit has declined considerably from 44.0 to 23.6 per cent while share

**Table 3.3: Flow of Institutional Credit to Agricultural Sector during 1997-98 to 2005-06**

(*Rs. in crore*)

| *Institutions* | *1997-98* | *1998-99* | *1999-2000* | *2000-01* | *2001-02* | *2002-03* | *2003-04* | *2004-05* | *2005-06* |
|---|---|---|---|---|---|---|---|---|---|
| *Production (Short-term) Credit* | | | | | | | | | |
| Cooperative Banks | 10895 | 12571 | 14845 | 16853 | 18828 | 19707 | 22697 | 27259 | NA |
| Regional Rural Banks | 1396 | 1710 | 2423 | 3245 | 3277 | 4775 | 6088 | 9901 | NA |
| Commercial Banks | 8349 | 9622 | 11697 | 13486 | 17904 | 21104 | 26192 | 34680 | NA |
| Sub-Total (A) | 20640 | 23903 | 28965 | 33314 | 40509 | 45586 | 54977 | 71840 | NA |
| *Medium/Long-term Credit* | | | | | | | | | |
| Cooperative Banks | 3190 | 3386 | 3518 | 4218 | 4776 | 4009 | 4262 | 4165 | NA |
| Regional Rural Banks | 644 | 750 | 749 | 974 | 1077 | 1295 | 1493 | 2503 | NA |
| Commercial Banks | 7482 | 8821 | 13036 | 14321 | 15683 | 18670 | 26249 | 46801 | NA |
| Sub Total (B) | 11316 | 12957 | 17303 | 19513 | 21536 | 23974 | 32004 | 53469 | NA |
| *Short-term+ Medium/Long-term Credit* | | | | | | | | | |
| Cooperative Banks | 14085 | 15957 | 18363 | 20801 | 23604 | 23716 | 26959 | 31421 | 37252 |
| Regional Rural Banks | 2040 | 2460 | 3172 | 4219 | 4854 | 6070 | 7581 | 12404 | 14076 |
| Commercial Banks | 15831 | 18443 | 24733 | 27807 | 33587 | 39774 | 52441 | 81481 | 106152 |
| Total (A+B) | 31956 | 36860 | 42628 | 52827 | 62045 | 69560 | 86981 | 125309 | 157480 |

*Sources*: 1. NABARD Annual Report (2005-06) pp. 49.
2. Agricultural Statistics at a Glance 2006 pp. 205.

of commercial banks has increased significantly from 49.5 to 67.4 per cent during the corresponding period, while share of RRBs has slightly increased from 6.4 to 8.9 per cent. The total ground level credit flow for agriculture and allied activities which was Rs. 31,956 crore during 1997-98 increased to Rs. 1,57,480 crore during 2005-06 registering an increase of 392.8 per cent.

### *Sectoral Growth of Agricultural Credit*

During the period of four years (2001-04), crop loans increased by 166.4 per cent while term loans recorded comparatively better growth (182.8%). Significant increase in credit flow was observed in case of minor irrigation, land development and hi-tech agriculture, while moderate increase was observed in respect of farm mechanization, fisheries and plantation and horticulture sector (Table 3.4).

**Table 3.4:** Ground Level credit Flow for Agriculture and Allied Activities: Sub-sectors wise

(*Rs. Crore*)

| *Sector/Sub-Sector* | *2001-02* | *2002-03* | *2003-04* | *2004-05* | *Annual Compound Growth Rate (2001-04)* |
|---|---|---|---|---|---|
| Crop loan (Short-term production credit) | 40509 | 45586 | 54977 | 76062 | 16.0 |
| Term loan (Medium-term and long-term investment credit) | 21536 | 23974 | 32004 | 49247 | 22.0 |
| A. Minor Irrigation | 1845 | 1976 | 2730 | 4186 | 22.0 |
| B. Land Development | 307 | 393 | 579 | 840 | 37.0 |
| C. Farm Mechanization | 3847 | 3600 | 3986 | 4555 | 2.0 |
| D. Plantation and Horticulture | 765 | 1195 | 1436 | 1720 | 37.0 |
| E. Animal Husbandry @ | 2221 | 2637 | 2928 | 3097 | 15.0 |
| F. Fisheries | 508 | 539 | 1142 | 1301 | 50.0 |
| G. Hi-tech Agriculture | 2257 | 2268 | 4017 | 6648 | 33.0 |
| H. Others# | 9786 | 11366 | 15186 | 26900 | 25.0 |
| Total | 62045 | 69560 | 86981 | 125309 | 18.0 |

Note: @ Includes Dairy Development, Poultry Farming and Sheep/Goat/ Piggery.

## Others include storage/market yards, forestry/WLD, RIDF, Bullock and Bullock carts, bio-gas and credit flow through private sector commercial banks for which sector-wise break-up is not available.

*Source*: NABARD Annual Report (2005-06), pp. 50.

The ground level credit flow which recorded an annual growth of 18 per cent during period 2001-04 increased by 44 per cent during 2004-05. During 2005-06, total disbursement by all agencies was at Rs. 157,479.57 crore recording 12 per cent increase over target of Rs. 141,000 crore set by Government of India.

### *Kisan Credit Card Scheme*

The Kisan credit card scheme introduced in August 1998 for short term loans for seasonal agricultural operations has been under implementation in all the states and union territories by public sector banks, regional rural banks and state cooperative banks/district cooperative banks facilitating smooth flow of ground level credit for crop loans. By the end of March 2006, cooperative banks, regional rural banks and commercial banks all-together have issued 5.71 million Kisan credit cards. The state wise position embodied in Table 3.5 revealed that maximum cards have been distributed in Uttar Pradesh followed by Andhra Pradesh, Maharashtra, Rajasthan, Madhya Pradesh, Tamil Nadu, Orissa and Karnataka. During 2005-06, cooperative banks, commercial banks and regional rural banks issued 25.98 lakh, 41.65 lakh and 12.49 lakh cards, respectively (Table 3.6). Of the 5.91 million cards issued by the banking systems since inception of the scheme, cooperative banks accounted for the largest share (51 per cent) followed by commercial banks (37 per cent) and RRBs (12 per cent). Cooperative banks and RRBs have been routing a major portion of their crop loans through Kisan credit cards having recognized it as a widely accepted mechanism for delivery of credit to the farmers.

**Table 3.5:** State-wise Number of Kisan Credit Cards issued upto 31 August 2006.

| *Sl. No.* | *States* | *Cooperative Banks (CB)* | *Regional Rural Banks (RRB)* | *Commercial Banks** | *Total* |
|---|---|---|---|---|---|
| 1. | Andhra Pradesh | 3592011 | 1249599 | 4790213 | 9631823 |
| 2. | Assam | 5424 | 80088 | 202158 | 287670 |
| 3. | Arunachal Pradesh | 980 | 1334 | 10009 | 12323 |
| 4. | Bihar | 775438 | 289074 | 740593 | 1805105 |
| 5. | Gujarat | 1160965 | 160130 | 830494 | 2151589 |
| 6. | Goa$ | 3632 | 0 | 7613 | 11245 |
| 7. | Haryana | 1194877 | 259207 | 507855 | 1961939 |
| 8. | Himachal Pradesh | 48643 | 19909 | 131973 | 200525 |

*(Contd.)*

*(Contd.)*

| Sl. No. | States | Cooperative Banks (CB) | Regional Rural Banks (RRB) | Commercial Banks* | Total |
|---|---|---|---|---|---|
| 9. | Jammu & Kashmir | 48351 | 9376 | 5677 | 63404 |
| 10. | Karnataka | 1274319 | 696753 | 1477071 | 3448143 |
| 11. | Kerala | 969403 | 310217 | 951527 | 2231147 |
| 12. | Madhya Pradesh | 2738713 | 313151 | 896576 | 3948440 |
| 13. | Maharashtra | 4104630 | 192836 | 1332151 | 5629617 |
| 14. | Meghalaya # | 5299 | 9582 | 24170 | 39051 |
| 15. | Mizoram # | 2104 | 5100 | 7996 | 15200 |
| 16. | Manipur # | 491 | 1037 | 15672 | 17200 |
| 17. | Nagaland # | 1664 | 898 | 10534 | 13096 |
| 18. | Orissa | 2573753 | 345210 | 598735 | 3517698 |
| 19. | Punjab | 848851 | 74647 | 867926 | 1791424 |
| 20. | Rajasthan | 2724069 | 292905 | 875412 | 3892386 |
| 21. | Sikkim #$ | 2447 | 0 | 3321 | 5768 |
| 22. | Tamil Nadu | 1535488 | 162267 | 2215825 | 3913580 |
| 23. | Tripura # | 2898 | 15846 | 21461 | 40205 |
| 24. | Uttar Pradesh | 5416102 | 2501834 | 3761554 | 11679490 |
| 25. | West Bengal | 1174593 | 177904 | 796220 | 2148717 |
| 26. | A & N Islands #$ | 2554 | 0 | 874 | 3428 |
| 27. | Chandigarh $ | 0 | 0 | 935 | 935 |
| 28. | Daman & Diu @# | 0 | 0 | 71 | 71 |
| 29. | New Delhi #$ | 1915 | 0 | 3044 | 4959 |
| 30. | D & N Haveli @$ | 0 | 0 | 16 | 16 |
| 31. | Lakshdweep @$ | 0 | 0 | 396 | 396 |
| 32. | Pondicherry $ | 6499 | 0 | 22882 | 29381 |
| 33. | Jharkhand | 117390 | 174634 | 222575 | 514599 |
| 34. | Chhattisgarh | 731878 | 168977 | 136735 | 1037590 |
| 35. | Uttaranchal | 278094 | 21721 | 144773 | 444588 |
| | *Break-upnot available for CBs (1998-99)* | | 188005 | | |
| | Total | 31343495 | 7534236 | 21803042 | 60680773 |

# SCB functions as CFA., @ No Cooperative Banks in these UTs. $ No RRB in these States/UTs.

*Note*: No. of banks implementing the Scheme, Amount sanctioned data provisional, CBs data received from RBI upto June 2005.

*Source*: Credit Division, Ministry of Agriculture, New Delhi and *Agricultural Statistics at a Glance* 2006. pp. 2005.

## *Region-Wise Trends in Growth of Credit*

There is a wide regional disparity in India in the disbursement of agricultural credit by scheduled commercial banks (excluding Regional Rural Banks). On comparing the agricultural credit as proportion of Net

State Domestic Product (NSDP), it is found that the Southern states stood out with a substantially higher share of agricultural credit followed by Northern and Central Regions (Table 3.7). Whereas the ratio for the Southern Region increased during the latter part of the 1990's, it remained stationery for the Northern, Central and North-Eastern Regions. The share of agricultural credit in the Southern States is likely to be higher due to active cooperative movement. The low share of the Western States can be attributed to very active role of cooperatives in the region. The Eastern and North Eastern Region have a very low share.

**Table 3.6:** Agency-wise Kisan Credit Cards issued.

(*Lakh*)

| *Years* | *Cooperative Banks* | *RRBS* | *Commercial Banks* | *Total* |
|---|---|---|---|---|
| 2001-02 | 54.36 | 8.34 | 30.71 | 93.41 |
| 2002-03 | 45.79 | 9.64 | 27.00 | 82.43 |
| 2003-04 | 48.78 | 12.74 | 30.94 | 92.46 |
| 2004-05 | 35.56 | 17.29 | 43.95 | 96.80 |
| 2005-06 | 25.98 | 12.49 | 41.65 | 80.12 |
| Total* | 304.12 | 68.78 | 218.03 | 590.93 |

*Since inception of the scheme.

*Source*: NABARD Annual Report (2005-06).

**Table 3.7:** Region-wise share of Agriculture and Allied Sector Credit (Short-term and long-term) Disbursements by Scheduled Commercial Banks and Credit per Capita.

| *Region* | *Credit Disbursement (%)* | | | *Credit per Capita (Rs.)* | |
|---|---|---|---|---|---|
| | *1990-91* | *1995-96* | *2001-02* | *1991-95* | *1996-2001* |
| Northern | 12.9 | 11.6 | 19.9 | 60 | 153 |
| North-Eastern | 0.4 | 0.4 | 0.5 | 9 | 17 |
| Eastern | 8.3 | 6.4 | 7.4 | 21 | 42 |
| Central | 16.9 | 16.4 | 14.1 | 36 | 86 |
| Western | 13.6 | 17.1 | 14.4 | 67 | 134 |
| Southern | 47.9 | 48.0 | 43.8 | 157 | 280 |
| Average India | 100.0 | 100.0 | 100.0 | 67 | 128 |

*Note*: Ratio obtained by dividing the average direct finances to agriculture and allied activities of All-India Schedule Commercial Banks during the period 1991-95 and 1996-2001 by the total region with population in 1991 and 2001 respectively.

*Source*: Reserve Bank of India; *Economic Survey* various issues. Mohan Rakesh (2004).

Regional trends in agricultural and allied sector credit per capita also revealed that per capita credit was the highest in the Southern states followed by Northern and Western States. It was extremely low in case of Eastern and North Eastern Regions (Table 3.7).

The data of average number of accounts: size-wise embodied in Table 3.8 revealed that number of accounts has increased in all the categories. There has actually been continuous growth in the number of accounts in all categories of term size in the case of commercial banks. Data on average share of loan outstanding by land size depicted in Table 3.9 revealed that percentage share of loan outstanding has not changed significantly over the past two decades across all the categories.

**Table 3.8:** Average Number of Size wise Accounts

| *Size of Holding* | *Number of Accounts (000's)* | | |
|---|---|---|---|
| | *1980's* | *1990's* | *2000-01* |
| Upto 2.5 acres | 1771 | 1084 | 849 |
| Above 2.5 acres to 5 acres | 2047 | 1563 | 1341 |
| Above 5 acres | 2382 | 1860 | 1599 |

*Source*: *Handbook of Statistics on Indian Economy*: 2002-03.

**Table 3.9:** Average Share of Loan Outstanding.

| *Size of Holding* | *No of Account (000's)* | | |
|---|---|---|---|
| | *1980s* | *1990s* | *2000-01* |
| Upto 2.5 acres | 27.5 | 23.7 | 48.7 |
| Above 2.5 acres to 5 acres | 26.5 | 24.7 | 48.4 |
| Above 5 acres | 25.8 | 25.1 | 49.2 |

*Source*: *Handbook of Statistics on Indian Economy*: 2002-03

## *Problems of Institutional Sources of Agricultural Credit*

### *A. Cooperative Banking System*

Many PACSs are at present dependent on DCCBs and have failed miserably in mobilizing rural savings. It has made the cooperatives a "mediocre, inefficient and static system". The cooperative credit institutions are plagued by the problems of high level of overdues. The proposition of overdues to demand in case of DCCBs was 30 per cent in 1995 and 31 per cent during 1996. In the case of SLDBs, the proportions of overdues to demand were 38 per cent in 1995 and 39 per cent in 1996. These overdues have clogged the process of credit recycling since they have drastically reduced the capacity of cooperatives to great loss. The profitability of the cooperative is a matter of serious concern. According to a sample study conducted by a consultant of Agricultural Credit Review Committee, the average net margin of PACSs on their agricultural credit was negative at (-) Rs. 3.2 per Rs. 100 worth of business. Margin becomes positive (+1.22) only as a result of their non-credit business like distribution of fertilizer *etc.* Large land owners have accrued maximum benefits from the cooperatives due to their strong socio-economic status, while the share of poorest and needy like tenants, share-croppers and landless labourers is only meagre. The restricted access of small farmers to cooperative credit can also be substantiated by the fact that only 30 per cent of farmers holding less than one ha land are member of PACSs whereas almost all the farmers holding above 4 ha are members of PACSs. Clear regional disparities in the distribution of credit by the cooperative societies have been witnessed. Six States (Andhra Pradesh, Gujarat, Maharashtra, Kerala, Punjab and Tamil Nadu) received as much as 78.8 per cent of the loans provided by PACSs, Kerala alone received almost one fourth of the loans. The cooperatives have metamorphoses into Government directed, Government controlled and Government regulated enterprises giving rise to red tapism and administrative interference by the Govt. in day to day working of cooperatives. Not only that, it has led to interference in recovery of dues or promised to write off dues if elected to power and determination of interest rates on consideration other than financial returns. Management of most of the cooperative societies by the large farmers to their advantages and negligence of small and marginal farmers dampens the faith in and sprit of the cooperation.

### *B. Commercial Banks*

Although nationalized banks increased the flow of credit to weaker sections and rural areas, but deterioration in the quality of scheme preparation particularly under antipoverty programme and quality of lending have been major problem of such expansion. There is a lack of adequate staff in rural branches of commercial banks. Consequently supervision of rural advances is neglected many a times. Establishing a large number of rural branches without adequate business potential rise in establishment expenses and increase in non-performing advances affected the profitability of banks adversely. Recovery position of commercial banks is not satisfactory. The agricultural loan waived during 1990 had seriously accentuated the problem of recovery. Recovery has varied between 54 and 62 per cent indicating in turn that overdues have been as high as 38 to 46 per cent. Commercial banks have failed to provide their services in the areas not covered by the cooperatives. While there are a number of branches of different nationalized banks in one area resulting in unhealthy competition. There was a regional imbalance in the credit disbursed by banks. For instance, only southern region bags the lion's share.

### *C. Regional Rural Banks*

Multi-agency control of RRBs, restricted area of operation and restricted cliental, lack of proper system to avoid or minimize the scope for overdues, the faulty recruitment system of RRB staff and unplanned growth of these banks and branches created problems in control and management of these banks. Although overall dues as a percentage of demand is declining, but there is still a high incidence of overdues due to defective policies of loaning, weak supervision and monitoring, failure to link lending with development, political interference, useful default, drought and floods, lack of legal and administrative support from State Governments in loan recovery. Most of RRBs are running into losses for a number of years due to confinement of their lending to weaker sections, low margins coupled with high cost of servicing, no scope for cross-subsidization and increasing overhead costs without proportionate increase in income due to opening a number of new branches.

## ***Prospects***

### *A. Cooperative Banking System*

The essence of basic feature of cooperative banking system must be a larger reliance on resources mobilized locally and lesser and lesser dependence on higher credit institutions. So rural savings should be mobilized by the cooperatives to achieve the projected level of growth.

There have been huge overdues. Efforts should be made for affected recovery and transaction cost for recovery must be minimized. The tenants, share-croppers and landless labourers who are the poorest and therefore, the neediest should receive greater share of total loans advanced by PACSs. Efforts should be made to pursue all the poorest people to join PACSs as members. Regional disparities should be removed. Due to lack of adequate business expertise among the employees, PACSs are not capable of carrying their business in competition with money lenders and agents. The management of these societies should be efficient. The manager should be well educated and trained. The government should least interfere in the functioning of the societies so that societies may become self-dependent. But government assistance to the societies should be continued as such. The cooperative feeling among the members should be inculcated by proper education by organizing seminars and literature distribution. The cooperative education should be disseminated so that manager, officers and employees can be trained. For that, a nation-wide programme should be chalked out with full cooperation of central and State Governments.

*B. Commercial Banks*

For operating efficiently particularly in rural areas, the commercial banks must tackle point of major concern like reduced productivity of staff, increase in overdue and lower staff motivation *etc.* A greater autonomy should be accorded in their functioning. There rural branches need to be strengthened. They should be allowed to have a higher margin and their equity base should be fortified. The problem of increasing overdue is an alarming situation and calls for immediate corrective action. If this trend is not reversed and banks are reduced to institutions providing grants rather than recycling scarce resources to get the maximum benefits for the country as a whole, the banking system will be unable to provide more credit to meet the growing demand of credit by the farmers. Regional imbalances in the credit disbursed by the banks should be corrected. There should be proper coordination between commercial banks, cooperative credit structure and the government departments.

*C. Regional Rural Banks*

The sponsor banks should properly monitor functioning of RRBs.

Area of operations and cliental should not be restricted. Proper procedures should be followed to avoid any scope for overdues right from the start. Adequate attention should be paid for recruiting and training RRB staff. Recovery position of RRBs should be improved by all means. By providing greater flexibility in their lending operations, option of lending to non-target groups, permission to issue drafts and allowing deregulation of interest rates, a level playing field has been provided to RRBs like the rural branches of the commercial banks. RRBs are eminently suitable to do the job envisaged for them (*i.e.* taking banking closer to the rural households) and they can exist side by side with cooperatives and commercial banks. In the latter role, RRBs can keep on doing the good work of providing resources to the weaker section of the society.

In short, there has been a substantial increase in institutional credit to agriculture in the planned era. The increase has been particular during the last three of the five decades with the nationalization of major banks in 1969, setting up of RRBs in 1975 and NABARD in 1982. Yet there is a significant gap between the demand for and supply of credit and this gap will widen further if appropriate steps are not taken in time for expansion of agricultural credit. To meet these challenges, revamping of agricultural credit is urgently required. Some steps have already been undertaken in this direction. These include linking up of Self-Help Groups (SHGs) and Voluntary Organizations (VOs) with banks and the setting up of Local Area Banks (LABs) in the private sector and the Farmers' Club Programme initiated by NABARD. The area of operation of LABs can be a maximum of three geographically contiguous districts and branches can be opened only in the area of operation.

## REFERENCES

Anonymous (2005) *Agricultural Statistics at a Glance*. Directorate of Economics and Statistics, Department of Agriculture and Cooperation, Ministry of Agriculture, Govt. of India, New Delhi.

Anonymous (2005) *Annual Report* 2005-06. National Bank for Agriculture and Rural Development, Mumbai.

Kumar, Ranjana (2005) Credit Institutions: Empowering Small Farmers. *The Hindu Survey of Indian Agriculture* 2005. pp. 199-201.

Nair, P.K.K. (2000) Farm Credit: Policy Needs Revamp. *The Hindu Survey of Indian Agriculture* 2000 pp. 203-204.

Report of the *Expert Group on Investment Credit* (2005) National Bank for Agriculture and Rural Development, Mumbai. June 2005. pp. 69.

Mohan, Rakesh (2004) Agricultural Credit in India: Status, Issues and Future Agenda. *Indian Journal of Agricultural Marketing* 18(1): 1-25.

Thorat, Y.S.P. (2006) Rural Credit in India: Issues and Concerns. *Indian Journal of Agricultural Economics* 61(1): 1-10.

Sidhu, R.S. and Gill, Sucha Singh (2006) Agricultural Credit and Indebtedness in India: Some Issues. *Indian Journal of Agricultural Economics* 61(1): 11-35.

4

# Rural Co-operative Credit Institutions in India

H. SHIVAPPA

*The co-operative movement in India started and originated as a measure against poverty and exploitation of farmers by money lenders. Agrarian disturbances in 1875 in the Deccan against the money-lenders necessitated the enactment of Taccavi Legislation by Government and also led to the concept of the co-operative approach. The Northern India Taccavi Loan Act 1875, the Land Improvement Loans Act 1883, the Agricultural Loans Act 1884 etc., were all enacted to facilitate the availability of credit to farmers. In 1892 Sir Federick Nicholson recommended the establishment of rural co-operative credit societies on German pattern. The Famine Commission (1901) recommended introduction of Co-operatives in the country. In 1904, the Co-operative Credit Societies Act was enacted by the Imperial Government to facilitate organization of credit co-operatives and confer upon them special privileges and facilities, the scope of which was subsequently enlarged by the more comprehensive Co-operative Societies Act of 1912. These Acts were framed to combat rural indebtedness and supply credit to farmers. Under the Government of India Act 1919, the subject of co-operation was transferred to the then provinces, which were authorized to enact their own co-operative laws. Under the Government of India Act 1935, co-operatives remained a provincial subject.*

*As the societies were not in a position to supply sufficient loan to farmers to liquidate their past debts, and to make permanent improvement upon their land for improving the incomes, the necessity of long-term loans for the farmers was felt. This realization led to the establishment of the Co-operative Land Mortgage Banks (CLMBS) in the early 20s. The first CLMB was set up in Punjab in 1920. The All India Rural Credit Survey Committee also favoured the establishment of LMBS and this led to the establishment of Agricultural Refinance Corporation in 1963 and established the long term structure. In 1980 the scope of the banks was enlarged with a view to extending loans for farming and non-farming activities. As a result the banks were renamed Agricultural and rural development banks.*

*The rural cooperative credit institutions have been structured into two separate arms namely Short-term Co-operative Credit Structure (STCCS) and the Long-term Co-operative Credit Structure (LTCCS). The STCCS comprising Primary Agricultural Credit Societies (PACS) at the village level, District Central Co-operative Banks (DCCBS) at the intermediate level and the State Co-operative Banks (SCBS) at apex level provides crop and other working capital loan primarily for short-term purposes to farmers and other rural people. The LTCCS comprising State Co-operative Agricultural and Rural Development Banks (SCARDBs) at the State Level and Primary Co-operative Agriculture and Rural Development Banks (PCARDBs) at the district/block level has been providing medium and long-term loans for investment in agriculture, rural industries and housing. However the structure of rural co-operative banks is not uniform across all states of the country. NABARD is the apex institution entrusted with a pivotal role in policy planning and providing refinance facilities to rural financial institution to augment their resource base.*

*Before independence there was not much improvement in regard to the distribution of credit by these co-operative credit societies due to paucity of resources, lack of managerial skill, indifferent attitude of farmers and lack of interest of the Government. As a result moneylenders continued to enjoy the same status and farmers remained dependent upon the money-lenders for credit. After the attainment of independence, great stress was laid on the development of co-operative credit with a view to protecting the farmers against exploitation by money-lenders and to increase the credit flow to the agricultural sector. The rural co-operative banks with their vast numbers, regional out-reach and significant amount of assets is an important segment of the financial sector.*

**Genesis:** The co-operative movement in India started and originated as a measure against rural poverty, aggravated by chronic indebtedness of the farmers and practice of usuary at its worst by the money-lenders. Agrarian disturbances in 1875 in the Deccan against the money-lenders necessitated the enactment of Taccavi Legislation by Government and also led to the concept of the co-operative approach. The Northern India Taccavi Loan Act 1875, the Land Improvement Loans Act 1883, the Agricultural Loans Act 1884, etc., were all enacted to facilitate the availability of credit to farmers. In 1892 Sir Frederick Nicholson recommended the establishment of rural co-operative credit societies on German pattern. The Famine Commission (1901) recommended introduction of co-operatives in the country. In 1904, the Cooperative Credit Societies Act was enacted by the Imperial Government to facilitate organization of credit co-operatives and confer upon them special privileges and facilities, the scope of which was subsequently enlarged by the more comprehensive Co-operative Societies Act of 1912. These Acts were framed to combat rural indebtedness and supply credit to farmers.

Under the Government of India Act 1919, the subject of co-operation was transferred to the then provinces, which were authorized to enact their own co-operative laws. Under the Government of India Act 1935, co-operatives remained a provincial subject. In order to administer the operations of co-operatives societies membership was from more than one province, the Government of India enacted the Multi-Unit Co-operatives Societies Act 1942, which was subsequently replaced by the Multi-State Co-operative Societies Act 1984, under entry 44 of the union list.

The societies were not in a position to extend loans to farmers so that the farmers may liquidate past debts, redeem their land and other assets from usurious money-lenders. Loans from co-operative societies were also not enough to enable farmers to improve upon their land and augment their incomes. It was felt that the Long-Term (LT) loans needed by farmers for these purposes would have to be met by a separate set of institutions. This realization led to the establishment of the co-operative Land Mortgage Banks (LMBs) in the early 1920s. The first co-operative LMB was set up in Punjab in 1920 followed by two more in the Madras Presidency in 1925.

Later, the All India Rural Credit Survey Committee (AIRCSC) recommended establishment of a separate institution, which could LMBs, the resources for Long-Term lending to farmers for the development of agriculture. The recommendation led to the establishment of the Agricultural Refinance Cooperation in 1963 and established the LT structure to expand rapidly and change from being land mortgage banks to Land Development Banks (LDBs). In 1980 the scope of the banks was enlarged with a view to extending loan for agriculture and non-agricultural activities. As a result the banks were renamed agricultural and rural development banks.

Structure of Co-operative Societies/Banks.

The rural co-operative credit institutions have been structured into two separate arms namely Short-Term Co-operative Credit Structure (STCCS) and the Long-Term Co-operative Credit Structure (LTCCs). The STCCS comprising Primary Agricultural Credit Societies (PACS) at the village level, District Central Co-operative Banks (DCCBs) at the intermediate level, and the State Co-operative Banks (SCBs) at the apex level provides crop and other working capital loans primarily for short-term purposes to farmers, rural artisans etc. The LTCCS, comprising State Co-operative Agriculture and Rural Developments Banks (SCARBDs) at the State Level and Primary Co-operative Agriculture and Rural Development Banks (PCARDBs) at the district or block level has been providing typically medium and long-term loans for making investments in agriculture, rural industries and in the recent period, housing. However the structure of rural co-operative banks is not uniform across all states of the country. Some states have unitary structure with the state level banks operating through their own branches, while others have a mixed structure incorporating both Unitary and Federal System.

NABARD is the apex institution entrusted with a pivotal role in policy-planning and providing refinancing facilities to rural financial institutions to augment their resource base. NABARD is responsible for regulating and supervising the functions of Co-operative Banks. In this direction NABARD has been taking various initiatives in association with Government of India and RBI to improve the health of co-operative banks.

Before Independence there was not much improvement in regard to the distribution of credit by these co-operative credit societies due to paucity of resources, lack of managerial skill, indifferent attitude of farmers and lack of interest of the Government. As a result money-lenders continued to enjoy the same status and farmers remained dependent upon the money-lenders for credit. The condition of the farmers was so pitiable, which was beautifully summed up the Royal Commission on Agriculture:

*Indian farmer takes birth in debt, lives in debt and dies in debt.*

After the attainment of Independence, great stress was laid on the development of co-operative credit to achieve twin objectives. Firstly, to protect the farmers against exploitation by money-lenders and secondly to increase the credit flow to the agricultural sector to enable the farmers to introduce permanent improvements in land and adopt modern agricultural technology so that agricultural productivity may increase. It is also being conceived as an important factor in building up an egalitarian and non-exploitative economic and social order.

The rural co-operative banks with their vast numbers, regional out reach and significant amount of assets is an important segment of the financial sectors.

## Developments in Short Term Structure

*Primary Agricultural Credit Societies (PACS):* The PACS directly interface with the farmers and other rural people, provide short and medium credit, supply agricultural inputs, distribute consumer articles and arrange marketing of produce of its members through co-operative marketing societies. They also mobilize rural savings. Recently, they have diversified their activities to improve the economic viability. Further they have wider outreach unlike commercial banks.

*Growth:* Since the beginning of planning era in the country these societies have recorded an impressive growth in terms of membership, loans advanced, etc., as depicted in Table 4.1.

**Table 4.1:** Progress of PACS

*(Rs. in Crore)*

| *Year* | *1951-52* | *1974-75* | *1980-81* | *1985-86* | *1987-88* | *1993-94* | *2004-05 March 31st* |
|---|---|---|---|---|---|---|---|
| No. of Societies | 107925 | 153000 | 96000 | 92000 | 90000 | 91000 | 108779 |
| Membership | 47.77 lakhs | 36442000 | 57511000 | 72118000 | 87346000 | 89067000 | 127406000 |
| Deposits | 4.39 | 101.04 | 289 | 575 | 808 | 2367 | 1897604 lakhs |
| Working Capital | 45.22 | NA | NA | NA | NA | 15207 | 7540741 lakhs |
| Loans Advanced | 24.21 | 900.82 | 1746 | 3140 | 3687 | 7301 | 3921172 |
| Loans Outstanding | 33.66 | 1176.63 | NA | NA | NA | NA | 3844613 lakhs |
| Loans Overdues (Overdues to Demand) | NA | NA | NA | 44.1% | 40.02 | 41% | 33.6% |
| Borrowing Members | NA | NA | NA | NA | NA | NA | 45070000 |
| Borrowings | NA | 1040.70 | 2433 | 3927 | 4934 | 8487 | 4024949 lakhs |
| *Societies in Profit:* | | | | | | | |
| No. | NA | NA | NA | NA | NA | NA | 47015 |
| Amounts | NA | NA | NA | NA | NA | NA | 72802000 |
| *Societies in loss:* | | | | | | | |
| No. | NA | NA | NA | NA | NA | NA | 61323 |
| Amount | NA | NA | NA | NA | NA | NA | 198905000 |

*Source*: *Report on Trend and Progress of Banking in India* Supplement to RBI Bulletin, Mumbai.

Table 4.1 reveals the rapid development of PACS in the country as the membership rose from 47.77 lakh in 1951-52 to 127406000 lakhs in 2004-05, the loan advanced increased from Rs. 24.21 crore during 1951-52 to Rs. 3921172 lakhs during 2004-05, the deposits increased from Rs. 4.39 crore in 1951-52 to Rs. 1897604 lakhs in 2004-05, the working capital rose from 45.22 crore in 1951-52 to Rs. 7540741 lakhs in 2004-05.

The borrowing members accounted just for 35 per cent of the total membership in 2004-05. The number of societies increased from 107925 in 1951-52 to 155088 in 1974-75, but decreased to 94019 in 1980-81 due to amalgamation, which was undertaken to make the societies economically viable. However, in 2004-05 there were 108779 societies.

The working results of the societies reveal that 47015 societies were in profit which earned a profit of Rs. 7.28 crore while 61323 societies were in loss which incurred a loss of Rs. 19.89 crore in 2004-05. The loan over dues formed 33.60 to total demand in 2004-05.

## Districts Central Co-operative Banks (DCCBs)

The second-tier of the co-operative credit structure for short and medium-term loans is the DCCBs, which are, located either at taluk or district head-quarters. All the PACS in the district are its members. In addition, individuals can also become its members and can participate in the management.

*Progress:* The DCCBs have made rapid development in the country in terms of membership, loans issued etc., as illustrated in Table 4.2, which reveals the progress of DCCBs in the country. These banks are playing an important role as link between PACS and the SCBs and also in extending the flow of credit to the agricultural sector and other sectors either directly or through the PACS.

*State Central Cooperative Bank: SCBS:* The last-tier of the short and medium-term co-operative credit structure is the SCB—an apex body in the state. All the DCCBs in the state are its members and dependent heavily upon this bank for financial resources to meet agricultural credit and the credit requirements of other emerging economic activities in rural areas.

*Progress:* The success of the co-operative credit institutions in the state, to a large extent depends upon the viability of the SCBS as they provide capital resources to the DCCBs for meeting the credit needs of the cultivators. Table 4.3 shows the progress made by these banks.

**Table 4.2:** Progress of DCCBs

(Rs. in Crore)

| Year | 1951-52 | 1972-73 | 1975-76 | 1993-94 | 2000-01 | 2001-02 | 2002-03 | 2003-04 | 2004-05 | 2005-06 |
|---|---|---|---|---|---|---|---|---|---|---|
| No. of Banks | 509 | 344 | 344 | 361 | 367 | 368 | 367 | 365 | 367 | 365 |
| Owned Funds/Capital | 462 | 17629 | 360.49 | 2559 | 12180 | 14141 | 16398 | 19131 | 20495 | NA |
| Deposits | 3823 | 64664 | 984.92 | 16251 | 61745 | 68181 | 72344 | 78326 | 82098 | 86855 |
| Borrowings | NA | NA | 513.36 | 7223 | 16935 | 18820 | 19243 | 20882 | 22568 | 24622 |
| Working Capital | 6011 | 141184 | 2047.58 | 27586 | 87821 | 99424 | 101252 | 114702 | 111970 | NA |
| Loans Issued | 10564 | 124554 | 1721.66 | 17744 | 45016 | 55915 | 64665 | 48709 | 66266 | 64276 |
| Loans Outstanding | 3591 | 102832 | 1428.16 | 17758 | 52478 | 59316 | 63198 | 66696 | 73091 | 80090 |
| Recovery (as% to Demand) | NA | NA | NA | 33 | 67 | 66 | 61 | 63 | 71 | NA |
| CD Ratio | NA | NA | NA | NA | 85 | 87 | 87 | 85 | 89 | 92 |

Source: *Report on Trend and Progress of Banking in India* Supplement to RBI Bulletin, Mumbai.

**Table 4.3:** Progress of SCBS

| Year | *Rs. In Lakhs* | | | | *Rs. In Crore* | | | | | |
|---|---|---|---|---|---|---|---|---|---|---|
| | 1951-52 | 1973-74 | 1975-76 | 1993-94 | 2000-01 | 2001-02 | 2002-03 | 2003-04 | 2004-05 | 2005-06 |
| No. of Banks | 16 | 26 | 26 | 28 | 30 | 30 | 30 | 31 | 31 | 31 |
| Owned Funds/Capital | 190 | 5454 | 158.71 | 1528 | 5837 | 6712 | 7150 | 8473 | 9495 | NA |
| Deposits. | 2118 | 48867 | 723.68 | 11305 | 32626 | 36191 | 36658 | 43394 | 44316 | 45833 |
| Borrowings | NA | NA | 246.94 | 4749 | 11693 | 11672 | 11365 | 12416 | 14608 | 17054 |
| Working Capital | 3672 | 94200 | 1287.26 | 18919 | 49490 | 54262 | 57651 | 57936 | 65879 | NA |
| Loans Issued | 5527 | 116191 | 1514.81 | 14107 | 34307 | 34663 | 38642 | 39320 | 44452 | 43837 |
| Loans Outstanding | 2001 | 70623 | 893.60 | 9801 | 29861 | 32678 | 32798 | 35111 | 37346 | 39967 |
| Recovery (as% to demand) | NA | NA | NA | 17 | 84% | 82 | 79 | 83 | 84 | NA |
| CD Ratio | NA | NA | NA | NA | 92 | 90 | 89 | 81 | 84 | 87 |

Source: *Report on Trend and Progress of Banking in India* Supplement to RBI Bulletin, Mumbai.

Table 4.3 speaks the progress of SCBS in the matter of loan issued, deposits, working capital etc., in 2005-06 as compared to 1951-52.

## Working Results of DCCBs and SCBS

The DCCBS have improved their financial position in 2004-05 as compared to 2003-04 as shown in Table 4.4.

**Table 4.4:** Working Results of DCCBs.

| *Sl. No.* | *Item* | | *2003-04 March end* | *2004-05 March end* |
|---|---|---|---|---|
| 1. | Profit: | No | 263 | 296 |
| | Amount | | 863.79 | 1378.91 |
| 2. | Loss: | No | 102 | 71 |
| | Amount | | 755.64 | 404.83 |
| 3. | NPA as% to Loans Outstanding | | 23.94 | 19.87 |
| 4. | Recovery% to Total Demand (June end) | | 62.92 | 71.23 |

*Source*: *Report on Trend and Progress of Banking in India* Supplement to RBI Bulletin, Mumbai.

The wprking results of SCBS are presented in Table 4.5.

**Table 4.5:** Working Results of SCBS

| *Sl. No.* | *Item* | *2003-04 March end* | *2004-05 March end* |
|---|---|---|---|
| 1. | Profit/Loss | 373.24 | 291.21 |
| 2. | NPA as% Loans Ouststanding | 18.65 | 16.25 |
| 3. | Recovery% to Total Demand (June end) | 83.32 | 83.47 |

*Source*: *Report on Trend and Progress of Banking in India* Supplement to RBI Bulletin, Mumbai.

The NPA has decreased and credit recovery has improved in 2004-05 when compared to 2003-04. But the profit has decreased to Rs. 291.21 crore in 2004-05 from Rs. 373.24 crore in 2003-04.

### *Long-term Co-operative Credit Structure*

Before the establishment of long-term co-operatives, LT credit needs of the farmers were also met by the money-lenders who sucked their blood. To save the farmers from the exploitation of money-lenders need was felt for the establishment of a banking institution to cater to the LT credit needs of the farmers in the country. This thinking led to the establishment of LDBs which previously named as LMBS. Though the first bank was set up in Punjab at Jhang, the real break through in the development of these banks occurred during the five year plans.

## Progress of State Co-operative Agricultural and Rural Development Banks (SCARDBs)

These banks have made good progress in the matter of loan issued, no. of banks etc., as illustrated in Table 4.6.

**Table 4.6:** Progress of SCARDBs

*(Rs. in Crore)*

| *Sl. No.* | *Parameter/Item* | *1975-76* | *2000-01* | *2001-02* | *2002-03* | *2003-04* | *2004-05* | *2005-06* |
|---|---|---|---|---|---|---|---|---|
| 1. | Number | 19 | 20 | 20 | 20 | 20 | 20 | 20 |
| 2. | Owned Funds | 154.32 | 3034 | 2484 | 2892 | 4403 | 5022 | NA |
| 3. | Deposits | NA | 536 | 571 | 546 | 480 | 566 | 502 |
| 4. | Borrowings | 1383.82 | 13413 | 14846 | 15910 | 16891 | 17118 | 16964 |
| 5. | Working Capital | 1667.29 | 16896 | 18955 | 20613 | 27038 | 23187 | NA |
| 6. | Loan Issued | 204.93 | 2586 | 2746 | 2964 | 2812 | 3292 | 2819 |
| 7. | Loans Outstanding | 1068.70 | 12553 | 14147 | 15385 | 16357 | 17425 | 17895 |
| 8. | Recovery to Total Demand | NA | 58 | 55 | 49 | 44 | 44 | NA |

*Source*: *Report on Trend and Progress of Banking in India* Supplement to RBI Bulletin, Mumbai.

The loan issued was Rs. 204.93 crore in 1975-76 which increased to Rs. 2819 crore in 2005-06—an increase of 1281 per cent. In 1975-76 the working capital of banks was Rs. 1667.29 crore which rose to Rs. 23187 in 2004-05. The owned funds in 1975-76 was Rs. 154.32 crore which increased to Rs. 5022 crore in 2004-2005 (Table 4.6).

Progress of Primary Co-opersative Agricultural and Rural Development Banks: (PCARDBS). Table 4.7 Shows the performance of PCARDBS during 2000-06.

### *Working Results of SCARDBs and PCARDBs*

The working results of SCARDBS are incorporated in Table 4.8.

**Table 4.7:** Progress of PCARDBs

*(Rs. in Crore)*

| Sl. No. | Parameter/Item | 2000-01 | 2001-02 | 2002-03 | 2003-04 | 2004-05 | 2005-06 |
|---|---|---|---|---|---|---|---|
| 1. | Number | 732 | 768 | 768 | 768 | 727 | 697 |
| 2. | Owned Funds | 1628 | 2494 | 2730 | 3856 | 3494 | NA |
| 3. | Deposits | 210 | 256 | 222 | 341 | 365 | 298 |
| 4. | Borrowings | 8294 | 10334 | 11217 | 10680 | 12873 | 13238 |
| 5. | Working Capital | 10838 | 12290 | 15458 | 15812 | 17143 | NA |
| 6. | Loan Issued | 1865 | 2045 | 2151 | 2057 | 2569 | 2184 |
| 7. | Loans Outstanding | 8295 | 9982 | 10775 | 11378 | 12763 | 12792 |
| 8. | Recovery% to Total Demand | 53 | 48 | 44 | 44 | 51 | NA |

*Source*: *Report on Trend and Progress of Banking in India* supplement to RBI Bulletin, Mumbai.

**Table 4.8:** Working Results of SCARDBs

*(Rs. in Crore)*

| Sl. No. | Item | 2003-04 | 2004-05 |
|---|---|---|---|
| 1. | Profit or Loss | -118.57 | -162.57 |
| 2. | NPA as% to Loans Outstanding | 26.73 | 31.27 |
| 3. | Recovery% to Total Demand (June end) | 43.84 | 43.70 |

*Source*: *Report on Trend and Progress of Banking in India* supplement to RBI Bulletin, Mumbai.

**Table 4.9:** Workings Results of PCARDBs.

*Rs. in Crore*

| Sl. No. | Item | 2001-02 | 2003-04 | 2004-05 |
|---|---|---|---|---|
| 1. | *Profit:* | | | |
| | Number | 191 | 282 | 262 |
| | Amount | 47 | 76.75 | 665.10 |
| 2. | *Loss:* | | | |
| | Number | 577 | 489 | 465 |
| | Amount | 294 | 334.85 | 273.96 |
| 3. | NPA as% to Loans Outstanding. | NA | 35.80 | 31.9 |
| 4. | Recovery% to Total Demand (June end) | NA | 43.90 | 50.60 |

*Source: Report on Trend and Progress of Banking in India* supplement to RBI Bulletin, Mumbai.

In 2003-04 the SCARDBs incurred a loss of Rs. –118.57 crore which increased to Rs.–162.57 crore in 2004-05. NPA also increased to Rs. 31.27 crore in 2004-05 from Rs. 26.73 crore in 2003-04. The credit recovery during 2003-05 more or less remind at the same level.

The working results of PCARDBs during 2001-2005 have been shown in Table 4.9.

**Weaknesses of Rural Co-operative Credit Institutions**

The rural co-operative credit institutions have played a crucial role in reducing dependency of farmers on usurious money-lenders, in enabling farmers to use modern agriculture technology to increase crop productivity by advancing loans, in improving socio-economic status of rural population.

Inspite of these benefits and financial support from NABARD for the development of infrastructure of rural co-operative banks, the banks are suffering from the following weaknesses:

(1) Lack of owned funds/low resource base and absolute reliance on borrowings from upper-tier/NABARD.
(2) Interference of politicians in the working of the co-operative banks.
(3) Inability to issue sufficient credit to the big and medium farmers and poor response to credit requirements of marginal/ small farmers, landless labourers.
(4) Misuse of funds by the staff and elected body of the banks.
(5) Rise in the number of wilful defaulters on account of loan and interest waiver scheme of the State Governments.
(6) Huge accumulated losses, persistent NPA and low recovery level.
(7) Poor deposit mobilization.
(8) Lack of proper diversification of funds to meet the credit requirements of emerging economic activities.
(9) Poor business per PACS/PCARDB and high cost of management.
(10) Lack of sufficient, qualified and trained manpower.
(11) Lack of dynamic, impartial, honest, committed and educated Governing Body members of the Rural Co-operative Banks/ Societies.

***Suggestions***

The following suggestions are offered for improving the economic viability of the rural co-operative institutions and also in catering sufficient credit at right time, at low cost for all rural economic activities and for all credit needy people.

(1) The Government, the RBI, the NABARD, the staff of the co-operative banks should make all round efforts to provide sufficient credit to all farmers and other rural people for traditional and emerging economic activities at a low rate interest and at the right time. There is no point in waving of loan as it affects the economic viability of the institutions and increase willful defaulters.
(2) The rural co-operative banks/societies have to mobilize rural savings effectively.
(3) The Government should not nominate its own directors to the societies. This enables the elected representatives to run the institutions efficiently and impartially in the interest of all rural people.
(4) As there is some percentage of diversion of loan by the farmers, credit utilization should be monitored properly and if any farmers are involved in the diversion of credit they should be restricted from borrowing loan in future.
(5) The credit recovery has to be improved by changing the recovery schedule, recovering in installments and offering rebate on interest.
(6) Adequate provision has to be made for consumption loan for farmers with view to avoiding diversification of loan taken for productive purpose.

## Conclusion

Rural co-operative credit institutions have played a unique role in terms of issue of loans to farmers to enable them to adopt modern agricultural technology, in reducing the reliance of farmers on money-lenders etc. These institutions are the best ones to achieve 100 per cent financial inclusion in rural India, as they are familiar with rural people and their economic conditions. But even today about 50 per cent of the farmers do not borrow loan from institutional source. The farmers have expressed that the credit issued is inadequate, not available for emerging economic activities and untimely and some times costly. The resource base of these institutions have to be strengthened, the politicians should be kept away from the working of these institutions, the Government, the RBI, the NABARD and the personnel of the Co-operative Banks have to take appropriate measures from time to time to supply sufficient loan at reasonable rate of interest at right time for all economic activities for all credit needy people in rural areas.

## REFERENCES

Government of India, *Economic Survey* 2006-07.

P.S. Grewal (1991), *Rural Banking in India*, Kalyani Publishers, New Delhi.

Patnaik and Mishra (1983), *Rural Banking in India*, Anmol Publications Pvt. Ltd., New Delhi.

RBI Bulletin Annual Report 2006-07, Mumbai.

*RBI Bulletin*—Various issues, Mumbai.

Report on *Trend and Progress of Banking in India*, supplement to RBI Bulletin—Various issues, Mumbai.

Satya, Sundaram (1999), *Rural Development*, Himalaya Publishing House, Delhi.

Supplement to RBI Bulletin October 2007, Mumbai.

*The Hindu*—Daily Newspapers.

# 5

# Credit Planning in the Context of Rural Financial Intermediation in India: An Overview

PRABAL K SEN

*Banking system acts as a conduit for transfer of financial resources from net savers to net borrowers and plays a key role in mobilization and allocation of domestic savings. In a resource-scarce country like India, balanced development of the economy necessitates speedier and heftier transfer of financial resources to the sectors relatively more starved of the same. Hence there is a need to align the rural financial system to the developmental goals. Attempts to secure this alignment through institutionalization of the system were not efficacious, on account of largely inherent challenges facing the Rural Financial Market (RFM). The challenges of RFM arose from factors like (i) seasonality of agricultural business cycles, (ii) absence of traditional forms of collateral, (iii) inadequate linkage with other markets impeding information flow and risk diversification, and (iv) low population density coupled with high marginal propensity to consume (MPC), resulting in low average sizes of savings and loans, and consequently high transaction cost. A system of credit planning was therefore introduced under Lead Bank Scheme to help address these challenges.*

*Measures were taken to refine the process from time to time. Attempt was made to decentralize the exercise under Service Area Approach (SAA) in late 1980s. Notwithstanding these measures, credit planning in India continues to be afflicted by a variety of operational and management deficiencies. Also, with introduction of prudential accounting standards as a part of financial sector reforms, recovery of loans has assumed critical significance, often influencing size of the credit plans. The paper traces the evolution of credit planning in rural financial system in India, discusses various inadequacies still affecting the process and offers suggestions for addressing the issues related to these inadequacies. It concludes that efficacy of the system hinges critically on effective co-ordination among all stakeholders in the development process including notably the lending institutions, the Government and the civil society.*

## Introduction

Banking system acts as a conduit for the transfer of financial resources from net savers to net borrowers and plays a key role in mobilization and allocation of domestic savings. In an economy characterized by an overall constraint of resources, the government and the private corporate business are generally in financial *deficit*, which in accordance with the flow of funds terminology refers to a situation where the claims issued by these sectors exceed the claims acquired by them.

Imperatives of sustained economic development call for investment of resources of a gradually higher order by the government as well as the private corporate business inspite of their *deficit* status. This makes it incumbent on them to complement their investment capacity through borrowings from the third sector of the economy, namely, the households. Such borrowings from the household sector however are invariably effected through intermediation done by the banking system.

Gains to the real sector, which are manifested in the levels of development registered by the economy, are therefore dependent much on the efficiency with which the financial sector discharges its function of intermediation (Rangarajan and Jadhav: 1992). By the same token, the patterns and kinds of development (of an economy) would depend *inter alia* upon whether or not the financial system is attuned to the developmental goals of that economy.

In India the role of financial intermediation in economic development was unambiguously articulated at the very beginning of its planning process. To quote from the First Five Year Plan (GOI 1952: pp. 38-9):

> *Central banking system in a planned economy can hardly be confined to the regulation of the overall supply of credit or to a somewhat negative regulation of the flow of bank credit. It would have to take on a direct and active role, firstly, in creating or helping to create the machinery needed for financing developmental activities all over the country, and, secondly, in ensuring that the finance available flows in the directions intended......The proper discharge of its functions by the banking system will necessitate its operation more and more in the light of the priorities for development indicated in the Plan and less and less in terms of returns on capital.*

The need for alignment of the financial system to the developmental priorities is more pronounced in the case of the rural sector as historically this sector has received flows of investible resources on a considerably lower scale.

## Challenges of Rural Financial Intermediation

Orienting the Rural Financial Market (RFM) to the goals of development is acknowledged as a difficult task. That is so because it can hardly be achieved without addressing the challenges which the RFM typically faces. Studies indicate that these challenges arise out of a variety of factors (including notably the following) which usually characterize the rural sector (Yaron *et al.* 1997):

(i) Low density of population and high Marginal Propensity to Consume (MPC) resulting in low level of household savings and small size of average loans, which in turn contribute to high transaction cost,

(ii) Absence of traditional forms of collateral required by commercial banks,

(iii) Seasonality of rural agricultural business cycle and the high probability of co-variant production price and income shocks adding to the risks of financial intermediation; and

(iv) Inadequate communication and lack of integration with other markets leading to information barriers and limited scope for risk diversification.

**Attempts at Addressing the RFM Challenge: Institutionalization of the System**

A process of institutionalization of the rural financial system was embarked upon in India over a century ago for meeting the challenges of RFM, so as finally to align it to the objectives of development. It practically began with disbursement of taccavi loans by the native Governments at times of natural calamities (under Taccavi Acts, 1871-79) and was continued with enactment of the Land Improvement Loans Act, 1871, empowering the local governments to advance long term loans to the farmers for improvement of land from State funds. It was followed by introduction of the Co-operative Societies Act of 1904 in terms of which village agricultural co-operative credit societies were formed.

The process of institutionalization was reinforced by introduction of the so called Integrated Scheme of Rural Credit (ISRC) in 1954 in pursuance of the recommendation of the Committee of Direction on the All India Rural Credit Survey (AIRCS). The ISRC heralded the era of partnership between the Government and co-operative credit institutions through contribution by the former to the equity capital of these institutions. It also led to the conversion of the erstwhile Imperial Bank of India (which was then in the private sector) into the public sector State Bank of India by an Act in 1955, facilitating the association of the largest commercial bank in the country with rural credit operations (RBI 1954). Most of the policy initiatives which were launched in India after the 1950s vis-à-vis rural financial system were inspired by the report of the Committee of Direction on AIRCS (Dandekar: 1993).

## Areas of Continuing Concern–Need for Credit Planning

Successive measures taken by the Government both before and after Independence facilitated the process of institutionalization and regulation of the rural financial market to some extent. The system, however, continued to be dominated by the informal sector characterized largely by the same old medieval/exploitative features on both supply and demand sides of the credit equation.

### *Supply Side*

Lendings were made with the predominant intention to attain super normal profits based on usurious rates of interest. These were predominantly security-oriented, and the purpose for which credit was demanded was hardly a consideration. The All India Rural Credit Review Committee (AIRCRC), 1969, observed that the ultimate object in supplying credit by the money-lenders was apparently to grab the assets—moveable or immoveable—furnished as security by the borrowers. The money-lenders thus amassed considerable wealth, which was in effect either the agricultural surplus or funds created out of disinvestment of assets related to agriculture (RBI 1969a).

### *Demand Side*

Demand for credit in the rural areas arose largely for meeting the consumption requirements of the borrowers and not for carrying out any production activities. Demand for credit on investment account was insignificant inasmuch as use of capital in Indian agriculture was nominal (Singh and Asokan: 1988). Chemical fertilizers were almost unknown till the middle of 1960s, and the indigenous sources of nutrients involved hardly any cost. Ploughs, bullocks, bullock carts and a few crude implements were the only fixed assets needed. Big farmers and landlords could after all managr all these from their own resources. Only a modest part of the demand for credit on this account originated from the small farmers. Investment activities like renovation of land and dredging of ponds carried out occasionally by the small farmers were made almost exclusively with their own and family labour. Studies indicate that the major component of overall credit demand on investment account emanated largely for the purpose of purchase of land by bigger landholders from the poor peasants, and hence generated hardly any multiplier-accelerator effect.

### *The Net Outcome*

The vast mass of rural borrowers devoid of basic economic sense and bereft of general education thus remained invariably bound to a 'debt trap'. Major part of their income continued to be taken away by moneylenders through the mechanism of 'pseudo repayment' of their perpetual debt. Low level of agricultural productivity added with the requirement for payment of interest at an enormously high rate generated negative surplus for the majority of Indian farmers, which made them approach the moneylenders again and again (Ghatak 1976). To quote the National Agricultural Commission (1976), "*innumerable people are born in debt and they die in debt passing on their burden to those who follow*". Much of the indebtedness in India's countryside was thus ancestral.

In other words, some degree of institutionalization of the Indian rural financial system achieved through the measures taken towards this end notwithstanding, the Rural Financial Market (RFM) did not contribute positively to the growth and development of Indian agriculture and activities allied to it. Rather it had a disquieting effect insofar as it encouraged disinvestment of agricultural assets, funds generated out of which were mostly spent extravagantly (by the moneylenders) in luxurious consumption.

It was thus recognized at the policy level that alignment of the financial system to the development planning exercise, which aimed at economic growth combined with equitable distribution of the fruits of such growth, could hardly be achieved without a conscious introduction of a process of credit planning into the system.

There are a number of sources of finance for sustaining the process of formulation and implementation of development plans at the levels of district and sub-district units. The major among these sources are (a) revenues mobilized by the local self government institutions, (b) funds received from the state government and (c) the resources allotted under centrally sponsored schemes of employment generation and poverty alleviation. Quite a few of these centrally sponsored schemes including, notably, the *Integrated Rural Development Programme* (IRDP), since restructured as *Swarnjayanti Gram Swarozgar Yojana* (SGSY), the *Self Employment Programme for the Urban Poor*

(SEPUP), modified as the *Swarna Jayanti Shahari Rozgar Yojana* (SJSRY), the *Prime Minister's Rozgar Yojana* (PMRY) and the *Scheme of Liberation and Rehabilitation of Scavengers* (SLRS) consist of significant linkage to institutional credit. It is therefore in the fitness of things that bank credit is recognized as yet another major source of funds besides (a), (b) and (c) above, utilized for achieving the goals of the national planning process. With pronounced increase in the emphasis on programme launched for generation of employment and alleviation of poverty—success of which hinges critically on flow of credit extended by the banking system– credit plans have become important arms of the development planning exercise at district and sub-district levels (Nanjundappa: 1991).

## Evolution of Credit Planning in India

### *The Origin*

A systematic approach to credit planning for the rural sector was for the first time conceived under the Lead Bank Scheme (LBS), introduced by the Reserve Bank of India (RBI) in December 1969 in accordance with the recommendation of the "Study Group on Organizational Framework for Implementation of Social Objectives" (better known as Gadgil Study Group). The Study Group had identified serious gaps (both spatial and functional) in banking development, and recommended adoption of an area approach to banking for bridging these gaps (RBI 1969b). It was suggested that a system be evolved whereby commercial banks, particularly those in the public sector, could be entrusted with the responsibility of 'leading' the process of extending banking facilities in specified geographical areas, say, districts.

Lead banks were advised to formulate comprehensively drawn-up District Credit Plans (DCPs), which were to be implemented by banks operating in the respective districts. District credit planning, was preceded by massive expansion of bank branches, particularly in the relatively backward rural and semi-urban areas, so that the necessary framework required for implementing the Credit Plans could be put in place in hitherto neglected pockets.

### *Four Rounds of Credit Planning under LBS*

The first round of District Credit Plans (DCPs) which were expected to provide a blueprint of action on the part of the banking institutions for sub-serving the objectives laid down under the Five Year Plans, were prepared by the lead banks for their respective 'lead' districts during 1976-79. Targets for disbursement of credit for different viable sectors/activities in the district were set out in a DCP, which were reallocated among banks operating in that district, on the basis, among other things, of branch network and financial resource-base of the latter.

Three subsequent rounds of credit plans and a few independent annual plans were formulated and implemented till March 1989. These plans covered the following periods:

| | | |
|---|---|---|
| 2nd round of DCPs | : | January 1980—December 1982 |
| 3rd round of DCPs | : | January 1983—December 1984 |
| Annual Plans | : | Calendar years 1985, 1986 and 1987 |
| 4th round of DCPs | : | January 1988—March 1989 |

### *Decentralization of the Credit Planning Process*

Following the policy announcement made by the Union Finance Minister in his Budget Speech for 1989-90, the concept of 'Service Area Approach (SAA)' to rural lending was introduced by RBI in April 1989.

Under this approach, a number of villages were allocated to each of the rural and semi-urban branches of scheduled commercial banks including Regional Rural Banks (RRBs). The villages assigned to a branch constitute the *Service Area* of the Branch. According to the new dispensation put in place under SAA, each rural/semi-urban bank branch was required to prepare a credit plan, separately for each of the villages allotted to it. Such village-wise credit plans were expected to be consolidated into Branch (Service Area) Credit Plans. The credit plans thus arrived at the branch-level were aggregated into Block Credit Plans (BCPs) which, in turn, were summed up to form the District Credit Plan (DCP).

The entire credit planning exercise under SAA was thus expected to be gone through in a bottom-up process, based on the socio-economic and agro-climatic status of the service areas of the respective bank branches. Like under the previous dispensation, credit plans prepared according to SAA also were expected to have a correspondence with the development plans initiated by the government for the respective areas, and the resource-base of the bank branches concerned.

It was recognized that while national, state or even district—level planning can be based on abstraction of field-level realities, planning at the grassroots (say village)—level has to be fully informed of the ground realities. While the macro-level planning sees the forests, grassroots-level planning has of necessity to see the trees. In case of the latter each tree is important for the quality of the forest is ultimately determined by individual trees. It was generally felt that such decentralization in the matter of credit planning would help attain the objectives of the national planning exercise of reducing spatial and functional disparities in socio-economic development more effectively than hitherto.

### *Latest Development*

In pursuance of the announcement made by the Governor, Reserve Bank of India in course of mid-term review of the annual policy statement of the Bank for the year 2004-05, the 'restrictive provisions' of the service area approach have been done away with (RBI 2004a, RBI 2004b). Accordingly, the allocation of villages among the rural and semi-urban branches of banks would not be applicable for lending operations of these branches except under the Government-sponsored schemes. While the commercial banks and RRBs would be free to lend in any rural and semi-urban areas, the borrowers would have the option of approaching any bank branch for meeting their credit requirement. In view of this, RBI has dispensed with the need for preparation of village credit plans by the bank branches.

The Annual Credit Plans of bank branches would therefore now be based largely on the Potential Linked Credit Plans (PLPs)[1] prepared by the National Bank for Agriculture and Rural Development (NABARD). The particulars of potential available in different sectors (as contained in the PLPs) would be communicated to bank branches by the Conveners of the respective Block Level Bankers' Committees (BLBCs). The branches would then formulate the Branch Credit Plans with reference, among other things, to the communications received from the Conveners of BLBCs referred to above (RBI 2004b).

## Modality of Credit Planning

### *Concept of a Credit Plan*

A credit plan irrespective of whether it is prepared with reference to a district, a branch or a village, consists essentially of finalization of credit disbursement targets for a set of what are known as bankable schemes/activities. A bankable scheme is one which is technically feasible and financially viable. By technical feasibility one means that the economic activity under consideration is capable of being implemented in a given area, having regard to the interrelationship between the resources and resultant production income possibilities relevant to that activity.

All activities which are technically feasible in a given area may not be financially viable. A viable scheme is one where the aggregate income generated through operation of the scheme outweighs the cost incurred in implementing it. The surplus of income over cost should be of such a magnitude as to enable the borrower not only to repay the loan with interest from out of the surplus, but also to set apart adequate amounts for elevating his standard of living and for reinvestment in the project when necessary.

### *Estimation of Credit Demand*

Based on a comprehensive survey of their respective service areas and with reference to the potential of different activities as communicated in PLPs, the bank branches are expected to develop an insight about the demand for credit likely to emanate from different sections of the community in such areas for pursuing diverse economic activities. It has been observed that the pattern represented in the following chart corresponds closely to the ground reality of a typical Indian village. Bank branches therefore more often than not take such a scenario into account for estimating the number of units (in physical terms) of various bankable activities which are expected to require credit support (RBI 1988).

The sum of units of any given economic activity represented by item numbers (1), (3), (4) and (6) above gives the total number of physical units of the activity which may require credit in a village. It is through this process that the aggregate demand in physical terms is estimated for all possible activities having potential for development in the village. The demand for credit (on physical basis), measured in terms of number of units, when multiplied by the scale of finance/ unit cost of the respective activity, leads to the demand for credit in financial terms for that activity.

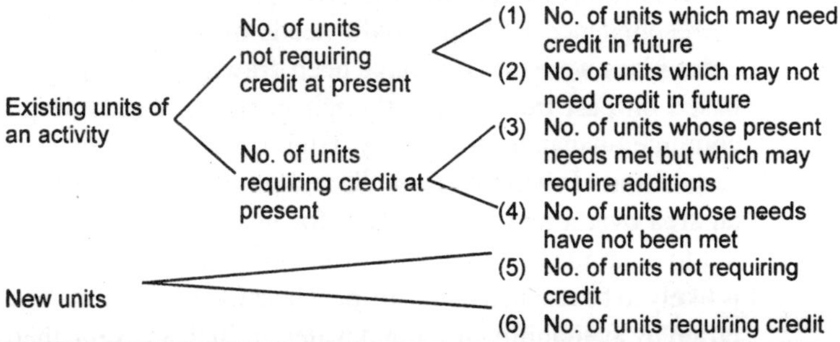


**Fig. 5.1:** Estimation of Credit Demand in Physical Terms for a Given Economic Activity

### *Assessment of the Supply Side*

No planning exercise is complete with an appraisal of the demand side only. Targets fixed without reference to the availability (i.e. supply) of resources with the lending institutions concerned will be anything but realistic. As such, a credit planner after making a comprehensive assessment of the demand for credit expected to originate from an area under reference, is required to balance the demand so estimated against the availability of financial and organizational resources with the institutions concerned, so as to arrive at realistic activity/scheme-wise targets of credit disbursement, which would constitute the basic framework of the credit plan.

## Insights Gained

Studies undertaken by the author across a number of States in the eastern, north-eastern and western regions of the country indicate that the quality of plans prepared varied from area to area and also from bank to bank within the same area. The credit planning exercise also appeared to suffer from a number of management and operational deficiencies and general infirmities. These inadequacies as revealed in course of the studies made by the author, some of which are enumerated below, affected the plans in different districts and across banks in varying degrees.

(i) Inadequate appreciation by the credit planner of the socio-economic realities of the area under reference has often led to formulation of unrealistic plans having little correspondence with the credit needs of the area. In such cases plans were found to have been drawn up mechanically based on past trends only, though in reality trends do not continue unabated indefinitely. High demand for credit for acquisition of shallow tubewells and pump sets registered in an area over a number of years, for instance, is only likely not to continue to be relevant after some time, as saturation is likely to be reached in this respect because of the limitations posed by availability of ground water. In such an event, there would rather be requirement in the subsequent years for service enterprises carrying out repairs of these items of irrigation equipment rather than for additional units of the said equipment.

(ii) Another infirmity witnessed in the credit planning exercise was that instead of allocating targets separately for the various activities comprised in a broad sector like agriculture, industries or services, credit outlays were set broad sector-wise. No allocation was made, for instance, for production of crop, investment in farm mechanization, minor irrigation or land development etc., all of which are comprised in the broad sector of agriculture and allied activities. Similarly separate targets were not set for retail trade, small business, education or road/water transport operations comprised in the services sector. Instead, credit outlays were fixed for the services sector as a whole. Essential intra-sector details were thus missing, resulting in a plan which was anything but reflective of the ground-level realities.

(iii) Credit Plans in most cases were not seen to have been dovetailed with development plans inasmuch as even a semblance of development planning (at district and sub-district levels) was found missing in most districts of the country. Post-Independence India adopted the path of planned economic development. However, for most part of the planning process the economic policy of the country was characterized by a centralized model. Studies indicate that India has not been an exception in this regard, for development initiatives in most countries have been observed to have followed a top-down approach rather than a multi-level planning model (Nanjundappa 1991). The move toward a decentralized and micro-planning regimen in this country has been slow and tortuous.

Decentralization in the planning process was for the first time seriously attempted at the national level, though only in a rudimentary form, as a part of the Sixth Five Year Plan 1980-85. Subsequently in the approach to Eighth Five Year Plan, decentralized planning was accepted as the major tool for achieving the development goals and a participatory process through transfer of both planning and implementation responsibilities to the local democratic institutions was emphasized. The approach paper expected that the process of democratic decentralization would be completed within the first year of the eighth plan. Shortly after commencement of the Eighth Five Year Plan, came the 73rd and 74th Constitution Amendment Acts which accorded statutory sanction to the decentralized planning process in the country. Notwithstanding these efforts, the system of development planning at district and sub-district levels has not yet stabilized in most parts of the country as a result of which the desired integration of credit plans with development plans at the grassroots level is yet to be achieved across the board.

(iv) In some cases where information on a few development programmes was available (even though a systematic district development plan was not in existence), bank branches failed to capture the potential created by such development programmes, as a result of which the targets fixed in the credit plans prepared by them were less than realistic. Establishment of a chilling plant in the vicinity of a village or the plans for construction of roads linking the village to nearby towns/market places, for instance, cannot but improve the potential for development of a number of activities including, notably, dairy farming, leading, in turn, to an increased demand for credit for these activities. Such possibilities, if not taken into account, can only result in underestimation of the overall demand for credit.

(v) The studies also revealed that in a large number of cases the extent of financial resources (required to be assessed in terms of inflow of deposits and recycling of funds etc.) and organizational strength (needed to be measured in terms of complement of field staff and vehicular support etc.) which would be available with the lending institutions concerned was either not assessed at all or assessed in a perfunctory manner, as a result of which allocations made in the credit plans did not necessarily have effective operational relevance.

(vi) Strategies required to be adopted and responsibilities needed to be discharged by different agencies for ensuring successful implementation of a credit plan were rarely delineated

Because of the deficiencies in the credit planning process, targets envisaged under these plans have in many cases remained arbitrary. This has been a major factor responsible for over or under-achievement of the targets at the end of the plan period. It was also observed that for the same reasons, actual disbursement of credit made in a given area during a specified time period across activities did not conform to the weightages accorded to them in the plan document. In a large number of districts covered by the author's studies, agriculture and industry sectors though assigned with higher weightages in the allocation of targets vis-à-vis service sector, actually ended up with receiving much lower shares of credit compared to the latter.

## Tasks Ahead: Ways for Improvement

### *Need for Formulation of and Integration with Development Plans at the Grassroots Level*

A credit plan at the district or sub-district level presupposes the existence of a development plan for the same level, so that the former can sub-serve the objectives of the latter (RBI 1981). With the introduction of the Constitution (73rd Amendment) and the Constitution (74th Amendment) Acts it is now the statutory requirement for development plans being formulated by the *Panchayati Raj Institutions* (PRIs) and the Urban Local Bodies (ULBs) respectively. However, the fact remains that so far development planning has by and large remained limited to the national and State-levels only, where the broad sectoral outlays are fixed in the light of accepted priorities. Allocations under various sectors for a State are disaggregated for Districts/Blocks. Steps are therefore called for to ensure that a credible framework of development planning at the grassroots (district and sub-district) levels is put in place, so that there can be a meaningful integration of credit plans–which are prepared on a bottom-up basis–with the development plans for the respective geographical entities. Decentralization of development planning is often found to be circumscribed by inflexibility in allocation of funds, which in turn is occasioned by the emphasis historically attached to the sectoral plans at the national and state levels. Also lack of credible socio-economic data often impede the process of planning at sub-State levels. These issues need to be addressed in right earnest if the overall objective of credit plans sub-serving the goals of development planning is to be achieved.

### *Backward and Forward Linkage Support*

A plan in the ultimate analysis is as good as it is implemented. One needs therefore to lay equal if not higher emphasis on availability of linkage support required for successful operation of the schemes included in a credit plan. It is not difficult to appreciate that success of any credit scheme depends not only on the adequacy and timeliness of disbursement of the financial input, but also on the availability of non-credit inputs in the form of backward and forward linkages. Disbursement to the farmers of crop loans even when made strictly as envisaged in the credit plan, may not for instance see the farmers carry out their agricultural operations successfully, if they are not able to avail themselves of seeds and water and fertilizers (backward linkages) and are not provided with proper market (forward linkage) in time. Coordinated efforts are therefore called for between the financing institutions and the development agencies in order to ensure that the schemes contained in a credit plan do not fail because of non-availability of back-up support.

### *Monitoring of Implementation*

Successful operation of a credit plan depends also on how closely its implementation is monitored on the ground. That is so because these plans more often than not envisage covering small borrowers quite a few of whom are first-generation entrepreneurs. It is only likely that such entrepreneurs would need hand-holding support. In order to enable the banks to provide such support and thus facilitate effective monitoring of implementation of the credit plans, the bank branches need to be provided with adequate complement of field staff. Also a comprehensive information system is required to be put in place. Studies made by the author indicate that there is need for modification in the Service Area Monitoring and Information System (SAMIS) in such a manner as to have the effect of simplifying the returns required to be filled in by bank branches in rural and semi urban areas and also of making these returns more conveniently amenable to computerization and analysis.

### *Reform-Driven Imperative*

Financial sector reforms introduced in India in 1992 onward have brought in their wake not only significant reduction in pre-emption of banks' funds in the form of Cash Reserve Ratio (CRR) and Statutory Liquidity Ratio (SLR) and deregulation of the interest rate structure on both credit and deposit sides, but also prudential standards of accounting for the banking system. Prudential norms have put in place a system of asset classification, income recognition, provisioning (against bad and doubtful debts) and capital adequacy stipulations, which have raised the significance of recovery of loans manifold. Incomes can now be recognized only when the same are realized and not merely when they accrue to the banks' books of accounts. Also provision is required to be made for overdue loans unless recovery is forthcoming within a stipulated time frame.

In other words, with the launching of financial sector reforms, recycling of funds has become much more important than hitherto. The limitation suffered by the Rural Financial Institutions (RFIs) on account of incidence of default and emergence of Non Performing Assets (NPAs) has, therefore, to be addressed on an urgent basis, failing which these institutions may not indefinitely be in a position to pump in credit in adequate measure. The size of credit plans is thus likely to be influenced by the rate of recovery registered by the RFIs.

## Conclusion

Institutional credit plays a key role in financing the development plans, particularly at the district and sub-district levels. It is in this context that optimum allocation of this scarce financial resource assumes critical importance. To the extent that credit plans are envisaged to accomplish this objective, there is an imperative need for addressing in right earnest all issues connected to the deficiencies identified in the process of credit planning. Efforts need also to be made to ensure that the much-desired integration of the credit plans with the development plans is accomplished across the board. It is widely recognized that the objectives of development and credit planning can hardly be achieved unless there is a perceptible improvement in the socio-economic infrastructure of the country—only which can ensure the availability of the linkage support on both backward and forward sides. There is need also for streamlining the overall credit discipline in the system, so as to secure a turn-around in the repayment climate vis-à-vis bank loans. These imperatives cannot be realized without concerted action by all stakeholders in the development process, including, notably, the lending institutions, the Government agencies and the civil society. Success in formulation as well as implementation of credit plans therefore hinges critically on effective and meaningful co-ordination among all these agencies.

## END NOTE

1. A Potential Linked Credit Plan (PLP) prepared separately for each district of the country by the National Bank for Agriculture and Rural Development (NABARD) is expected to "map the existing potentials for development and evolve an appropriate mechanism through which such potentials could be exploited over a specified time-frame. These plans presented an effort at making projections of the credit requirements in different sectors in a district, taking into account the long-term physical potential, availability of infrastructure, marketing support, absorption capacity and other strengths and weaknesses of the rural credit institutions. These plans are aimed at reflecting in a more realistic way, the micro (local) needs and potentials and linkages with development agencies" (NABARD 1995: pp. 1-2).

## REFERENCES

1. Dandekar, V.M. (1993), "Limits of Credit, Not Credit Limits", *Economic and Political Weekly,* 28 (39), September 25.

2. Ghatak, S. (1976), *Rural Money Market*; Delhi: Macmillan.
3. Government of India (1952), *The First Five Year Plan*. New Delhi: Planning Commission, Government of India.
4. Gurdev Singh and S.R. Asokan (1988), *Institutional Finance in Rural India: Efficiency and Efficacy*. New Delhi: Oxford and IBH.
5. NABARD (1995), *Handbook of Guidelines for Preparation/Updation of Potential Linked Credit Plan*, pp. 1-2. Mumbai: National Bank for Agriculture and Rural Development.
6. Nanjundappa, D.M. (1991), "Concepts, Approaches and Techniques of Decentralized Planning" in Yugandhar, B. N. and Amitava Mukherjee (Eds) (1991) *Readings in Decentralized Planning* Vol 1, pp. 13-19. New Delhi: Concept Publishing Company.
7. Rangarajan, C. and Narendra Jadhav (1992), "Issues in Financial Sector Reform" in Bimal Jalan (1992) (Ed) *The Indian Economy: Problems and Prospects*. New Delhi: Penguin Books.
8. Reserve Bank of India (1954), *All India Rural Credit Survey—Report of the Committee of Direction, Vol I (General Report)*. Mumbai: Reserve Bank of India.
9. ——— (1969 a), *Report of the All India Rural Credit Survey Committee*. Mumbai: Reserve Bank of India.
10. ——— (1969b), *Report of the Study Group on Organizational Framework for Implementation of Social Objectives*: (Chairman: D.R. Gadgil). Mumbai: Reserve Bank of India.
11. ——— (1981), *Report of the Committee to Review Arrangements for Institutional Credit for Agriculture and Rural Development (CRAFICARD)*. Mumbai: RBI.
12. ——— (1988), *Service Area Approach: Formulation of Credit Plan*. Mumbai: RBI, May.
13. ——— (2004a), *Mid-term Review of the Annual Policy for the year 2004-05*. Mumbai: Reserve Bank of India.
14. ——— (2004b), *Circular No. RBI/2004-05/293. RPCD. LBS (SAA) BC No. 62/08.01.00/2004-05* dated December 08, 2004.
15. Yaron, Jacob, McDonald P. Benjamin Jr. and Gerda L. Piprek (1997), *Rural Finance: Issues, Design, and Best Practices*. Washington, DC: The World Bank.

6

# Micro-Finance in India: New Mantra of Rural Finance

GURSHARAN SINGH KAINTH

*Rural India has not been getting as much attention as warranted from the banking sector. The flow of credit from the banking sector has grown with the banks only in the recent years after a phase of stagnation. Rural credit has suffered from high level of non-performing assets. The number of formal sector outlets that were catering to the rural people has declined due to the closure or relocation of the Regional Rural Banks which were mandated to work in these areas. The phase in which the mainstream banking services have flowed down has seen an aggressive growth of the micro-finance sector comprising to distinct strands—Self-Help Groups (SHGs) and Micro Finance Institutions (MFIs). The study has highlighted the performance of the micro-finance movement in India. It is noted that the micro-finance movement has penetrated into the client groups that a mainstream agency had not been able to reach effectively in the past. It has added a new set of clients of not only the poor, but also, to a large extent, women. It has worked under a credit culture, which bore a legacy of write-offs and political intervention and has till now proved to be an insular system with very high repayments rates. It has worked under a paradigm of social collateral, trust and local systems thereby reducing significant amount of transaction cost. It has looked at activities other than of agriculture helping people to diversify there source of livelihoods. But the progress of micro-finance sector is in the segment termed as small, short, and unsecured. This implies that the loans are really small amounts given for short duration without any security. Therefore it is unlikely that micro-finance would complete the Indian banking system. Rather, these two segments are playing complementary roles.*

Recent change in the world economy coupled with Structural Adjustment Policies (SAP's) has particularly hit hard the poorest and the most vulnerable group and also created new ones in the process. The growing mistrust of State is an obvious contributing factor in all this, particularly donor agencies. The role played by the State in dealing with poverty exacerbated the situation due to widespread political corruption and misuse of resources, thus making the poverty much more grim and serious. *"Underdevelopment"* refers to a particular type of situation, which perpetuates and reinforces the *"culture of poverty and deprivation"*: what Nurkse called a vicious circle and is at the centre of Myrdal's circular cumulative causation thesis. Economics growth alone cannot solve the grim issues of such a culture. It requires a commitment, a clear understanding of the realities of the phenomenon of underdevelopment, *a Political Will* and also clearly defined objective. Above all, it needs creation and development of institute, which can deal with the realities of underdevelopment. It is the culture of poverty and despair that needs to be replaced by the culture of hope. Tadaro has very aptly summarized all this under the heading of *"Economics as Social Systems: the Needs to Go Beyond Simple Economics"*. This is especially true today with the spread of market economics and the rapid globalization of trade, finance, technology, and labour migration. Sizeable sections of the population are trapped in poverty and have no hope of getting out unless specific and deliberate steps are taken to address this problem. The gap between the rich and poor, urban and rural is widening too. The group and communities caught in the poverty trap are clearly visible and identifiable and have historical, political as well as social backgrounding. Here comes the role of NGOs—what is sometimes labelled as the third or voluntary sector to perform very distinct function of filling the gaps ignored or bypass by the other two agencies—private as well as public sectors.

The Indian rural context has altered significantly in the last decade or so. The term small is no longer synonymous with agriculture. Services sector in the rural economy is growing rapidly and hence a growing demand for rural finance. While one can be rightly proud of the banking sector's achievements over the last few decades at the same time, one is also left with a deep sense of failure. Rural India has not getting as much attention as warranted from banking sector. The flow of credit from banking sector has grown with banks only in the recent years after a phase of stagnation. Rural credit has suffered from high levels of non-performing assets (NPA's). The number of formal sector outlets that were catering to the rural people was reducing specially with the closure or relocation of the rural branches (around 370) originated from RRBs which was mandated to serve in these areas. The policy of forcing banks to open more branches in rural areas using 1.3 rule (banks get a license to open one branch in a location that already has a branch of another bank only if they open branches in three other unbaked location) was instrumental in making significant impact on poverty. This rule was abandoned in 1990 and since then there was stagnation in expansion of bank branches especially in the rural areas. The number of rural branches has reduced from 32918 in 1997 to 32212 in 2004; a decline of 2.15 per cent while the rural population is on the increase, bank outlets in the rural area has been slowly going down. This certainly has implication on the ability if the branches to reach out to the small customers. On the other hand, the formal banking sector has moved toward large customers meeting their targets for lending to the priority sectors. The average size of direct loans to agriculture in portfolio of Commercial Banks has increased from Rs. 13,500 in 1997 to Rs. 31,585 as on March 2003. In contrast, average size of loans of the cooperative sector is currently Rs. 6640 per borrower only.

Micro-finance is defined as the provision of thrift (savings), credit and other financial services and products of very small amounts to the poor for enabling them to raise their income levels and improve living standards. Micro-finance has in recent times, comes to be recognized and accepted as one of the new development paradigms for alleviating poverty through social and economic empowerment of the poor, with focus on empowering woman. experience of different anti-poverty and other welfare programmes within the country and else-where have shown that the key to its success lies in the participation of community based organizations at the grass roots level people's participation in credit to delivery recovery and linking of formal credit institutions to borrowers through the inter-medication of Self Help Groups (SHGs) have been recognized as a supplementary mechanism for providing credit support to the rural poor. From the prevalent international point of view, micro-finance means providing the low and middle-income strata with small amounts of credit through sustained credit service activities. The essential characteristics of micro-finance, which distinguished it from the conventional financial service of formal financial institutions and traditional ways of aiding the poor, is that the poor or low and middle-income groups are the designated target customers and that customers on the designated target groups are provided with a financial products service. Such a project or institution providing particular financial service to specific target customers aspires to financial interdependence and constant goals. A type of banking service that is provided to unemployed or low-income individuals or groups who would otherwise has no other means of gaining financial services. Themes Ditcher, sketches out the dynamics of micro-credit as: "It emerges that the clients with the most experience got started using their own recourses and though they have not progressed very far. They can not because the market is just too limited—they have enough turnovers to keep buying and selling, and probably, would have with or without the micro-credit. For them loan are often diverted to consumption since they can use the relatively large lump-sum of the loan, a luxury they do not come by in their daily turnover"

Hence micro-credit is a great tool as a *Survival Strategy*. The awarding of the Noble Peace Prize to Muhammad Yunus, regarded as the father of micro-credit comes at a time when micro-credit has become something like a religion to many of the powerful rich and famous. Hillary Clinton regularly speaks about going Bangladesh Yunu's homeland and being "inspired by the power of these loans to enable even the poorest of women to start business lifting their families and their community out of poverty." The Asian and Pacific Regional Agricultural Credit Association (APRACA) presented a platform, the basic concern of which was traditional banking cannot any longer ignore the creative human potential of the poor in Asia. They should not remain wasted, as they are potential motor for grassroot level development. The APRACA, with special programme support by German Technical Assistance (GTZ, Germany) played the role of a lead agent in promoting SHG—Banking in Asia. APRAÇA is an association of Central Banks, Rural Development Banks and Rural Commercial Banks established in 1977 with support from FAO and a mandate to promote innovations in rural finance. It was at the fifth General Assembly of the (APRACA) in the Bangkok (Dec 1984) and subsequently in Kathmandu (Dec. 1986) that solutions on how to improve the access of rural poor and micro-entrepreneurs to a cost-effective financial intermediation system were discussed. Finally in Kathmandu in 1986 an agreement was signed in order to undertake national level studies on existing Self-Help Groups of the rural poor and to initiate project activities on "promotion of linkages between Banking Institution and self-help groups in rural savings mobilization and credit delivery to the rural poor."

In India, micro-finance is provided by apex development financial - institutions (such as National Bank for Agriculture and Rural Development–NABARD, Small Industries Development Bank of India, and Rashtriya Mahila Kosh), Commercial Banks, Regional Rural Banks, Co-operative Banks, Non-Banking Financial Companies (NBFCs) and various not-for-profit entities. There are different mechanisms through which the delivery of micro-credit loans takes place. Banks may lend directly to customers. Second, NABARD sponsors the Self Help Group-Bank Lending Programme (SBLP). Under SBLP, Self-Help Groups (SHGs) need to save regularly for a minimum of six months and maintain prescribed records and accounts in order to become eligible to be linked to local banks. Third, commercial banks or apex institutions lend to Micro Finance Organizations (MFOs) for further lending to groups or individuals as depicted below.

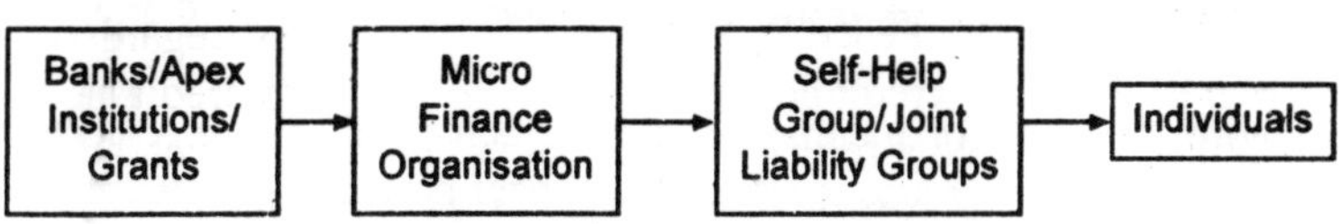


Institutional Flow of Micro-Finance

MFOs lend to SHGs and Joint Liability Groups (JLGs, which are also known as Grameen Groups). The number of MFOs in India involved in lending activities is estimated to be around 800. These MFOs vary significantly in size, outreach and credit delivery methodologies. Presently, the lending activities of MFOs are not regulated except for those registered as NBFCs.

***SHGs-Bank Linkage***

The phase in which the main-stream banking service have slowed down has also seen an aggressive growth of Micro-Finance {MF} sector. The MF-sector comprises of two distinct strands:

- The Self-Help Groups {SHGs} movement that has emerged from the mid-1980's and is actively promoted by the States and banking system.
- The Micro-Finance Institutions {MFIs} that have emerged in the 1990's and are largely coming up at the initiative of the Non-Government Organizations (NGOs) and supported by International Donors.

NGOs and Banks interact with such people, especially women from such families, to form small homogenous group. These small groups are encouraged to meet frequently and collect small thrift amounts from the members. They are taught simple accounting methods so that they maintain their own accounts. Although individually these poor could never have enough saving to bank account, the pooled saving help those to open a formal banking account in the name of the group. This is the first step to have link with the formal banking system. The group meets often and uses the pooled thrift to give small loans to members to help meet their small emergent needs. This saves them from usurious debt traps. And thus begins their empowerment through group dynamics, decision-making and funds management. Gradually, the pooled thrift grows and soon they are ready to receive external funds in multiple of the groups' saving. Such bank loans to the group help them to give larger loans to member for income generating activities. The transparent decisions taken in-groups meetings build peer pressure and ensure use of funds. Member takes up both traditional and non-traditional activities, individually or ingroup. And their income rise. These SHGs also take social action, building common pathways and cleaning village tanks or wells and participate in literacy, child care and health related programme. All this builds up their confidence, skills and entrepreneurship and they begin their march to become a part of the social and economics mainstream. The cheer on their faces is not then restricted to an occasional festival only. As the late Mahbub ul Haq said,

*"Human destiny is a choice and not a chance".*

Both these sub-strands of MF have achieved something that was difficult for the formal sector to achieve. NABARD had set a mission of credit linking one million SHGs by 2007 and the mission was achieved 3 years ahead of the schedule. The Budget for 2004-05 has emphasized the need for promoting the programme more vigorously and for the graduation of SHGs from consumption or production credit to credit for starting micro-enterprises. The Budget for 2005-06 has set an indicative target of credit linking 5.85 lakh SHGs by end of March, 2007. The programme of linking SHGs of the rural poor with the banking system was launched as a pilot project in 1992. Over the years the SHGs-Bank Linkage programme has emerged as the major micro-finance programme in the country. Currently, 560 banks including 48 Commercial Banks, 196 RRBs and 316 Cooperative Banks are actively involved in the operation of this programme. The programme has been providing the rural poor access to the formal banking system and has achieved several milestones in terms of gender sensitization, empowerment and poverty alleviation. The programme provides thrift linked credit support to the members of SHGs. While the programme directly benefits the members, it also helps banks in reducing their transaction costs as well as risk in delivering small loans.

The SHG-Bank Linkage Programme launched by NABARD continues to be the predominant MF model in the country. It is a proven method of financial inclusion, providing unbanked rural clientele with access to formal financial services from the existing bank infrastructure. During 2006-07, 686408 new SHGs were credit linked with banks as against 620109 during 2005-06, taking the cumulative number of credit linked SHGs to 2924973. The phenomenal outreach of the programme has enabled as estimated 409.5 lakhs poor households to gain access to MF for banking system as on 31 March 2007, registering a growth of 24.2 per cent over the previous year. The cumulative progress in financing SHGs from 1992 onwards, both, in physical and financial terms is presented in Table 6.1 along with Fig. 6.1 and Fig. 6.2. Bank loans aggregating Rs 39,042 million was disbursed to 2924973 SHGs covering more than 16.7 millions household with refinance support of Rs. 21,242 million from NABARD up to 31st March 2007. The cumulative number of SHGs has increased at annual growth of 62.7 per cent during 2000 through 2007. On the other hand cumulative bank loan to these SHGs increased at a much lower growth rate of only 15.1 per cent.

Apparently majority of SHGs had not availed of bank facility of banking loan. A redeeming feature of programme is that about 90 per cent of the SHGs were exclusively that of women. Furthermore on-time repayments of SHGs loans were around 95 per cent. Though cent per cent refinance from NABARD was available to all banks for SHGs; some banking did not utilize this facility to full extent. To give new life and strength to the SHGs-Bank Linkage programme during 2000-01, Rs. 100 (MFDF) crores Micro-Finance Development Fund was created with NABARD. The RBI has been taking a pro-active role in promoting micro-finance movement. It set up four groups in 2002 to look into various aspects of micro financing, based on the recommendations made by these groups, the RBI announced that banks should provide adequate incentives to their branches in making the procedures for financing the SHGs simple and easy. Based on the recommendation of the Vyas Committee, the RBI, in its annual policy statement for 2004-05, indicated that micro-finance institute would not be permitted to accept public deposits unless they comply with the extent regulatory framework.

At present, Micro Finance Institutions (MFIs) obtain finance from banks according to guidelines issued by RBI.

MFIs seek to provide small-scale credit and other financial services to low income household and small informal businesses. Government intends to promote MFIs in a big way. The way forward is to identify MFs classify and rate such institutions, and empower

**Table 6.1:** Progress of SHGs-Bank Linkage in India: 1992-2007.

| Up to March End | *Total SHGs Financed* | | | *Bank Loan* | | |
|---|---|---|---|---|---|---|
| | *During the Year* | | *Cumulative Number* | *During the Year* | | *Cumulative (Rs. Million)* |
| | *Amount (Number)* | *Per cent Growth* | | *Amount (Rs. Million)* | *Per cent Growth* | |
| 1992-99 | 18,678 | 226.60 | 32,995 | 333 | 182.20 | 571 |
| 1999-00 | 81,780 | 337.84 | 114,775 | 1359 | 308.11 | 1,930 |
| 2000-01 | 1,49,050 | 82.26 | 263,825 | 2879 | 112.85 | 4,809 |
| 2001-02 | 1,97,653 | 32.61 | 461,478 | 5454 | 89.44 | 10,263 |
| 2002-03 | 2,55,882 | 29.46 | 717,360 | 10224 | 87.46 | 20,487 |
| 2003-04 | 3,61,731 | 41.37 | 1,079,091 | 18555 | 81.48 | 39,042 |
| 2004-05 | 5,39,365 | 49.11 | 1,618,456 | 29943 | 61.37 | 68,985 |
| 2005-06 | 6,201,09 | 14.97 | 2,238,565 | 44990 | 50.25 | 113,975 |
| 2006-07 | 6,86,408 | 24.20 | 2,924,973 | 66432 | 47.35 | 180,407 |

*Source*: NABARD

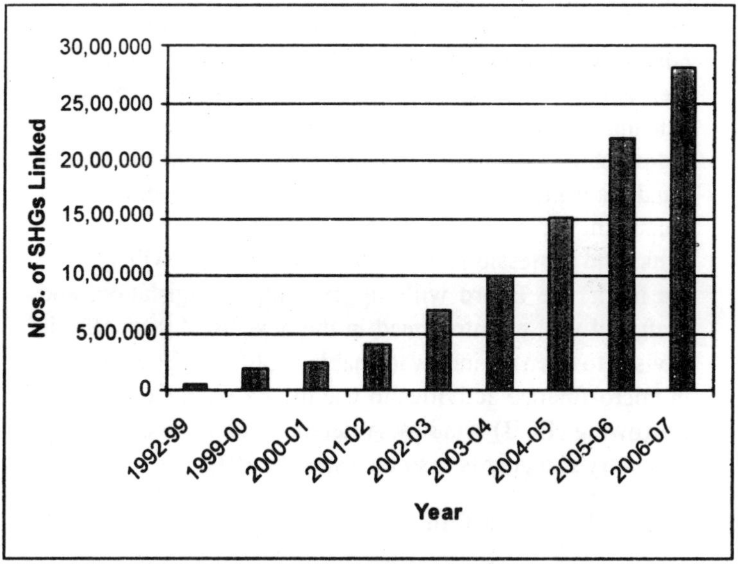


**Fig. 6.1:** Growth of SHGs-Bank Linkage in India

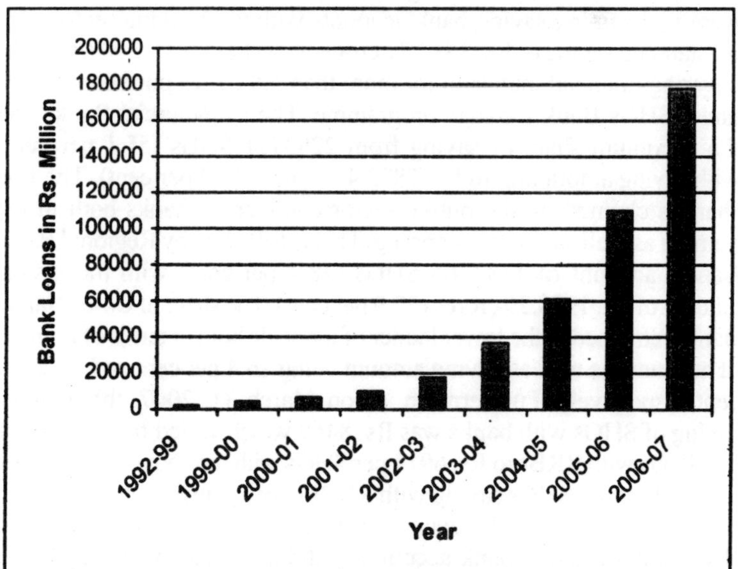


**Fig. 6.2:** Progress of Bank Loans of SHGs-Bank Linkage in India.

them to intermediate between the lending banks and the beneficiaries. Commercial banks may appoint MFs as *banking correspondents* to provide transaction services on their behalf. Since MFIs require infusion of new capital the existing Rs. 100 crore Micro-Finance Development Fund is redesignate as the "Micro-Finance Development and Equity Fund" and increased the corpus to Rs. 200 crore. A Board consisting of representatives of NABARD, commercial banks and professional with domain knowledge will manage the fund. The Board will suggest suitable legislation, and draft Bill will be introduced in the next fiscal year. RBI is advised to open a window to enable qualified NGOs engaged in micro-finance activities to use the External Commercial Borrowing (ECB) window. A detailed guideline containing necessary safeguards is to be issued by RBI.

## Savings of SHGs with Bank

The agency-wise saving of SHGs with banks as on March 31, 2007 are reported in Table 6.2 along with Fig. 6.3 and 6.4. 4160584 SHGs were maintaining saving bank accounts with the banking sector with outstanding saving of Rs. 3512.71 crores as on March 31, 2007, thereby covering financial inclusion for more than 5.8 crores poor households under SHGs Bank Linkage programme. The Commercial Banks had the maximum share of saving from 2293771 SHGs (55.1 per cent) with saving amounting to Rs. 1892.42 crores (53.9 per cent). The lion share is claimed by the public sector commercial banks both in the number as well saving outstanding. This is followed by Regional Rural Bank's account of 1183065 SHGs (28.4 per cent) with the saving amount of Rs. 1158.29 crores (32.9 per cent). The share of Co-operative Banks remained at the lower ladder of the scale both in terms of number of accounts as well as saving amount being 16.4 per cent and 13.2 per cent respectively. Furthermore, as on March 31, 2007, the average saving of SHGs with banks was Rs. 8469 which varied from Rs. 9791 per SHGs with RRBs to Rs. 6914 per SHGs with the cooperative banks. The highest per SHGs saving with RRBs may be attributed to localized nature of the banks. The exclusive women SHGs claimed the major share both in saving bank accounts with banks (78.25 per cent) with the saving share of 86.12 per cent. Per exclusive women SHGs saving was estimated at Rs. 9247 as compared per SHGs saving of Rs. 8469.

**Table 6.2:** Saving of SHGs with Banks: Agency-wise.

| Agency | *SHGs Savings as on 31 March 2007* | | | | *Saving per SHG* | *Saving of Exclusive Women SHGs* | | | |
|---|---|---|---|---|---|---|---|---|---|
| | *No* | *Per cent Share* | *Amount* | *Per cent Share* | | *No of SHGs* | *Per cent Share* | *Amount* | *Per cent Share* |
| Commercial Banks (Public Sector) | 2206335 | 53.0 | 1815.00 | 51.7 | 8226 | 1718637 | 77.90 | 1582.86 | 87.21 |
| Commercial Banks (Private) | 87436 | 2.1 | 77.42 | 2.2 | 8854 | 76083 | 87.02 | 68.61 | 88.62 |
| Commercial Banks | 2293771 | 55.1 | 1892.42 | 53.9 | 8250 | 1794720 | 78.24 | 1651.47 | 87.27 |
| Regional Rural Banks | 1183065 | 28.4 | 1158.29 | 32.9 | 9791 | 974811 | 82.40 | 1042.99 | 89.99 |
| Cooperative Banks | 683749 | 16.4 | 462.00 | 1.2 | 6914 | 501708 | 73.38 | 330.52 | 71.56 |
| Total | 4160584 | 100.0 | 3512.71 | 100.0 | 8469 | 3271239 | 78.25 | 3024.98 | 86.12 |

*Source*: NABARD.

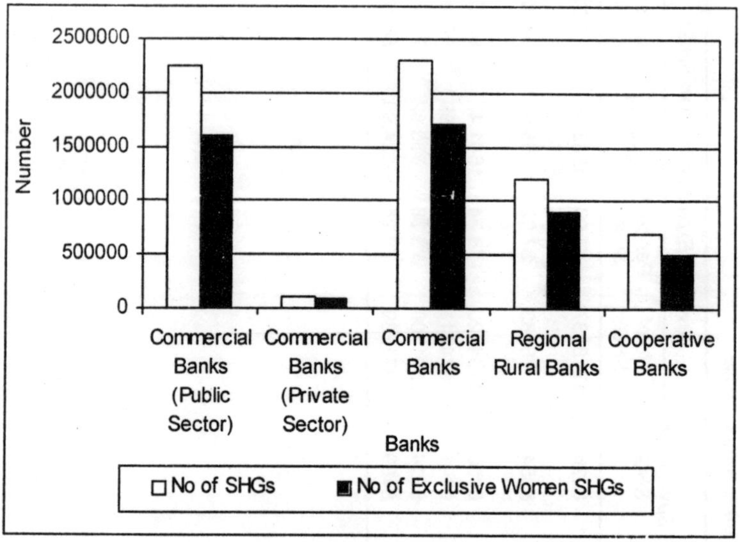


**Fig. 6.3:** No of SHGs having Saving Bank Accounts in India

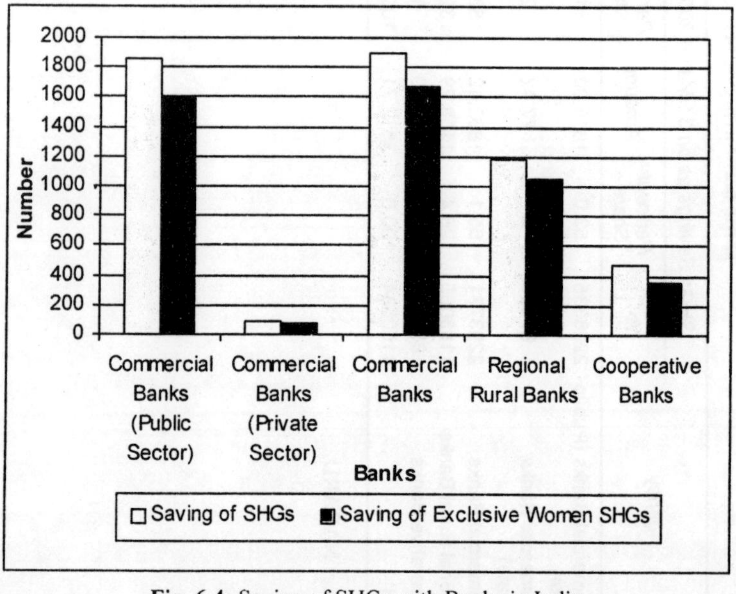


**Fig. 6.4:** Saving of SHGs with Banks in India

### Regional Spread

The year 2006-07 witnessed the spread of the MF programme in resource-poor regions of the country indicating a marked shift from its initial concentration in the southern region. (Table 6.3 and Fig. 6.5). The cumulative share of non-southern region rose from 29 per cent as on March 2001 to 48 per cent as on March 2007. Southern region continued to have the lion's share, though its share had marginally declined from 66.90 per cent as on March 2000 to 52.04 per cent as on March 2007. On the other hand North-Eastern region was on the lowest ladder of the scale claiming only 3.14 per cent of SHGs as on March 2007. This percentage has however increased from 0.20 per cent as on March 2000. This region had showed highest growth rate of 130 percent annum during the study period. The share of the Central and Western region had declined during the reference period because of slow growth rate of 58.2 per cent and 47.6 per cent respectively per annum. Similar situation was observed in respect of bank loan. Southern region continued to claim the lion's share of cumulative bank loan of 78.73 per cent as on March 2007, which was also highest at 78.34 per cent as on March 2000. On the other hand North-Eastern regions remained on the bottom ladder of the scale with a share of 0.52 per cent as on March 2007 which increased from 0.21 per cent as on March 2000.

**Table 6.3:** Progress of SHGs Bank Linkage in India: Region-wise

| Region | Per cent SHGs Financed | | Per cent Bank Loan | |
|---|---|---|---|---|
| | 2000 | 2007 | 2000 | 2007 |
| Northern | 3.41 | 5.95 | 2.33 | 3.50 |
| North-Eastern | 0.18 | 2.79 | 0.24 | 1.45 |
| Eastern | 8.43 | 17.62 | 4.84 | 8.21 |
| Central | 10.94 | 11.96 | 6.63 | 7.06 |
| Western | 5.89 | 7.43 | 8.67 | 4.61 |
| Southern | 71.15 | 54.25 | 77.29 | 75.17 |

The share of cumulative bank loan in the Northern regions had increased from 3.42 per cent as on March 2000 to 6.22 per cent as on March 2007 inspite of significant increase in the SHGs formed during the same period (from 1.94 per cent to 6.22 per cent). Further though the share of SHGs formed in Central region declined from 13.55 per cent as on March 2000 to 11.37 per cent as on March 2007, their relative share in bank loan increased from 6.90 to 7.08 per cent. Special emphasis is given by NABARD to the North-Eastern region for the implementation of SHGs bank linkage programme by collaborating with local MF agencies to bring about a synergy of interests for the development of the region. But still North-Eastern region accounts for only three per cent share of SHGs-Bank Linkage programme.

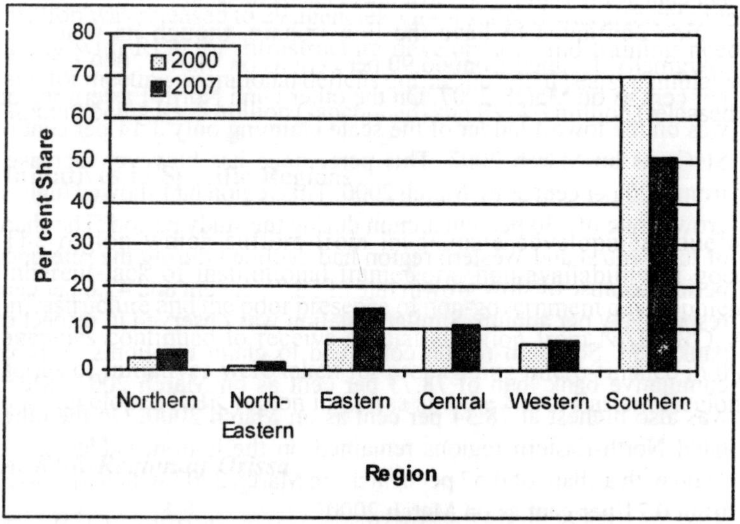


**Fig. 6.5:** Progress of SHGs Bank Linkage in India: Region-wise.

In order to reduce the regional imbalance in the spread of SHGs-Bank linkage programme, NABARD identified 13 states, which have a large poor population for focused attention. The cumulative number of SHGs credit linked in these 13 states increased from 10.05 lakhs in 2005-06 to 13.75 lakhs in 2006-07. During 2006-07, the number of SHGs credit linked in these 13 states constituted 53.9 per cent in the all India credit linked of 686408 SHGs.

***State-wise Outreach***

The spread of SHGs-Bank linkage programme has not been uniform across region of Indian Union, rather it is skewed. Even within the region, the spread and performance of MF programme varied. After the year 2004 witnessed a perceptible increase of SHGs-Bank in state, which had not shown significant progress in the past. During 2006-07 alone, some states showed an increase in the number of SHGs credit linked which was equal to or even more then the cumulative number of SHGs credit linked in those states up to March 2006.

For example, Orissa 35316 SHGs, West Bengal 19038, Rajasthan 11104; Madhya Pradesh 11824 and Bihar 8085 SHGs. The States, which already had growth record, continued to maintain the trend during 2003-04 as well. For example Andhra Pradesh 1,0 4,328 SHGs, Tamil Nadu 51,851; Karnataka 41,688, Uttar Pradesh 25,514, Maharashtra 10,470 and Kerala 12,716 SHGs. All-round growth was also witnessed during the year in the States of Himachal Pradesh 4353; Jharkhand 4882 and Chhattisgarh 3033 SHGs.

The positive growth of SHGs-Bank linkage in some of the regions and States was facilitated by the State and region-specific strategies developed by NABARD in consultation with its Regional Offices at State -level, banks, NGOs, and the State-Governments, Promotional efforts were launched by NABARD through its Regional Offices in these States, participating agencies and other specific step to identify district-level bottlenecks in expansion of SHGs Bank linkage in the State of Bihar, Uttar Pradesh, Rajasthan, Assam, Madhya Pradesh, West Bengal and Orissa, by conducting Goal of Oriented Project Planning (GOPP) programme for the district officers of NABARD in these State. This enabled NABARD to widen its network partnership beyond the NGO sector in formation and nurturing of SHGs in these States. The partners including RRBs, farmers' clubs, government organizations and development department which have effectively taken up the role of promoting and nurturing SHGs. Almost all Commercial Bank (48), RRBs (196) and Co-operatives (316) participated in SHGs-Bank linkage. Encouragingly the micro-finance outreach is also expanding from its southern stronghold to undeserved States like Uttar Pradesh, Madhya Pradesh, Rajasthan, Jharkhand, Orissa and Assam. We are now present in over 200 districts of 14 States, including 133 districts that are among the poorest in India.

**Differrent Models of Linkage**

Three broad models of SHGs-Bank linkage which have emerged over the past few years are as under:

**Table 6.4:** Progress of SHG-Bank Linkage Programme: Agency-wise

| Regions | Commercial Banks | | | | Regional Rural Banks | | | | Co-operative Banks | | | |
|---|---|---|---|---|---|---|---|---|---|---|---|---|
| | % of SHGs | | % Bank Loan | | % of SHGs | | % Bank Loan | | % of SHGs | | % Bank Loan | |
| | 2000 | 2007 | 2000 | 2007 | 2000 | 2007 | 200s0 | 2007 | 2000 | 2007 | 2000 | 2007 |
| Northern | 54.03 | 46.23 | 58.48 | 47.16 | 43.18 | 34.38 | 37.68 | 31.52 | 2.79 | 19.37 | 3.83 | 21.3 |
| North-Eastern | 11.11 | 38.17 | 13.4 | 61.64 | 87.83 | 56.15 | 82.15 | 34.45 | 1.05 | 5.66 | 4.40 | 3.89 |
| Eastern | 36.06 | 39.75 | 30.42 | 46.19 | 40.84 | 40.48 | 48.43 | 39.31 | 23.08 | 19.75 | 21.13 | 14.49 |
| Central | 19.07 | 44.61 | 44.40 | 50.48 | 79.33 | 47.92 | 52.99 | 43.74 | 1.59 | 7.46 | 2.60 | 5.77 |
| Western | 69.73 | 54.34 | 75.49 | 60.40 | 27.19 | 20.70 | 21.23 | 22.10 | 3.06 | 24.94 | 3.26 | 17.48 |
| Southern | 62.51 | 60.60 | 69.67 | 64.67 | 35.06 | 27.72 | 27.03 | 26.88 | 2.418 | 11.67 | 3.28 | 8.43 |
| Total | 54.54 | 53.07 | 66.24 | 61.31 | 41.20 | 33.06 | 29.77 | 29.15 | 4.26 | 13.87 | 3.99 | 9.54 |

*Source*: NABARD

**Table 6.5:** Progress of SHG-Bank Linkage in India: Model-wise

| Region | Model I | | | | Model II | | | | Modal III | | | |
|---|---|---|---|---|---|---|---|---|---|---|---|---|
| | No of SHGs | | Bank Loan | | No of SHGs | | Bank Loan | | No of SHGs | | Bank Loan | |
| | 2000 | 2006 | 2000 | 2006 | 2000 | 2006 | 2000 | 2006 | 2000 | 2006 | 2000 | 2006 |
| Northern | 19.08 | 8.86 | 34.47 | 7.66 | 78.40 | 90.99 | 64.55 | 92.23 | 2.50 | 0.142 | .97 | .102 |
| North-Eastern | 14.81 | 75.77 | 13.20 | 83.13 | 37.03 | 16.11 | 27.13 | 13.70 | 48.14 | 8.108 | 59.65 | 3.16 |
| Eastern | 37.13 | 32.84 | 45.73 | 36.55 | 22.70 | 58.01 | 29.23 | 56.38 | 40.16 | 9.14 | 25.03 | 7.05 |
| Central | 36.38 | 19.69 | 44.76 | 17.43 | 60.55 | 78.39 | 49.73 | 81.39 | 3.05 | 1.91 | 5.50 | 1.175 |
| Western' | 29.30 | 31.70 | 26.25 | 30.71 | 66.97 | 62.73 | 67.93 | 61.71 | 3.72 | 5.56 | 5.810 | 7.56 |
| Southern | 4.75 | 12.78 | 12.24 | 9.62 | 77.64 | 80.02 | 73.72 | 85.23 | 17.60 | 7.19 | 14.02 | 5.13 |
| Total | 14.32 | 20.07 | 17.60 | 14.36 | 69.34 | 73.53 | 69.43 | 80.71 | 16.32 | 6.39 | 12.95 | 4.92 |

*Source*: NABARD

**Table 6.6:** Grant Assistance Extended to Various Partners in SHG-Bank Linkage Programme

| Agency | Sanctions during the Year | | | Cumulative Sanctions | | | Cumulative Progress | | |
|---|---|---|---|---|---|---|---|---|---|
| | No. | Amount | No of SHGs | No. | Amount | No. of SHGs | Amount Released | SHGs Formed | SHGs Linked |
| Cooperative Banks | 8 | 64.10 | 6200 | 78 | 380.52 | 41010 | 125.25 | 28811 | 16546 |
| RRBs | 1 | 12.30 | 850 | 110 | 346.25 | 42040 | 159.28 | 49475 | 32112 |
| NGOs | 352 | 1110.66 | 40562 | 1656 | 3675.65 | 205112 | 1619.78 | 149464 | 95856 |
| Farmers' Clubs | X | X | X | X | X | X | 57.77 | 13002 | 6825 |
| IRVs | 23 | 216.90 | 12050 | 46 | 347.54 | 21110 | 18.69 | 3934 | 1589 |
| Total | 384 | 1403.96 | 59662 | 1890 | 4749.96 | 309272 | 1980.77 | 244686 | 152928 |

*Source*: NABARD

### *Model-1: Bank-SHGs-Members*

In this model, the bank itself acts as Self-Help Group Promoting Institutions (SHGIs). It takes initiatives in forming the group, nurturing them over period of time, opening of their saving accounts and then providing credit to them after satisfying itself about their maturity to absorb credit. Under this model despite significant increase in the share of SHGs formed, their relative share had declined from 17.61 per cent as on March 2000 to 14.08 per cent as on March 2006. Cumulative numbers of SHGs formed increased at an annual growth rate of 74.2 per cent while bank loan showed as increase of 74.5 per cent per annum during in reference period. This implies that per borrower loan has declined considerably during the study period. Similar situation was observed in Eastern and Southern region of India. Highly significant increase in the share of cumulative SHGs formed and bank loan was noticed in North-Eastern regions. In Northern and Central region the share under this Model had considerably declined both in SHGs formed and bank loans.

### *Model-2: Bank-(Facilitating Agency)—SHGs-Members*

In this Model, facilitating agencies like NGOs, government agencies or other community based organizations form groups. The groups are trained by these agencies. The bank open saving accounts and then provide credit directly to the SHGs after observing their operations and maturity to absorb credit. While the bank provides loan to the groups directly, the facilitating agencies continue their interaction with the SHGs. Most linkage experiences begin with this model with NGOs or other agencies playing the facilitator's role. The share of SHGs financed under this model has significantly increased to 72 per cent as on March 2006 as against 69 per cent as on March 2000. As a result their share in bank loan jumped to 81.06 per cent as on March 2006 from 69.43 per cent as on March 2000. Apparently per borrower loan sanctioned improved under this model. Similar pattern was noticed in Northern, Central, Eastern, Western and Southern region of India. On the other hand, North-Eastern region of India observed a decline in both the SHGs financed and bank loans under this Model during the reference period. The increase is attributed to the participation of more number of NGOs as also the wider involvement of Sate Government through their development agencies like the DRDA, DWDA, and some of the centrally sponsored social sector mission.

### *Model-3: Bank-NGOs-MFIs—SHGs-Members*

Due to various reasons, banks in some areas are sometimes not in a position to even finance SHGs promoted and Micro-Finance intermediaries (MFs). First, they promote the groups, nurture and train them approach banks loans for on-lending to the SHGs. Under this model, NGOs have also been found to federate the SHGs and gradually equip the SHGs federations to take on this role. Other agency like NBFCs is also coming up to take up this role. The share of cumulative number of SHGs supported under this model continue to be relatively small which declined to 7.8 per cent as on March 2006 from 16.32 per cent as on March 2000. As a result, the share in cumulative bank loan under this model declined from 12.96 per cent as on March 2000 to 4.86 per cent as on March 2006. Similar situation was noticed in all the regions of India, except Central region. In Central region, despite increase in share of cumulative SHG formed, their share in cumulative bank loan had declined as on March 2006. However, this model is likely to be found more convenient by banks for credit linkage in the coming years, when very large number of SHGs would be required to be linked by small sized branches of banks.

### Partner Agency

During the year 2006-07, 35294 branches of 560 banks–48

Commercial Banks, 196 RRBs and 316 Cooperatives participated in the SHGs-Bank linkage programme. Agency-wise numbers of SHGs financed are presented in Table 6.2. Commercial Banks claimed one-half of the SHGs formed as on March 2006 with a share of 53.9 per cent in Bank loan. On the other hand, the share of Cooperatives remained at the lowest ladder of the scale being 16.4 and 1.2 per cent as on March 2006. However there exist wide variations across different regions of the country. In Southern and Western regions Commercial Banks remained on the top of the scale, both in the SHGs formed and bank loans. However, in Northern, North-Eastern, Eastern and Central regions, RRBs dominated SHGs-bank linkage scenario. However, Cooperatives remained at the lowest ladder of the scale in all the regions.

### *Commercial Bank*

The SHGs–bank linkage became part of business for all the 27 public sector banks and 21 private sector banks. During the year, with NABARD refinance, SBI has credit linkage the highest number of SHGs (48473) during 2006-07 followed by Andhra Bank (20,164) and Indian Bank (14,320). The other banks having a significant share in the programme were Canara Bank, Indian Overseas Bank, State Bank of Hyderabad, Syndicate Bank and Bank of India. The private-sector banks which supported SHGs-Bank linkage programme was ICICI Bank (4741) followed by the Vysya Bank (1202).

### *Regional Rural Banks*

Regional Rural Banks financed SHGs in a very significant way during the study period. All the 196 RRBs in the country participated in SHGs-Bank linkage programme. During 2006-07, minimum numbers of SHGs have been linked by Pandyan Gramin Bank in Tamil Nadu (9171 SHGs) in Andhra Pradesh. The other RRBs showing significant achievement were Kolaput-Panchabati Gramin Bank, Kalahandi Anchalik Gramya Bank in Orissa and Gorakhpur Kshetriya Gramin Bank in Uttar Pradesh.

### *Cooperatives*

Cooperative Banks, though comparatively late starters, have begun making forays into the MF sector on a large scale. The amendments made by many of the States in their respective Co-operative Societies Acts enables Co-operative Banks to take up the activity of promotion and nurturing of SHGs. Influenced by the pioneering performance of DCCBs like Bidar (Karnataka), Mugberia and Hoogly (West Bengal) in the SHGs-bank linkage programme, many DCCBs evinced keen interest in SHGs-Bank linkage programme. The number of partner of the SHGs-Bank linkage in the Cooperatives banking sector increased to 516 upto March 2007. During the year, maximum number of SHGs have been linked by Hoogly DCCB (2,286 SHGs) in West Bengal, followed by Tiruchirapalli DCCB (1,940 SHGs) in Tamil Nadu and Hassan DCCB (1,850 SHGs) in Karnataka. The other DCCBs showing significant achievements cumulatively were Bidar DCCB, South Canara DCCB in Karnataka and Mugberia DCCB in West Bengal.

**Micro-Finance Institutions and Bank Linkage**

Micro-finance Institutions (MFIs) are playing an important role as financial intermediaries to micro-finance sector. MFIs operate under various legal forms:

1. NGO-MFIs registered under Societies Registration Act, 1860 and/or Indian Trust Act, 1880.
2. Cooperative-MFIs.
3. NBFC-MFIs under Section 25 of Company Act 1856 and not for profit.
4. NBFC-MFIs incorporated under Company Act 1856 and registered with Reserve Bank of India.

Following RBI guidelines in its circular of 18 February 2000, MFIs are availing bank loans from banks for on-lending to group and other smaller borrowers. The first MFI in India was set up in 1974, but the momentum was achieved only during the 1990s. Initially the formal financial institutions were reluctant to be involved with the MFIs, and social entrepreneurship was also in short supply. In recent years banks and other institutions, helped by supportive public policies, have become more aware of the commercial viability of the micro-finance services. Innovative partnership models have been developed between the banks and the MFIs. These have increased

**Table 6.7:** Bank Loans Provided to MFIs: 2006-07 (Amount in Rs. Lakh)

| *Agency* | *Amount of Loan Disbursed in 2006-07* | | | *Loan Outstanding as on 31 March 2007* | | | *Percentage of Recovery of Loans* |
|---|---|---|---|---|---|---|---|
| | *No. of Banks* | *No. of MFIs* | *Amount* | *No. of Banks* | *No. of MFIs* | *Amount* | |
| Commercial Banks (Public) | 327 | 126 | 82059.54 | 12 | 226 | 45080.26 | 92 |
| Commercial Banks (Private & Foreign) | 12 | 201 | 82059.54 | 12 | 315 | 113347.30 | 100 |
| Commercial Banks | 24 | 327 | 115133.81 | 24 | 541 | 158427.56 | |
| RRBs | 2 | 7 | 22.55 | 2 | 8 | 19.79 | 90 |
| Cooperative Banks | X | X | X | 1 | 1 | 0.60 | 100 |
| Total | 26 | 334 | 115156.36 | 27 | 550 | 158477.95 | |

availability of funding to the sector and have subsequently enabled MFIs to increase their scale of operations and outreach. On the basis of return received from banks for 2006-07, 12 public sector commercial banks, 12 private sector commercial banks, 2 Regional Rural Banks and one State Cooperative Bank have financed MFIs for on-lending. The progress of MFI Bank linkage as on March 31, 2007 is reported in Table 6.7.

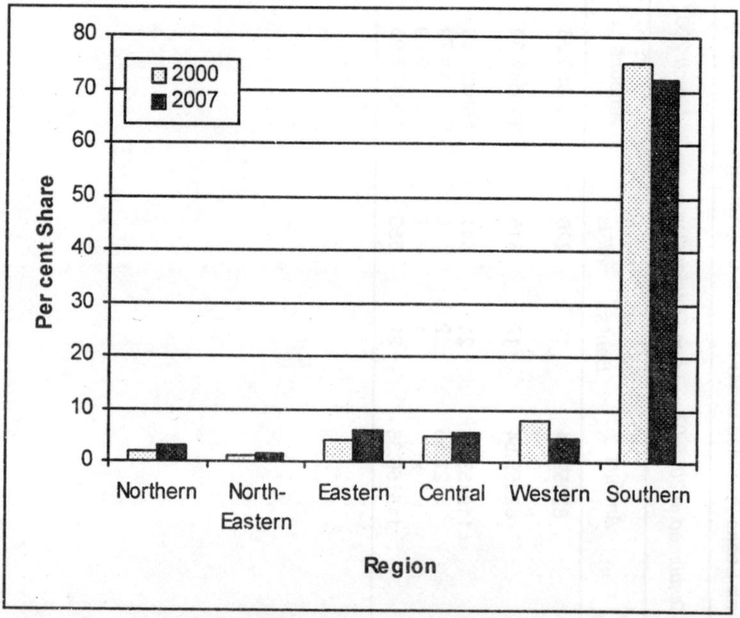


**Fig. 6.6:** Progress of Loan Disbursed: Region-wise

With a view to providing holistic support to Micro-Finance Sector and recognizing the important role played by MFIs working in remote unbanked areas of the country, NABARD provides grant and loan based assistance to these institutions.

### *(a) Capital/Equity Support*

The overall objective of the scheme, which was remodelled in February 2007, is to promote linkage between banks and MFIs so that the poor can have better access to financial services by MFIs. The specific objective of the scheme is to provide capital/equity support to MFIs so as to enable them to leverage capital/equity or accessing funds from banks, for providing financial services at an affordable cost to the poor and to enable MFIs to achieve sustainability in their credit operations over a period of 3 to 5 years. Micro Finance Organizations (MFOs), Micro Finance Institutions-Non Banking Financial Companies (MFI-NBFCs) are eligible for capital/equity support from Micro Finance Development and Equity Fund (MFDEF). Capital support would be provided in the form of soft loan at an interest rate of 3.5 per cent subject to change from time to time with tenure of seven years inclusive of moratorium of two years. The maximum capital support available under the scheme is linked to the outreach and/or amount of loan outstanding subject to a ceiling of Rs. one crore. The equity support would be restricted upto 10 per cent of the total paid up capital of the entity with a ceiling of Rs. 2 crores. MFI-NBFCs would be provided equity support in the form of Cumulative Redeemable Preference Shares with coupon rate of 3.5 per cent subject to change from time to time. During 2006-07, three MFIs viz. Rashtriya Gramin Vikas Nidhi (RGVN), Guwahati (Assam); Shri Kshetra Dharamsala Rural Dev. Project (SKDRDP), Mangalore (Karnataka) and Sangamitra Rural Financial Services, Mysore (Karnataka) have been sanctioned equity/capital support of Rs. 100 lakhs each.

### *(b) Rating of Micro-Finance Institutions*

In order to identify, classify and rate MFIs and empower them to intermediate between the lending banks and the clients, NABARD has introduced a scheme for providing financial assistance by way of grant to Commercial Banks, RRBs and Cooperative Banks to avail of the services of accredited rating agencies for rating of MFIs. Banks can avail the services of credit rating agencies viz. CRISIL, M-CRIL, ICRA, CARE and Planet Finance for rating of MFIs and avail financial assistance by way of grant to the extent of 100 per cent of the total professional fee of the credit rating agency subject to a maximum of Rs. one lakh. The facility is available for the first rating of MFIs with a minimum loan outstanding of Rs. 50 lakhs and maximum loan outstanding of Rs. 500 lakhs. The scheme will be operational up to 31 March 2010. So far only one commercial bank has availed the assistance for rating of MFIs, that is, Bharat Integrated Social Welfare Agency in Orissa.

### *(c) Revolving Fund Assistance*

NABARD provides loan funds in the form of Revolving Fund Assistance (RFA) on a very selective basis to MFIs. The RFA provided to these agencies is necessarily to be used for on-lending to SHGs or the individuals and the amount is to be repaid along with the service charges within a stipulated period of five to six years. This enables them to build a *Credit History,* which would help them to access credit facilities through the regular banking channels. During 2006-07, RFA of Rs. one crore was sanctioned to Rashtriya Gramin Vikas Nidhi, Guwahati (Assam). Cumulatively, RFA of Rs. 2832 lakhs was sanctioned to 32 agencies and Rs. 2163.8 lakhs has been released against which Rs. 615.2 lakh stands outstanding against 9 agencies.

## Promotional Efforts by NABARD

### *Grand Support to Partner Agencies for Promotion and Nurturing of SHGs.*

NABARD has been instrumental in the formation and nurturing of SHGs by means of promotional grant support to NGOs, RRBs, DCCBs, Farmer' Clubs and individual volunteers and in developing capacity-building of various partners, which have brought about excellent result in the promotion and credit linkage of SHGs. Further, increasing number of partner institutions functioning as Self-Help Promoting Institutions (SHPIs) over the years resulted in the expansion of the programme throughout the country. The financial support provided by NABARD to its partner institutions and their progress in SHGs promotion/linkage is indicated in Table 6.6.

#### *A. Support to Regional Rural Bank (RRBs)*

The local character and regional spread of RRBs give them an advantage in providing promotional and nurturing support to SHGs. Therefore, NABARD has been encouraging RRBs for this purpose from 1999 onwards. During the year 2006-07, RRBs were sanctioned a grant assistance of Rs. 12.30 lakhs for promotion and linkage of 850 SHGs taking the cumulative total of grant sanctioned to Rs. 346.25 lakhs to 90 RRBs in 20 States for promotion and linkage of 42040 SHGs. Out of this, grant assistance aggregating Rs. 159.29 lakhs was availed by banks, which resulted in formation of 49475 SHGs, of which 32112 were provided with bank loans. Highest grants was sanctioned for the Central region at Rs. 76.22 lakhs but only 24.57 lakhs was availed which resulted in the formation of 4123 SHGs. This was followed by Eastern region with Rs. 67.55 lakhs sanction and only Rs. 11.63 lakhs availed resulting in the formation of 6984 SHGs. On the other hand North-Eastern and Southern region remained at the bottom of the scale with the formation of 686 and 1490 SHGs respectively.

*B. Support to Cooperative Banks*

NABARD has been supporting capacity-building, exposure and awareness creation initiatives of the co-operatives to mainstream SHGs-Bank linkage in the co-operative banking sector. A specific initiative has been taken from last year to encourage CCBs to function as SHPIs. During the 2006-07, 28 DCCBs in 9 States have been sanctioned grant assistance of Rs. 64.10 lakhs for promotion and linkage of 6200 SHGs, taking the cumulative total grant assistance to Rs. 380.52 lakhs for 29 DCCBs for promotion and linkage of 41010 SHGs. Out of this grant assistance, an amount of Rs. 125.25 lakhs has been released for promotion of 28811 SHGs and linkage of 16546 SHGs. Highest assistance was availed by the southern region at Rs. 34.61 lakhs followed by Western Region with Rs. 14.90 lakhs. The assistance availed was minimum in North-Eastern and Northern region. Specific visits to Bidar DCCB or such other DCCB, which have successfully taken up SHGs-Bank linkage programme are also being supported. The team from the visiting CCB may comprise the President, a few directors, the CEO, other key official and even union leaders in a single batch, so that they start evolving their strategy at the training institute itself.

*C. Support to Non-Governmental Organizations (NGOs)*

Recognizing the core competences of the non-governmental agencies in formation and nurturing of good quality SHGs. NABARD continued to involve an increasing number of NGOs partner to take up the function of Self-Help Promoting Institutions (SHPIs). The NGOs, which act as SHPIs as an add-on function, were provided with supplementary assistance in the form of promotional grant and infrastructural support.

During the year, promotional grants aggregating Rs. 1110.66 lakhs were sanctioned to 352 NGOs for promotion and credit linkage of 40562 SHGs as against Rs. 36.5 million sanctioned to 243 NGOs for promotion and credit linkage of 24,332 SHGs during the year 2003-04. The amount of cumulative grant support sanctioned for promotion and linkage of SHGs aggregated Rs. 3675.65, covering 1656 NGOs towards 205112 SHGs. As against this, a cumulative grant of Rs. 1619.78 lakhs was so far, drawn by the NGOs, which resulted in promotion of 149464 SHGs and credit of 95856 SHGs.

*D. Support to Farmers' Clubs*

The Farmer's Clubs, promoted by banks under the Farmer's Club Programme—popularly known as Vikas Volunteer Vahini (3Vs) programme of NABARD enjoy local acceptability and goodwill by they being informal ambassadors of the village to the banking system. They spread the message of development through credit and inculcate repayments ethics among borrowers. Cumulatively, Farmers' Clubs were so far provided assistance of Rs. 57.77 lakhs as on March 2007 and they promoted 13002 SHGs. Of these, 6825 were credit linked as on 31 March 2007.

*E. Support to Independent Volunteers*

Based on the feedback received in respect of a pilot scheme for encouraging socially committed Individual Rural Volunteers (IRVs) in organizing the rural poor into SHGs, it was decided to extend the scheme to 13 States which account for bulk of the rural poor. During 2006-07, financial assistance of Rs. 216.90 lakhs was sanctioned to 23 IRVs for promotion of 12050 SHGs. As on March 2007, the progress under the pilot scheme has been modest, with 21110 SHGs promoted and 1589 credit linked with Rs. 18.69 lakhs of amount released. Highest SHGs linked was in the Eastern region at 968 followed by Western region at 485 and Central region at 136. No SHGs was linked in the Northern and North-Eastern region as on March 31, 2007.

## INNOVATIONS IN MICRO FINANCE

### Pilot Project on SHG-Post Office Linkage Programme

The Pilot Project on SHG-Post Office linkage programme was initially launched in 5 select districts of Tamil Nadu, viz. Sivaganga, Pudokotai, Tiruvannamali, Thanjaur and Tiruvarur with the objective of examining the feasibility of utilizing poor on agency basis. The progress under the project has been encouraging. As on date 831 SHGs have opened zero interest saving account with select post offices in Tamil Nadu and 371 SHGs have been credited linked with loan amounting to Rs. 88.23 lakhs as on march 31, 2008. Based on the success of the SHG-Post Office linkage project in Tamil Nadu, extension of pilot project to few more States is being considered. An RFA of Rs. 5 lakhs has been sanctioned to Department of Posts, Shillong in Meghalaya State for on-lending to 50 SHGs in East Khasi hills.

### *Micro Enterprise Development Programme for Skill Development*

Micro Enterprise Development Programme (MEDP) programme was launched in March 2006 with the basic objective to enhance the capacities of the members of matured SHGs to take up micro enterprises through appropriate skill upgradation/development in existing or new livelihood activities both in farm and non farm sectors by way of enriching knowledge of participants on enterprise management business dynamics and rural markets programme. The duration of training programme can vary between 3 to 13 days depending upon the objectives and nature of training. During 2006-07, a total of 297 Micro Enterprises Development Programmes were conducted covering 7579 members of matured SHGs in both the farm and non-farm sectors. Training was imparted in goat rearing, mushroom cultivation, and preparation of papad, agarbatti, candles and jute products micro enterprises.

### *Training and Capacity Building*

NABARD continued to organize/sponsor training programme and exposure visits for the benefit of officials of banks, NGOs, SHGs and government agencies to enhance their effectiveness in the field of micro-finance. Training supplements and material were supplied to banks and other agencies. Best practices and innovations of partner agencies were widely circulated among government agencies, banks and NGOs. During 2006-07, funds support of Rs. 5.80 crores was provided for capacity building, exposure and awareness building.

During the current year 5173 training/capacity building programmes were conducted covering 268078 participants. Maximum participants were in the Eastern region with 149855 participants followed by Southern region with 37020 participants. On the other hand, Northern and North-Eastern Region remained at the bottom of the ladder in 9546 and 16781 participants. Accordingly, the cumulative participations as on March 31, 2008 was highest for Eastern region at 648736 followed by Southern region at 48455. Northern region followed by Western region was at the bottom of the scale with 87920 and 123120 participants respectively.

### Social Security System for SHG Members

the pilot project launched during 2004-05 in two villages covering 500 poor house-holds from Betul district of Madhya Pradesh with a view to developing a community based social security system for SHG members in rural areas is being implemented by a NGO-Organisation for Awareness of Integrated Social Security (OASIS) - with a grant assistance of Rs 8 lakh. The scheme envisages providing a single package covering health and life insurance by paying premium generated through discounts offered by service providers like grocery shops, cloth merchants, etc, in the project area.

### Financial Assistance for Developing software-MYRADA

The Nabard had sanctioned a financial assistance of Rs. 10.29 lakh to MYRADA a NGO, managing rural development programmes, for the development of a software for NGOs. The software nabyukti is being made freely available to all NGO partners involved in the promotion and linkage of SHGs.

### Pilot Project on Processor Cards and Branch Automation

The pilot project envisages introduction of processor cards for active clients like kisan credit card (KCC) holders and SHGs as also automation of bookkeeping in SHGs with a view to reducing paper work, time saving and maintaining upto-date accounts, thus improving the efficiency levels of the field workers. The pilot project was launched with Sri Visakha Grameena Bank in the first phase and a grant assistance of Rs 25 lakh was sanctioned for implementing the project in five of its branches. In the second phase, five branches of Krishna Grameena Bank in Gulbarga have been selected.

**Piloting Alternative Mechanisms for Bookkeeping and Accounting in SHGs - Setting Up of Computer Munshi**

The project envisages entrusting the tasks of maintaining SHG Accounts, preparation of relevant reports for use by the groups as well as bankers (at a cost) by training a skilled youth from a block/ taluka/town as a computer munshi. For this purpose, Professional Assistance for Development Action (Pradan), an NGO has been sanctioned a grant assistance of Rs. 6.10 lakh. The Project is being implemented in four districts (nine units) in Orissa. So far 10 youths have been trained under the project and their services are being availed of by 1,329 SHGs in these states.

***Grain Banks and SHGs***

The pilot project enables the poor to save in kind, raise resources against such savings and provide access to self-managed, participative food security systems. Encouraged by the successful establishment and maintenance of three grain banks by SHGs formed by tribal communities covering 17 villages in two blocks of Kalahandi district, Orissa, NABARD extended the pilot project in the predominantly tribal area of Chhattisgarh. A grant assistance of Rs. 2.4 lakh has been sanctioned for construction and establishment of 10 grain banks in Bastar and Kanker districts in the state.

**Loanable Fund Assistance to NGOs and MFIs**

NABARD provides loan funds in the form of Revolving Fund Assistance (RFA) on a very selective basis to NGOs, SHGs Federations (NBFCs) and Credit Union which undertake financial intermediation. The RFA provided to the NGOs is necessarily to be used for on –lending to SHGs or individuals and the amount is to be repaid along with the service charge within a stipulated period of 5 to 6 years. This enables them to build a 'credit history', which would help them in future, while trying to access credit facilities through the regular banking channels. The RFA support also helps the NGOs and MFIs to supplement their immediate lending needs.

During the year, RFA of Rs. 84 million was sanctioned to two NGOs, viz. Friends of World Women Banking, India (Rs. 74 million for on-lending to small NGOs), and Kalanjiam Development Financial Services (Rs. 10 million for on-lending to SHGs). Cumulatively, RFA of Rs. 273 million was sanctioned to 32 agencies of which Rs. 152 million was released to 29 agencies. Grant support was also extended along with RFA for infrastructure development and training needs and for meeting operational deficits during the initial years; cumulative amount being Rs. 5 million (sanctioned) and Rs. 4.3 million (released).

## Initiatives in Specific Regions

The region which suffers from inadequate development due to inherent lack of institutional framework, non-availability of good infrastructure and the poor presence of non-government development agencies continued to receive special attention from NABARD. A series of initiatives were taken for propagating micro-finance in the less developed KBK region in Orissa and the North Eastern Region.

### *A. KBK Region of Orissa*

The Kalahandi-Bolagir-Koraput (KBK) region in Orissa continued to receive thrust in micro-finance from NABARD. During the year 12,798 SHGs were provided with bank loan, ruining the cumulative number of groups credit linked to 31,732. During the year 2003-04 six new NGOs were sanctioned promotional grant assistance of Rs. 1.9 million for promotion and linkage of 1,070 SHGs. Besides, under the scheme of associating individuals rural volunteers for SHGs promotion and linkage, Kalahandi Anchalik Gramin Bank was sanctioned a grant assistance of Rs. 0.39 million for promotion of 300 rural volunteers over a period of two years in Kalahandi, Nuapara, Kandhamal and Boudh Districts of Orissa.

### *B. North Eastern Region (NER)*

During the year, 8,209 SHGs were provided with Rs. 141.82 million as loans by banks in the NER. The cumulative number of SHGs credit linked in the NER rose to 12,278 with bank loan of Rs. 202.14 million disbursed to them. Grant assistance aggregating Rs. 1.54 million was sanctioned to 11 NGOs during the year, taking the cumulative amount of grant assistance sanctioned to Rs. 3.88 million to 25 NGOs for promotion and linkage of 2,415 SHGs in the region. As against this, grant amount of Rs. 2.04 million was released so far, resulting into promotion of 3,111 SHGs. In order to ensure that needy SHGs are not loans due funds due to poor banking infrastructure in the NER, RFA of Rs. 65.89 million was sanctioned to 6 NGOs for lending to groups for individuals. An amount of Rs. 21.5 million, has so far been released to 6 NGOs. Further, 6 RRBs in the region have been sanctioned grant support of Rs. 1.63 million to function as SHPIs.

## Micro Finance Development and Regulation Bill: 2007

India's micro-finance movement—arguably the most comprehensive attempts ever at achieving financial inclusion for poor Indian, is pacing ahead. That is despite regulatory imbroglio and amid intensifying debate over real and imagined conflicts between social and commercial objectives of micro-finance. Micro finance industry caters financial services to the poor in both rural and urban areas reaching to millions of households who were otherwise thought to be un-bankable. As an industry, it has been growing like any other sectors. But as it grows, it also needs to sustain its growth to serve the poor, women, and marginalized section of the society in a sustainable way. To sustain the growth and its services in an orderly manner, the microfinance sector requires action and co-ordination of activities to benefit stakeholders. The micro financial sector has great potential to assist in the national goal of financial inclusion and to add depth to India's financial and capital markets. There has been growing recognition for greater professionalism in the micro-finance sector. This has been fuelled by the urge for making-financial inclusion effective. Increasing outreach has underlined the need for regulation to ensure further orderly growth. The micro-fina nce sector faces other challenges as well on its road to further growth. First, there is scope for substantially improving the quality and efficiency of service delivery by the organizations providing micro-financial services. Secondly, micro-finance sector has begun to offer insurance, pensions and remittance products. As more complex products get added to the MFIs suite, professional management becomes very important. Thirdly, increasing urbanization poses new challenges and opportunities at a rate higher than the world average. Nearly

41 per cent of India's population will be urban by 2030 as per United Nation Population Fund report on *State of World Population.* MFIs need to gear up to cater to the needs of expanding urban sector. Fourthly, there is disproportionate reliance on group lending. MFIs need to offer individual-based lending which require focus on modern management information system and appraisal skills. The regulation of the sector should encourage MFIs to meet the challenges successfully. Keeping in view of the objective of creating an orderly growth, the Finance Minister introduced Micro Financial Sector Development and Regulation Bill 2007, in Lok Sabha on 20th March, 2007, henceforth the Bill as a first step in trying to regulate the sector. The Bill has since been referred to Parliamentary Standing Committee on Finance (Chairperson: Shri Ananth Kumar). The Bill was further referred to Group of Minister headed by Shri Shard Pawar, Minister of Agriculture. The Micro Financial Sector (Development and Regulation) Bill, 2007, would provide a legal framework for entities engaged in micro-finance and facilitate flow of financial services to the un-banked population of the country. The Bill has two broad objectives: (a) to promote and regulate the micro- finance sector; and (b) to permit MFOs to collect deposits from eligible clients.

> *The Preamble to the Bill sets the objective: "to provide for promotion, development and orderly growth of the micro financial sector in rural and urban areas to facilitate universal access to integrated financial services by the population not having banking facility and thereby securing prosperity of such areas and regulation of Micro Finance Organizations (MFOs) not being regulated by any law for the time being in forces and for matters connected therewith or incidental thereto".*

**Micro Finance Organizations**

The Bill defines an MFO as any organization that provides micro-finance services and includes societies, trusts, and co-operative societies (except co-operative banks, agricultural co-operative societies, and co-operative societies engaged in industrial activity or sale of any goods and services). The definition of MFO excludes SHGs and groups of SHGs. An MFO may provide micro-finance services to an 'eligible client'. Such services may be in the form of financial assistance which cannot exceed (a) Rs. 50,000 in aggregate per individual for small and tiny enterprise, agriculture, and allied activities, or (b) Rs. 1.5 lakh in aggregate per individual for housing purposes. These services also include insurance and pension services, and such other services as may be specified by NABARD. An '*eligible client*' is defined as any member of an SHG or any group formed to provide micro-finance services to certain categories of people. The categories include (a) any farmer owning a maximum of two hectares of agricultural land; (b) agricultural cultivators such as oral lessees and share-croppers; (c) landless and migrant labourers; (d) artisans and micro entrepreneurs; and (e) women.

It speaks of the sector and affirms to regulate only the MFOs and not MFIs as the latter in the shape of NBFCs are already being regulated by the RBI. Section 2(e) (i) is silent about the societies that are registered/incorporated under various state laws that have been enacted by several states for registration of societies in their respective States (e.g. Rajasthan 1958; Karnataka 1960; West Bengal 1961; Madhya Pradesh 1973; Tamil Nadu 1975; Meghalaya 1983; Andhra Pradesh 2001). Does it mean that societies in these states are excluded from the purview of this Bill, since the Societies Registration Act 1860 is not applicable in these states? Which are the other entities claimed in the Bill as not being regulated by any law? These are societies, trusts and cooperatives. These three forms are already covered by the Societies Act, Trusts Act and Cooperative Acts of both the Centre and States and these Acts have been mentioned under the Chapter on Definitions. Therefore, the very premise is wrong. The Bill excludes from its purview HUFs, NBFCs, Section 25 Companies, scheduled banks including RRBs presumably because they are already being regulated by RBI.

Second, there is lack of clarity on the scope of the Bill. The Indian micro-finance sector is characterized by a diversity of legal forms. The Bill defines a Micro Finance Organization (MFO) as "including" societies, trusts and cooperatives, leading to varying interpretations. One possible interpretation is that the Bill does not include in its scope legal forms other than those mentioned. This implies that NBFCs (Non Banking Financial Companies) and Section 25 Companies (Not for profit companies) are excluded from its scope. The largest 20 MFIs in India account for around 90 per cent of the loans outstanding and many of them are NBFCs. Of the MFI channel, NBFCs account for about 70 per cent of total loans distributed and for 70 per cent of total MFI membership (M-CRIL, 2007). Thus, excluding NBFCs is pretty much like excluding most people who are using microfinance in this country. Moreover, as NBFCs are regulated by the Reserve Bank of India (RBI), the Bill introduces differential legislation in the micro-finance sector which could lead to regulatory arbitrage. This involves structuring operations in such a manner that organization comes under the jurisdiction of a weaker regulator. Another possible interpretation is that the definition of MFO given in the Bill is not an exhaustive one and hence the Bill does in fact cover NBFCs and Section 25 companies. This will lead to dual regulation with its attendant distortions and complexities.

Section 2(c) defines "Financial Assistance" as "any loan, advance, grant or any guarantee given or any other credit facility extended in cash or kind with or without security or guarantee." Facility extended in kind becomes financial assistance and this gets regulated. The Bill provides to regulate only those groups where the individual loan assistance does not exceed Rs. 50,000 for purposes other than housing and Rs. 1.50 lakh for housing. NABARD actually went on record at number of places that the self-help group effort is an add-on or incrementalistic and not a stand-alone effort to enhance the standards of living of the poor. How these figures of Rs. 50,000 and Rs. 1.50 lakh have arrived at? No clue exists in the law.

## *Registration*

Chapter 3 provides for mandatory registration of MFOs with NABARD and periodic report submission by all MFOs seeking to accept deposits. The latter also need to submit annual audited financial statements. This has the potential to build a robust database of the sector over time; and help institute greater professionalism in the functioning of MFOs. The 'liberalistic' economy ushers in license or permit raj once again through this Bill. Section 10 seeks to recognize those MFOs which are in operation for a minimum of three years having net owned funds of at least Rs. 0.5 million and satisfactory management having net owned funds of at least Rs. 0.5 million and satisfactory management would be extended the Certificate of Registration by NABARD and would be, of course, subject to audit (Chapter 4). The Registrar of Cooperative Societies is given responsibility to scrutinize the returns for submission to the regulator. Suddenly, this odd man comes into the picture. It would be odd to find this official playing some role in micro-finance sector. The Bill provides for inspection of MFOs by the regulatory authorities in case of complaints of harmful practices. There is also a mention that a dispute resolution mechanism for disputes between MFOs and consumers may be put in place. These steps can serve as important consumer protection mechanisms.

### *Regulators*

For regulation and supervision, we need to understand some of the basic questions. First—Is regulation and supervision really necessary and why? If yes, what does it mean to "Regulate and Supervise"? To answer this, it is important to recognize the key stakeholders in micro finance. These are:—(a) Institutions (MFIs) promoted by social entrepreneurs (b) donors, banks and investors (c) the clients—poor, women and marginalized population. These stakeholders have their own expectations and goals to obtain and achieve. In fact, these different expectations and goals, if not regulated can harm the interest of the other for an orderly and sustainable growth. MFIs expect that they should be able to recover the cost of delivery. Moreover they also expect that their social mission be achieved. Likewise, donors expect that they make a profitable business by investing in MFIs and at the same time, they want that poor people improve their income standard of living through their investment. Further, the clients expect that donors and MFIs are reasonably co-operative and helpful in their dealings by availing financial education, and skills to manage and engage profitably and are able to repay their loans. These expectations needs careful management otherwise, this could lead to conflict of interest as one of them may behave opportunistically, thus ruining their relationship and the sector. Regulation can help check these expectation held highly by each of the stakeholders. Regulation and supervision is thus, said to be creating a win-win situation by preventing vested interest or the opportunistic behaviour of the investors or the promoter of MFIs or and the clients thereby providing a level playing field for all market participants.

The Bill designates NABARD as the regulator. But NABARD is already a key participant in this sector, and the developmental role envisaged in the Bill for this institution will further strengthen its role as service provider. It is widely recognized that combining the role of service provider and regulator is not a good governance practice as it could lead to serious conflict of interest. Further, NABARD has been implementing self-help group bank linkage programme for the past one-and-a-half decades and is also co-regulating the cooperative banks and RRBs sectors with serious operational and governance challenges. Can an interested party become the regulator? Which country's law allows breach of such a fundamental tenet of law except this democratic nation?

There are concerns that NABARD's regulatory capacity may be over stretched. Its own governance structure does not sufficiently emphasize competence and professionalism, as well as transparency and accountability. The preamble contains a reference to MFOs in urban areas. There are also legitimate concerns that NABARD lacks expertise to regulate and develop MFOs in the urban sector as its role has been confined to rural areas and to agriculture. NABARD Act preamble restricts its operation to rural areas. NABARD for this purpose therefore would move into operation in urban areas for regulation purpose. NABARD Act would also be amended to provide the regulatory teeth to the organizations because MFDR Bill cannot seek to confer a power primarily absent in its mandate through an extra territorial legislation. Urban micro-finance is potentially a high growth segment which needs appropriate development. It is therefore strongly suggested that designation of NABARD as regulator be reconsidered.

### *Micro Products Innovations*

The Bill defines 'micro financial services' to include insurance and pension services without specifying to whom such services are to be provided. This implies that every insurance and pension company would be regulated by NABARD. But insurance companies are regulated by the IRDA (Insurance Regulatory and Development Authority), and the pensions are proposed to be regulated by the Pension Fund Regulatory and Development Authority (PFRDA). The PFRDA Bill is waiting passage in the Parliament. The jurisdictional aspects need to be explicitly addressed in the Bill. The Bill should leave room for regulating future micro-finance product innovations.

### *Prudential Norms*

Presently, the Reserve Bank of India (RBI) regulates the collection of public deposits. Organizations authorized to do so are subject to the prudential norms set by RBI, with a view to the safety of the savings/deposit. Other than banks, NBFCs are allowed to accept public deposits if they follow the regulations prescribed by RBI. In addition, all deposits with banks are insured up to Rs. 1 lakh, i.e. if a bank is unable to honour its liabilities, deposits up to Rs. 1 lakh would be paid by the Deposit Insurance and Credit Guarantee Corporation of India. The Bill allows MFOs to offer thrift services if they meet certain prescribed provisions. The Bill has prescribed conditions that have to be met before an MFO can offer thrift services. They include: (a) the net owned funds of an MFO has to be at least Rs. 5 lakhs, and (b) the MFO has to be in existence for three years before it can offer thrift services.

There are two points of view on allowing MFOs to offer thrift services. The first point of view argues that such a provision would increase the outreach of micro-financial services. It would also offer an alternative to the poor, who had to rely on riskier and lower yielding savings instruments. The other point of view argues that if prudential norms for such MFOs are lowered it might put depositors' money at risk. Since MFOs offering thrift services mainly cater to the poor, allowing a lower level of protection for their savings might lead to further impoverishment, especially of women who form the majority of SHGs in the country. An Advisory Committee appointed by the RBI recommended that in view of the need to protect the interests of depositors, MFOs may continue to extend micro-credit services to their clients but should not be permitted to accept public deposits unless they comply with the extant regulatory framework of the RBI. The Committee further added that MFOs could play an important role in facilitating access of their clients to savings services from the regulated banks. But, the minimum net owned funds required are not related to the amount of deposits taken by the MFO. The prudential norms prescribed for the deposits collected by MFOs are inadequate. The Bill has introduced a single safeguard for savings which is the requirement that MFOs offering thrift need to create a reserve fund into which they should deposit 15 per cent of their net profit before dividend every year. The use of reserve fund as the single prudential norm has severe limitations. An MFO not making profit need not form the reserve fund, leaving no safety net for the depositors.

Further the reserve mechanism covers only savings collected through the group mechanism. But dynamically, one may expect MFOs to start offering individual loans and collect individual savings.

The requirements of protection of these saving also need to be addressed. The denial of power to MFIs to collect saving deposits has starved the sector of a source of funds that will be cheaper than raising debt at commercial rates of 10 to 14 per cent. Moreover, such savings are likely to constitute declining share. The share of client saving in sources of funds for MFIs has declined considerably from 25 per cent in 2003 to 11.2 per cent in 2005 and 8.4 per cent now. Cheaper funds will, of course, mean more affordable micro-loans and more borrowers. It's a simple equation the regulators need to get. This suggests that the Bill does not adequately take into account the future growth and development of the MFI sector.

Another serious concern is that the Bill does not specify prudential limit on the volume of deposits that an MFO can accept. The volume of deposits accepted by the MFO should be linked with its reserve fund or its capital. This anomaly may encourage undesirable elements to garner savings based on NABARD registration, which could be used to mislead customers into believing that the Government was backing these savings. It is essential to recognize that the ultimate contingent liability of micro-savings will be on the fiscal budget and therefore the taxpayers.

The bill would regulate only thrift and saving based institutions and deliberately excludes the donor-dependent and exclusive-credit purveying institutions. This is a patent inequity in the Bill. Furthermore, the Bill does not exempt registered MFOs offering thrift services from the Usurious Loans Act, 1918 or state laws which prohibit charging of excessive interest rates (such as Tamil Nadu Money Lenders' Act, 1957, Kerala Money Lenders' Act, 1958). This could lead to dual regulation of MFOs offering thrift services. The rate of interest charged by banks is exempted from the Usurious Loans Act, 1918 and any other law related to indebtedness in force in any state. This implies an uneven playing field between banks and MFOs as the latter will be subject to interest rate stipulations of the Act, but the banks are not.

### *Efficiency of MFOs*

Commercial banks have fixed costs per transaction. Therefore, the transaction costs as a percentage of the loan amount rises as the loan size decreases. This deters banks from lending small amounts. Typically, lending to small borrowers follows an indirect route.

Banks lend to MFOs who then lend to various SHGs and JLGs. Individual borrowers get funds through SHGs and JLGs. Proponents of this model claim that (a) it is characterized by low transaction costs and high repayment rates; (b) it provides access to credit to the under-served; and (c) the work of SHGs also builds livelihood capacity and social capital among the poor. However, there is an opposing view which suggests that MFOs do not incur lower transaction costs but transfer the cost to donors through subsidized borrowings or to borrowers through higher interest rates. For example, NABARD funds commercial banks at 7.5 per cent per annum, banks on-lend to MFOs at 10-15 per cent, MFOs then lend to SHGs at 12-24 per cent and the groups lend to individual members at 24-36 per cent. There is also evidence that repayment rates slacken as the size of the loan increases and as the frequency of borrowing rises. For example, in the Grameen Bank, the default rate was 0.4 per cent among first-time borrowers, 1.2 per cent among second-time borrowers, 6.6 per cent among third-time borrowers and 9.5 per cent among fourth-time borrowers.

### *Micro-Finance Development and Equity Fund*

NABARD shall constitute a Micro-Finance Development and Equity Fund to be utilized for the development of the micro-finance sector. The Fund would include (a) all grants received from the government and other sources; (b) any income received from investments made in equity of an MFO; and (c) the balance outstanding in the Fund maintained by NABARD before the commencement of the Act. The Fund would be managed by the Board of Directors of NABARD and would be used to provide any financial assistance to an MFO, invest in equity of an MFO, and meet any other expenses for the promotion of the micro-finance sector. Moreover, the Bill reveals that NABARD's is already operating Micro Finance Development and Equity Fund. Hardly anybody knew about its existence. How many MFOs received assistance or support under this Fund? Are such organizations better off than others in the conduct of their affairs?

Finally, the developmental role in the Bill is envisaged in a fairly bureaucratic manner. The central government may establish a Micro-Finance Development Council to advise NABARD on formulation of policies related to the orderly growth and development of the micro-finance sector. Chapter II specifies the composition of the Micro Finance Development Council to advise NABARD—one more advisory body for NABARD and to accommodate one more senior IAS officer to occupy the chair. Its composition queerly provides for the MFIs, the competitors of the MFOs to be in this Advisory Body. Can there be any thing odder than this? However, this is unlikely to be effective without ensuring that the members of the Council and the NABARD board members are selected on the basis of their professional competence. This is important as they will also be responsible for the Micro Finance Development and Equity Fund, a fund which is proposed to be used for providing financial assistance/equity to MFOs and for promotion of the sector. The role of financial education for all stakeholders, which is essential for the development of this sector, is conspicuously absent from the Bill. Though MFIs provide some basic training to members, financial education by independent outside agencies would help MFIs customers make more informed choices with regards to financial products. Special needs of the urban MFOs will also need to be taken into account.

### *Should Interest Rate Caps be Introduced?*

Some members of the Standing Committee of the Parliament examining the Micro-Finance Bill have suggested that a cap on interest rates on micro-finance loans be introduced. Interest rates are a function of risk, costs of funds and transaction costs. Transaction costs in micro-finance typically include cost of group formation, group training and cost of weekly collections. The costs in these loans are higher than that of corporate and personal loans because of its small values and weekly collections. Further the services are provided at the customer's door step which again adds to cost. The Finance Ministry has sensibly opposed the cap for several cogent and persuasive reasons.

First, financial transactions are complex and capping nominal interest rates may lead to repackaging of loan contracts such that effective interest rates remain the same, while adding to transaction costs. It is the effective interest rate which the borrowers must pay (and the effective cost of funds obtained by the MFOs) which is relevant. For a given nominal interest rate cap, the effective rate can be altered in many ways, e.g. by varying the definition of balances, on which the interest rate is charged, or by varying the timing of payment.

Second, interest rates should be based on risk, cost of funds and transaction costs. A cap will lead to exclusion of customers whose risk profiles call for interest rates in excess of the cap. In the context of micro-finance, a uniform interest rate would create incentives for MFIs to move away from difficult and new geographies where transaction costs are higher. Differing needs of the MFOs in rural and in urban areas may not be addressed by a single interest rate cap.

Third, interest rate caps could be detrimental in attracting private and foreign financial institutions to enter the sector and enhanced capital estimated to require funding of Rs. 500 billion annually, to the sector so that MFOs build scale and thereby reduce lending costs. Fourth, the caps complicate the task of effective supervision and regulation.

Finally, the implied subsidy on the cap is often likely to be borne by the taxpayers through the fiscal budget which is already constrained and the subsidy amounts could be better used elsewhere. If the caps are applied on Government of India or State Government mandated funds, this could lead to arbitrage opportunities with low interest funds being used to repay high interest borrowings with subsidies being met by taxpayers. Thus if effective interest rate from government mandated funds is 15 per cent, but the private MFO charges 18 per cent, there would be incentives to borrow from lower cost funds to pay-back loans with higher rates. If as a result, default rates of government mandated funds increases, the taxpayers my end up bearing the burden. The caps thus could create severe moral hazard and principal-agent problems.

Contrary to common belief, that micro-finance took its roots in the Bangladesh Grameen Bank, micro-finance organizations existed prior to the Bangladesh Grameen Bank. Starting with small chits at the household level, historically, it existed informally in the villages and organizations such as SEWA (1970s) and FWWB (1980s) in India, the Bank Rakyat in Indonesia (1970s), BANCOSAL in Bolivia which has a large clientele of small borrowers, both individual and collective. While BRI in Indonesia is owned by the Government, BANCOSAL in Bolivia is promoted by Government and the Government has invested in the Bangladesh Grameen Bank. In each of these countries and many others the governments have realized the potential of extending outreach to rural remote and marginalized populations through the means of micro-finance. The outreach of these organizations to the rural poor and strengthening the thinking that the poor have the innate ability to spur the growth of the self-help group movement since the 1970s. Despite its unequal spread in the country, more than 50 lakh groups of various hues are operating in this country. Informality is their strength. In fact, the Reserve Bank of India does not want to regulate them not because it is a burden on them but because they know that such informal groups lend better potential for growth and greater flexibility to replace the usurious money-lender. It is a fond hope that wisdom would be brought to bear on the powers to modify the Bill in a manner that would address the key issues adequately and appropriately or stop enacting the Bill for the time being. In its current form, the Bill's positive features are more than outweighed by the deficiencies. It does not satisfy either development or regulatory aspect. The Bill therefore needs to be reworked to address them. The watchwords should be professionalism, competence, financial and technical innovations, transparency and accountability. A regulator should promote social entrepreneurship and tap into the considerable expertise existing in the micro-finance sector. The aim should be to lower transaction costs and generate savings in real resource costs to the economy in delivering micro-finance services to both rural and urban sectors in a sustainable manner. Coordination with the other regulators is also essential, as so is the need for financial education. Unless the Bill is reworked to address the deficiencies discussed in the paper, it will not be able to achieve the professed objectives. The Parliament and the Government will be judged on the basis of the outcomes arising from the Bill and not by their public pronouncements. There is a plurality in regulatory mechanism—RBI, Government of India, State Governments. How should this plurality need addressing as plurality need be required in terms of the roles that different agencies need to discharge? Can these issues not be tackled by a dedicated regulatory widow? A professional regulatory structure is essential to instill confidence in the sector's stakeholders so that it is able to play a role in furthering the goals of financial inclusion and social entrepreneurship.

**Future Strategies**

The performance highlights of the micro-finance movement could be summarized as follows:

- The movement has penetrated into the client groups that a mainstream had not reached effectively in the past.

- It has added a new set of clients not only the poor, but also, to a large extent, women.
- It has worked under a credit culture, which bore a legacy of write-offs and political intervention and has tilled now proved to be an insular system with very high repayments rates.
- It has worked under a paradigm of social collateral, trust and local system thereby reducing significant amount of transaction cost.
- It has looked at activities other than of agriculture helping people to diversity their livelihoods.

But the progress of micro-finance sector is in the segment which can be termed as small, short and unsecured. This implies that the loans are really small amount given for a short-duration without any security. Therefore it was unlikely that MF would compete with the Indian banking system. Rather, it can be safely assumed that these two segments are playing complementary roles. More importantly the movement has promoted participate-decision-making; saving; a diversity of loans products for consumption; production and in some cases insurance and social security. An important lesson from MF movement is that peer pressure can be used effetely for recovery. These need to be considered in the context of extending the lesson of MF to the formal sector. Perhaps MF works on faith, which work in two ways—the person who borrows repays with the same faith because the client knows that if a person repays to the group, he/she gets a higher loan in the next cycle.

There is a need for even distribution of group formation and linkage efforts especially in the northern, central and north-eastern states and to put a check on the uneven spread to the southern region of the country. This is more important in view of higher concentration of rural poor in these regions. The critical constraining factor is that SHGs members face a lot of problems in marketing of their produce besides low level of appropriate skills. Hence, methodology for promoting micro-enterprises to create livelihood and employment opportunities among SHGs members be developed besides imparting relevant financial skill and risk taking abilities. Absorbing capacity of group members be increased by enhancing their level of skills, literacy levels, access to ICT. Nonetheless, challenges remains for all the stake-holders, viz., government, bankers, NGOs etc. to join hands in the collective efforts for the economic upliftment of the SHGs members through various repeat cycles of credit. Micro insurance products be introduce and bring together various players in the insurance sector for development of composite insurance products, which cater for life, health crops, assets and accidents on a cluster or community basis which will meet the requirements of poorer and vulnerable rural people at lower costs.

Furthermore, unless MF is tuned with livelihoods in production, manufacturing and service sectors, it would not be able to deliver anything. It is important that money is used productively. It has to produce something—goods or services that could be marketed. No doubt, MF has improved significantly, the credit delivery but the problem with the borrowers is to find marketing facilities. Institutions providing marketing supporting to these units need strengthening. It is important to recognize that state (Central, State, RBI and NABARD) has a role to play in regulation and development (at policy level) and in support infrastructure, but it should not be a player especially in loans. Micro—finance institutions need to emphasize saving, both equity and capacity—building funding and regional strategies to address the regional imbalance. Depositors need to have a large role in governance and financial institutions. No doubt MF movement is so far depoliticized, but one has to be cautions. If somebody really espouses its cause for purpose, which are political in nature, problems can arise in future. Another danger to MF movement is that the system is living on a life-prolonging ventilator and as the supply of oxygen stopped, it will collapse. The history of cooperative thrift and credit system reveals that one cannot claim even ten per cent of the primary agricultural cooperative credit society are vibrant and functional. Another limitation is that of regional imbalances. The need strategies to have much finance are accepted as a national awareness to some of major problem such as universal financial service and poverty alleviation. Interest rates charged by MFIs is a mater of concern, which charges high rates of interest to attain sustainability and pass on the higher costs of credit to their clients who are interest insensitive for small loans. It is therefore necessary for MFIs to develop strategies for increasing the range and volume of their financial services to attain sustainability while charging reasonable rates of interest to cover costs and risks. Many of MFIs face paucity of owned funds being socially oriented institutions having little access to financial capital and hence have high debt equity ratios. With the sanction of RBI to treat MFIs sector lending as a part of priority sector funding obligation, private sector banks have since designed innovative products such as the bank partnership model of ICICI banks and have also started viewing as a sound business proposition. Appropriate credit ranking of MFIs will help in increasing the comfort levels of banking system for bulk endings.

There is need to make micro-finance lending to MFIs an attractive business proposition for potential lenders, as the huge demand for financial services by poor can largely be satisfied through mobilizing capital from the formal sector. In addition to credit/financial inputs into the activities of the target group be required as credit alone cannot yield the expected results. This is possible only through close interaction with the target groups. Expansion of micro-credit programme by retailing all the distinctive managerial aspects is also a challenge to be squarely met.

Micro-finance is the key mantra for a sustained and long-term economic growth in India. The same is in sharper focus today with Government taking keen interest to ensure a comprehensive and visible uplift of rural people through effective implementations of various schemes. Therefore, it is clear that micro-finance is most important factor to attain sustainable rural development. The question then arises are: To what extent should government instrument and agents and structures get involved in this programme? How do we enlarge the role of micro-finance? Should we have a mass movement?

## REFERENCES


1. APMAS, *SHG Movement in Adilabad, Cuddapah and Vizag Districts,* Andhra Pradesh Mahila Abhivruddhi Society, APMAS, Hyderabad, 2002.
2. Chavan, P (2001), *Some feature of Rural Credit in India with special reference to Tamil Nadu: A study of the period after Nationalization,* M. Phil. dissertation, Indira Gandhi Institute of Development Research, Mumbai.
3. Friends of Women's World Banking, *Indian Self-Help Groups and Bangladesh Grameen Bank Groups: A Comparative Analysis.* Discussion Paper, Ahmedabad, 2002.
4. Harper A, 'Group-based management of savings and credit—the cases of AKRSP in Pakistan', *Small Enterprise Development*, Vol. 9 no. 2.
5. Harper M, Esipisu E, Mohanty AK and Rao DSK, *The New Middle Women, Profitable Banking through on-lending groups,* Oxford/IBH New Delhi, ITDG Publications London, 1998.
6. Harper M, *Empowerment through Enterprise,* Oxford/IBH, New Delhi 1996.

7. Hulme D, "Is Micro-debt good for poor people? A note on the dark side of micro-finance", *Small Enterprise Development*, Vol. 11, No. 1. 2000.
8. Jayaraman, B (2001) *Micro-Finance: Retrospect and Prospects*, Occasional Paper-20, National Bank for Agriculture and Rural Development, Mumbai.
9. Kainth, Gursharan Singh, (2005), "Rural Finance in India—Interface with micro-finance", paper presented at the 62nd Annual Conference of Indian Society of Agricultural Economics organized by Department of Economics, Punjab Agricultural University, Ludhiana, November 24-26, *Indian Journal of Agricultural Economics*, Vol. 60, No. 3, July-September.
10. Karmaker, K.G. (1999). *Rural Credit and Self-Help Groups: Micro-Finance Needs and Concepts in India*, Sage Publications, New Delhi.
11. Malhotra R and Chauhan SD, "Banking with the poor, Innovations by Oriental Bank of Commerce", in Basu K and Jindal K (Eds.), *Micro-finance, Emerging Challenges*, Tata McGraw Hill, New Delhi, 2000.
12. Majumdar, N.A. (1988), "Rapporteur's Report on Institutional Credit", *Indian Journal of Agricultural Economics*, Vol. 41, No. 3 July-September
13. Menon P, 'Micro-credit and mixed success', in *Frontline*, Vol. 19 No. 19, September 2000.
14. NABARD, *Annual Report of MICD*, various issues.
15. NABARD (1995) *Report of the Working Group on Non-Governmental Organizations and Self-Help Groups*, National Bank for Agriculture and Rural Development, Mumbai.
16. NABARD (2001). *NABARD and Micro Finance*, National Bank for Agriculture and Rural Development, Mumbai.
17. Puhazhendi, V. (2000): *Evaluation Study of Self-Help Groups in Tamil Nadu*, National Bank for Agriculture and Rural Development, Mumbai.
18. Puhazhendi, V and K.J.S. Satyasai (2000): *Micro-Finance for Rural People—An Impact Study*, National Bank for Agriculture and Rural Development, Mumbai.
19. Satish, P (2000). "Some Issues in the Formation of Self-Help Groups", *Indian Journal of Agricultural Economies*, Vol. 56, No. 3, July-September,
20. Shivamaggi, H.B. (1986), "Rapporteur's Report on Credit", *Indian Journal of Agricultural Economics*, Vol. 41, No. 3, July-September
21. Shergill, H.S. (1981), *Rural Credit and Indebtedness in Punjab*, Institute for Development Communication, Chandigarh.
22. Titus, M, "Costs, What do urban self-help groups tell us?," in *Beyond Micro-Credit, Putting Development Back into micro-finance*, Fisher T and Sriram MS, Vistaar Publications New Delhi, Oxfam, Oxford, 2002.
23. Zeller, M., M. Sharma, A. Ahmed, and S. Rashid. (2002) *Group-based Financial Institutions for the rural poor in Bangladesh: An institutional and household level Analysis*, Research Report No. 120, International Food Policy Research Institute. Washington, D.C.

7

# Repayment Capacity in Self-Help Groups *vs.* Co-operatives

A. MALAISAMY

*Despite the vast expansion of the formal credit in the country, the dependence of the rural poor on money-lenders continues in many areas especially for meeting credit requirements. Such dependence is pronounced in the case of marginal farmers, landless labourers, petty traders and rural artisans belonging to socially and economically backward class and tribes whose propensity to save is limited or too small to be mopped up by the banks. For various reasons, credit to these sections of the population has not been institutionalized. The Self-Help Group (SHGs) Credit has helped the beneficiaries to increase their asset, income, and employment and consumption expenditure. Results showed that the income of the beneficiaries had increased by more than three times the pre-loan income. Level of employment of SHGs beneficiaries in crop activity, livestock activity have increased by more than 184.32 man days in milk enterprises by 300.07 man days and in petty shop business by 255.00 man days. The repaying status is regular (84%) and only 16 per cent of beneficiaries are irregular.*

## Introduction

The key to economic development in general and rural development in particular, lies in identifying the sources of growth and efforts to push up the growth, the benefits have been made to step up the rate of growth, the benefits have not been equally distributed among the poor and rich. The due share of economic development benefits has not been reaching the poor and the poor have not been able to significantly contribute to the development. The concern for poverty and unemployment can be seen in the formulation and implementation of plethora of schemes and programmes for the poverty alleviation. As poverty has been attributed mainly to unemployment or lack of income yielding assets, poverty alleviation programmes hinge around provision of productive assets and creation of wage employment. The Integrated Rural Development Programme (IRDP), Rural Literate Employment Guarantee Programme (RLEGP) introduced during the past one and a half decades is yet to make an impressive dent on the rural poor. The eligibility for assistance under these programmes has been restricted. The norms of identification do not permit each and every poor being brought under the schemes. Evaluation studies of such programmes have highlighted deficiencies like improper identification, political interference, poor quality of assets and their management, inadequate technical support, loan mastication, and default in loan repayment etc.

Among the harsh realities constraining access of the poor to banks are legal or conventional requirements for the extension of credit, including the need to offer physical and formalities of documentation which they find difficult to satisfy. The extend of documentation at bank level reflects its eagerness to assess the credit risk. Social and physical distance between banks and the poor contribute to banks difficulties in associating credit worthiness. The aspect of exploitation of the rural poor is well documented. In order to release the rural poor from the clutches of money-lenders, cooperative movement was considered as the best solution. However, the poor could not derive the intended benefit mainly because the membership of a cooperative society was too large and people of diverse interests were grouped together. The economic and the caste barriers were too strong for all the people to work as one cohesive unit. Added to that, the movement was sponsored, managed and supervised by the state giving the impression that it was one of the Government's functions.

With the passage of time, the natural resource base of the village is diminishing. The land and the people are becoming poorer now, which drive them to seek alternative sources of income, diversify their production base and needs mobilization of all resources for self reliance. One of the greatest strengths that still remain largely untapped is the organising potential of a united group.

In order to remedy these defects a number of Non-Governmental Organizations (NGOs) have embarked upon the task of motivating the rural poor to form Self-Help Groups (SHGs), small and homogenous enough for successful functioning. Such groups were trained to build up financial resources through regular savings so that needy members could be given loan quickly for meeting any pressing requirements. SHGs need to be linked with banks once their activities and operations stabilize. This facilitates smoother and meaningful banking with poor. A pilot project for linking SHGs with this approach was launched by NABARD in February 1992, with Commercial Banks to actively participate in the linking programme.

There is now increased realization of the role of SHGs in meeting the credit needs of the poor both for consumption and productive purposes. Cohesiveness, mutual regard, identity of mutual interest, compliance to group discussions etc. have been acknowledged as the needed social requirement for rural development programme.

## Problem Focus

Despite the vast expansion of the formal credit in the country, the dependence of the rural poor on money-lenders continues in many areas especially for meeting credit requirements. Such dependence is pronounced in the case of marginal farmers, landless labourers, petty traders and rural artisans belonging to socially and economically backward classless and tribes whose propensity to save is limited or too small to be mopped up by the banks. For various reasons, credit to these sections of the population has not been institutionalised.

Based on the conditions prevailing in the country in regard to the credit availability to the poor, it is apparent that the SHGs have to play a crucial role in the process of economic upliftment and make a way from the vicious circle of poverty. It is also essential to have a comparative assessment of the SHGs with the cooperatives, which have made rapid progress in providing finance to the rural population with a well developed network in rural areas. Further cooperatives have been considered as an instrument for economic development of the disadvantaged, particularly in the rural areas. Under such circumstance cited above, it would be appropriate to take up a study on the lending programmes organized by the NGOs and Cooperatives for the rural poor. The present study highlights the impact of cost of credit and recovery performance of loans received by SHGs and PACB beneficiaries.

## Objectives

The overall objective of the study is to assess the impact of Self-Help Groups and Co-operatives on poorer sections of the rural populations. Specific objectives of the study are:

(i) to study cost of credit and recovery performance of loans received by SHGs and PACB beneficiaries;
(ii) to analyse the causes of defaults in repayment of loans by the beneficiaries of SHGs and Cooperatives; and
(iii) to suggest suitable policy measures.

## Methodology

Two NGOs (*PRADAN* and *ASSEFA*) which had the maximum coverage in the district were selected for the study. Three villages covered by each of these NGOs were selected by simple random sampling technique. In each village fifteen beneficiaries were selected from the list of beneficiaries availing financial assistance in the SHGs functioning in the village at random. Five Primary Agricultural Co-operative beneficiaries in each of the selected villages were also randomly selected. The ultimate sample size was 120 beneficiaries including 45 beneficiaries from SHGs organized by *PRADAN* and 45 beneficiaries from SHGs organized by *ASSEFA* and 30 beneficiaries from Co-operatives.

Conventional percentage analysis and multiple regression model was used to predict the factors responsible for cost of credit and recovery performance of loans received by SHGs and PACB beneficiaries

## Results and Discussions

The data collected from the sample respondents were analysed with reference to the specific objectives of the study. The results are presented and discussed here. The present study focused attention on the impact of SHGs on the living conditions of its beneficiaries as compared to Co-operative beneficiaries, factors influencing the recovery of loans from these beneficiaries, problems faced by the beneficiaries in availing the loans and their solutions to solve them. To study the factors influencing overdues of the beneficiaries following three variables namely debt-asset ratio, educational level of the respondent, member of SHGs, were identified as likely causes. The debt-asset ratio was dependent on the size of the family member, earning-dependent ratio of the households, educational status, transactional cost and occupational pattern. A comparison of these characteristics between the beneficiaries of SHGs and Co-operatives are presented below.

### *I. Size of Household*

The size of the beneficiaries household has a large bearing on their need for and ability to use credit. Large families with high dependency ratio might have little savings and so larger demand for credit. Most of the time it may need consumption loans as well. But a large family may also have a large workforce and credit may increase employment opportunities. For this reason size of household was studied.

It could be observed from Table 7.1 that in the case of SHG beneficiaries the average number of male adults were 2.11 and female adults 1.77. While among cooperative society beneficiaries the corresponding figures were 3.76 and 2.33 respectively. The average number of adults per family was 3.83 in the case of SHGs and 6.09 in Co-operative.

The average numbers of children in case of SHGs were 2.22 and in co-operative, it was 3.73. So total members per family in case of SHGs were 6.00 and in Co-operatives it was 9.82.

In case of SHGs household the average number of earning persons was 2.56 and it was 1.22 for beneficiaries of Co-operatives. Earner dependency ratio was higher for members of Co-operatives compared to SHGs. This might be due to the low earning potential of the beneficiaries of the SHGs.

### *II. Age and Educational Levels of Heads of Households.*

Age and education have a strong influence on any one through changes in his perception and attitudes. In case of borrowers it will help them to choose the source of finance and decide on the amount to be borrowed for the purpose chosen.

The age and education levels of the heads of the households are given in Table 7.2. It could be observed from the table that the average age of the head of the household in the case of SHGs and Co-operatives were 41.36 and 39.56 years respectively.

**Table 7.1:** Family Size, Composition and Earning Member per Household

| *Sl. No.* | *Particulars* | *SHGs* | *Co-operatives* |
|---|---|---|---|
| 1. | Adults | | |
| | Male | 2.11 | 3.76 |
| | Female | 1.77 | 2.33 |
| | Total Adults | 3.88 | 6.09 |
| 2. | Children | | |
| | Male | 1.22 | 1.33 |
| | Female | 1.00 | 2.40 |
| | Total Children | 2.22 | 3.73 |
| | Total Family Members | 6.00 | 9.82 |
| 3. | Earning Members | 2.56 | 1.22 |
| 4. | Dependent Members | 2.45 | 3.53 |
| 5. | Earner Dependency Ratio | 0.95 | 2.89 |

**Table 7.2:** Age and Educational Levels of the Heads of Households.

| *Sl. No.* | *Particulars* | *SHGs* | *Co-operative Societies* |
|---|---|---|---|
| 1. | Average age of the head of the household (in years) | 41.36 | 39.56 |
| 2. | Literacy level of the head of the household | | |
| | (a) Primary School | 61.00 (67.77) | 15.00 (50.00) |
| | (b) Middle School | 9.00 (6.00) | 8.00 (26.66) |
| | (c) High School | 6.00 (6.00) | 4.00 (13.33) |
| | (d) Total Literate | 76.00 (84.44) | 27.00 (90.00) |
| 3. | Illiterate | 14.00 (15.55) | 3.00 (10.00) |
| | Total | 90.00 (100.00) | 30.00 (100.00) |

Figures in parentheses indicate percentage to total.

Regarding the educational status, the co-operative beneficiaries had a better educational level than those of the SHGs. In case of co-operative beneficiaries the literacy percentage was 90.00 per cent while it was 84.44 per cent among SHGs beneficiaries. Only 16.00 per cent of the beneficiaries of SHGs were educated beyond primary level whereas it was 40.00 per cent for co-operative beneficiaries. This might be due to low economic status of SHG beneficiaries.

### *III. Occupational Pattern*

The nature of job determines the level of income and uncertainty in it. Therefore occupation pattern will be a likely variable to influence borrowings and repayments. Occupation pattern of sample beneficiaries is presented in Table 7.3, with the occupation defined based on their major activity. It could be observed that the occupational pattern of the sample respondents was not the same in both the groups. In the case of SHGs, 41.11 per cent of households were engaged in crop activities, 37.77 per cent in milk production activities and 21.11 per cent in petty shop business.

All the beneficiaries of Co-operatives were mainly engaged in crop activities. As such it could be noted that the income and employment potential of the members of the groups are likely to differ widely.

**Table 7.3:** Occupational Pattern of the Sample Households

| *Sl. No.* | *Occupations* | *SHGs* | *Co-operative Societies* |
|---|---|---|---|
| 1. | Crop Enterprise | 37<br>(41.11) | 30<br>(100.00) |
| 2. | Milch Enterprise | 34<br>(37.77) | 12*<br>— |
| 3. | Petty Shop Owners | 19<br>(21.11) | —<br>— |
| | Total | 90<br>(100.00) | 30<br>(100.00) |

Figures in parentheses indicate percentage to total.

* Household has both Crop and Milch Enterprise.

### *IV Amount Borrowed by Sample Beneficiaries*

An analysis of the pattern of borrowings by the members of the two groups is presented in Table 7.4 to get an insight into the income earning potential of the two groups. It could be noted that all the beneficiaries of Co-operatives availed more than Rs. 6000 as loan while only 15.56 per cent of the SHG beneficiaries were able to borrow a similar amount. More than 62.00 per cent of SHG beneficiaries were able to avail loan between Rs. 2000-4000. Only SHGs beneficiaries availed loan below Rs. 1000 perhaps another indicator of the low income earning potential of this group. Average borrowing per household amount was Rs. 4527.93 and Rs. 10065.40 for the beneficiaries of SHG and Cooperative respectively.

**Table 7.4:** Amount of Borrowing by Sample Beneficiaries

| *Sl. No.* | *Range of Borrowing* | *SHGs* | | *Co-operative* | |
|---|---|---|---|---|---|
| | | *No.* | *Average Amount Rs.* | *No.* | *Average Amount Rs.* |
| 1, | < 1000 | 12 (13.33) | 805.00 | — | — |
| 2. | 2000-4000 | 44 (48.88) | 3284.19 | — | — |
| 3. | 4001-6000 | 20 (22.22) | 5550.00 | — | — |
| 4. | Above 6001 | 14 (15.56) | 8042.85 | 30 | 10065.40 |
| 5. | Average | | 4527.93 | | 10065.40 |

Figures in parentheses indicate percentages to total.

## *V Transaction Cost*

Transaction cost has been studied with reference to the borrower. In general the cost of credit is identified with the interest charges. However the rate of interest formed only a part of the cost, as it includes a number of other items of expenses incurred by the borrower in travel to the institutions, documentation charges, commissions and unaccounted payments. The transaction cost of credit incurred by sample beneficiaries was arrived at the cost per Rs. 100 of borrowings and presented in Table 7.5.

It could be seen that the beneficiaries of SHGs incurred only interest charges for obtaining the loans, while the beneficiaries of co-operatives had incur expenses on travelling, documentation, unaccounted payment and loss due to interest on share capital. Despite these additional cost items beneficiaries of Co-operatives incurred Rs. 17.45 as against Rs. 24 by the beneficiaries of SHGs. These high rates of transaction cost of SHGs beneficiaries might be attributed to low asset status of these beneficiaries and the rigid interest rates fixed by the SHGs.

**Table 7.5:** Transaction Cost of Beneficiaries

*(Rs. 100 Rs of amount borrowed)*

| Sl. No. | Particulars | SHGs | Co-operatives |
|---|---|---|---|
| 1, | Interest Charge | 24 | 14.90 (984.39) |
| 2. | Loss due to Interest on Share Capital | — | 1.05 (6.03) |
| 3. | Travelling Cost | — | 0.35 (3.00) |
| 4. | Documentation Cost | — | 0.40 (2.29) |
| 5. | Unaccounted Payment | — | 0.75 (4.29) |
| | Total | 24 | 17.45 (100.00) |

## *VI. Repayment of Loans*

The distribution pattern of loan repayment by the beneficiaries of SHGs and Co-operative societies is shown in Table 7.6.

**Table 7.6:** Distributions of Loan Repayment by Beneficiaries

| Sl. No. | Repayment of Loans | No. of Respondents | | Percentage | |
|---|---|---|---|---|---|
| | | SHGs | Co-operatives | SHGs | Co-operatives |
| 1. | Regular | 78 | 12 | 86.66 | 40.00 |
| 2. | Irregular | 12 | 18 | 13.33 | 60.00 |
| | Total | 90 | 30 | 100.00 | 100.00 |

In SHGs, 86.66 per cent of the beneficiaries were regular repayers of loan whereas in co-operative societies only 40.00 per cent of the beneficiaries were regular repayers and the rest were irregular in repayment. This showed that among the Self-help group members repayment of loan regularly was insisted so that could avail loan in future otherwise the group become ineligible for future credit.

## *VII. Factors Influencing Overdue Position of Households*

Majority of the members of PACB availing loans were willful

defaulters which denied them future loans but also affected the regular repayers. This tendency was not observed in SHGs. To study the factors influencing overdues of the beneficiaries following three variables, namely, debt-asset ratio, educational level of the respondent, member of SHGs were identified as likely causes. A linear multiple regression function of the following form was estimated and the results are presented below.

$$OD = 4359.2964 + \underset{(1608.3312)}{9907.7246\, X1^{**}} - \underset{(75.2930)}{77.6446\, X2^{**}} - \underset{(492.2480)}{4193.3623\, X3^{**}}$$

$R^2 = 0.5293$; $N = 120$; $F = 43.4972^{**}$

*Note*: **-Significant at one per cent level;
*-Significant at five per cent level
NS—Non-significant.

The co-efficient of determination was (0.53) which indicated that 53 per cent variation in overdue position was explained by the above included explanatory variables. The function as a whole was significant at one per cent probability level. The signs of regression coefficients were as per the priori expectation. The debt-asset ratio, educational level of the beneficiaries and membership of SHGs significantly influenced the overdue position.

The increase in debt-asset ratio by one unit significantly increased the overdue position by Rs. 9907.72 which showed that debt could be effectively utilised by creating increase in income generating assets and productive use of availing capital. The SHG members properly repaid the loan because of group guarantee system and inoculation of thrift concept among members and hence these were significant reduction in overdue position of SHG beneficiaries by Rs. 4193.36 over the non-members.

## Policy Implications

The beneficiaries of SHGs incurred only interest charges for obtaining the loans while the beneficiaries of co-operatives incurred expenses on travelling, documentation, unaccounted payment and loss due to interest on these capitals. Despite these additional cost items beneficiaries of cooperatives had to incur only Rs. 17.45 as against Rs. 24 by the beneficiaries of SHGs because of high interest charges by the SHGs.

Debt-asset ratio, educational level and the membership of the SHGs significantly affected the overdue position of the beneficiaries. While debt-asset ratio exerted a positive impact on overdues, educational status and membership in SHGs significantly reduced the overdues. Of the SHGs beneficiaries 86.66 per cent were regular repayers of loans which showed the internal pressure of the group among borrowers while this is absent in cooperatives. Hence percentage of irregular repayments was more in the case of cooperative beneficiaries.

This study results recommends that subsidies can be routed through SHGs to minimize the cost of credit, which stands at 24 per cent for the SHGs beneficiaries and reduce the overdues. Policy measure can be initiated for promoting the SHGs credit to help the weaker sections.

# 8

# An Anotomy of SHG-DCCB Linkage in Maharashtra

V. M. RAO

*Based on the secondary data collected from the records of NABARD, a study was conducted in Chandrapur, Kolhapur, Latur and Thane districts of Mahashatra to assess physical and financial performance of SHG-DCCB linkage. At the national level, NABARD's emphasis on scaling up linkage programme in priority states resulted in two and half fold increase in number of SHGs linked with banks. Across states, Southern Region stood first in SHGs linked to banks, loans disbursed and refinance from NABARD. As Maharashtra, the performance is better in Vidharbha. Linkage programme helped selected DCCBs in improving recovery position with low transaction and risk costs. It was found that margins to DCCBs were high when provided loans through SHGs. Study suggested for giving impetus to linkage programme.*

## Setting

Rural credit, a vital tool for poverty-eradication, expanded considerably during the last 60 years. Nationalization of commercial banks, organization of regional rural banks, and policy support to cooperative banks are some of the initiatives in this direction. However, a large segment of underprivileged rural poor (unskilled farm workers, tenant farmers, SC/STs, and illiterate rural women) were inadvertently left out of purview of rural credit. People's participation in developmental efforts through community-based organizations was also considered as a tool to provide credit to these un-bankable or under-bankable clients. Further, policy dialogues of Asian and Pacific Regional Agricultural Credit Association (APRACA) to target new banking concepts became the entry point of SHG-banking (Erhard and Suran, 2002). NABARD is a pioneer in conceptualizing and implementing SHG-bank linkage programme in partnership with various stakeholders. This linkage programme was launched in 1992 as an experiment in providing hassle-free institutional credit *hitherto* un-reached rural poor. It is now acclaimed as the largest and fastest growing micro-finance programme in the world, and made rapid strides in Maharashtra during 2005-06, and reached a new height with credit linkage of 60324 new SHGs registering a growth of 85 per cent over previous year (NABARD, 2006). Besides SHGs, stakeholders of SHG-bank linkage programme are commercial banks, Regional Rural Banks (RRBs), District Central Cooperative Banks (DCCBs), Urban Cooperative Banks (UCBs) NGOs, and other agencies (farmers' clubs, and individual rural volunteers).

## Objectives

A modest attempt is made in this paper to assess SHG-DCCB linkage in select (Kolhapur, Latur, Thane, and Chandrapur) districts of Maharashtra to know ground realities of SHG-bank linkages. Specific objectives of the study are:

(i) to understand status of SHG-bank linkage at national level,
(ii) to assess performance of SHG-bank linkage in Maharashtra,
(iii) to analyze physical and financial performance of SHG-bank linkage in selected districts of Maharashtra,
(iv) to examine recovery, transaction costs, risk costs, and margins of DCCBs towards loans advanced to linked SHGs, and
(v) to observe training programme conducted for staff of DCCBs, and SHGs.

## Methodology

Maharashtra is purposively selected for the study, as it has been pioneer in introducing SHG-bank linkage programme through Maharashtra Rural Credit Project (MRCP, 1997)[1]. On the basis of performance of DCCBs in linkage of SHGs to credit, a best performing bank from each region (Western, Konkan, Marathwada, and Vidharbha) Kolhapur, Thane, Latur, and Chandrapur DCCBs respectively were selected. The study is based on secondary data collected from DCCBs and NABARD.

## Concept of SHG

The concept of SHG is to provide poor with economic and social entitlement to resources through their active participation. SHGs are formed on voluntary basis and characterized by small-size usually limited to less than 20 members per group.

### *Concept of SHG-Bank Linkage*

SHG-bank linkage is a programme that helps to promote financial transactions between formal rural banking system comprising of public and private sector commercial banks, regional rural banks, and co-operative banks with informal SHGs as clients (Erhard and Suran, 2002). The process of SHG-Bank Linkage programme in India has three models: a) SHGs formed and financed by banks, (b) SHGs formed by NGOs and formal agencies, but directly financed by banks, and c) SHGs financed by banks using NGOs and other agencies as financial intermediaries.

### *Growth of SHG-Bank Linkage in India*

NABARD, in partnership with various stakeholders, has been facilitating SHG-Bank Linkage programme. The programme provides a 'savings and credit history' for the members of SHG, auguring well at the time of taking loans from banks. Simultaneously, it helps banks in reducing their transaction as well as risk costs in delivering small loans. On account of these positive features, SHG-bank linkage programme caught imagination of not only financial institutions, but also governmental and non-governmental agencies who joined hands with NABARD in its efforts.

Over the last one and a half decade, micro-finance initiatives of NABARD through its SHG-bank linkage programme has passed through three phases (viz.) pilot testing (1992-95), mainstreaming (1996-98), and expansion (1998 onwards), and has assumed shape of a micro-finance movement in the country (Table 8.1). During 2005-06, more than 16 lakh SHGs were credit linked with banks as against 255 during 1992-93. The programme has enabled poor households in the country to gain access to micro-finance from formal banking system, and ranged from 23 to 77 per cent during 1994-06.

**Table 8.1:** Progress of SHG-Bank Linkage Programme in India

| *Year* | *SHGs (000) Linked with Banks* | *Growth of SHG-Bank Linkage (%)* |
|---|---|---|
| 1992-93 | 255 | — |
| 1993-94 | 365 | 30 |
| 1994-95 | 1502 | 76 |
| 1995-96 | 2635 | 43 |
| 1996-97 | 3841 | 31 |
| 1997-98 | 5719 | 33 |
| 1998-99 | 18678 | 69 |
| 1999-00 | 81780 | 77 |
| 2000-01 | 149050 | 45 |
| 2001-02 | 197653 | 25 |
| 2002-03 | 255882 | 23 |
| 2003-04 | 361731 | 29 |
| 2004-05 | 539385 | 33 |
| 2005-06 | 1699140 | 68 |

*Source*: NABARD (various years).

In order to balance uneven growth of SHG-bank linkage programme, 13 states have been identified as priority states, where SHG-bank linkage has been progressing slowly and incidence of poverty is high. SHG-bank linkage programme in 'priority states'[2] also witnessed (Table 8.2) phenomenal growth. NABARD's emphasis on scaling-up programme in these priority states resulted in two and a half-fold increase in number of SHGs linked with banks during 2003-05. Significant increase was observed in economically backward States like Assam, Bihar, and Orissa.

Regional status of SHG-bank linkage (cumulative) in India during 2005-06 is explained in Table 8.3. Southern region stood at first place in respect of number of SHG linked to bank, loans disbursed, and refinance from NABARD. Further, Southern region represents 54 per cent (12 lakhs) of total SHG-linkage in India, disbursed 75 per cent (Rs. 8567.69 crores) of total loans to SHGs and got 83 per cent

(Rs. 3449.96 crores) of total refinance from NABARD. On the contrary, share of north-eastern region constituted 3 per cent of total SHG-linkage.

**Table 8.2:** Cumulative Growth (000) in SHG-Bank Linkage in priority States.

| Sl. No. | State | Year | | |
|---|---|---|---|---|
| | | 2002-03 | 2003-04 | 2004-05 |
| 1. | Assam | 3477 | 10706 | 31234 (4.68) |
| 2. | Bihar | 8161 | 16246 | 28015 (4.20) |
| 3. | Chhattisgarh | 6763 | 9796 | 18569 (2.78) |
| 4. | Gujarat | 13875 | 15974 | 24712 (3.70) |
| 5. | Himachal Pradesh | 8875 | 13228 | 17798 (2.66) |
| 6. | Jharkhand | 7765 | 12647 | 21531 (3.22) |
| 7. | Maharashtra | 28065 | 38535 | 71146 (10.65) |
| 8. | Madhya Pradesh | 15271 | 27095 | 45105 (6.75) |
| 9. | Orissa | 42272 | 77588 | 123256 (18.46) |
| 10. | Rajasthan | 22742 | 33846 | 60006 (8.99) |
| 11. | Uttar Pradesh | 53696 | 79210 | 119648 (17.92) |
| 12. | Uttaranchal | 5853 | 10908 | 14043 (2.10) |
| 13. | West Bengal | 32647 | 51685 | 92698 (13.88) |
| | Total | 249462 | 397464 | 667761 |

Figures in parentheses indicate percentages to total of 2004-05.

*Source*: NABARD, (2005).

**Table 8.3:** Region-wise status of SHG-bank linkage (cumulative) in India, 2006 (Rs. Lakhs).

| Sl. No. | Region | SHGs Linked | Loans Disbursed | NABARD's Refinance |
|---|---|---|---|---|
| 1. | Northern | 133,057 (6) | 39844.13 (4) | 14,489.64 (4) |
| 2. | North-eastern | 62,517 (3) | 16569.97 (1) | 2,489.40 (1) |
| 3. | Eastern | 394,351 (18) | 93542.04 (8) | 25,509.36 (6) |
| 4. | Central | 267,915 (12) | 80500.85 (7) | 14,240.12 (3) |
| 5. | Western | 166,254 (7) | 52513.95 (5) | 14,232.36 (3) |
| 6. | Southern | 1,214,431 (54) | 856769.21 (75) | 344,995.83 (83) |
| | Total | 2,238,525 (100) | 1,139,740.14 (100) | 415,656.71 (100) |

Figures in parentheses indicate percentages to total.
*Source*: NABARD, (2006).

### *Status of SHG Linkage Programme in Maharashtra*

As rightly mentioned earlier, Maharashtra was pioneer in implementation of MRCP in India in 1995, SHG-bank linkage has spread to all districts of Maharashtra. Classification of districts according to number of SHGs linked is given in Table 8.4. Fifteen (46%) districts in Maharashtra fall in category of SHG-bank linked more than 3000, on the other hand only two (6%) districts linked less than 1000 SHGs. It indicates that more number of districts have been involved in scaling up of SHG-bank linkage programme in the state. Region-wise SHGs linked with credit in Maharashtra during 2005-06 is depicted in Table 8.5. Vidharbha region linked 46.5 per cent of total SHGs followed by Western Maharashtra (31.6%), which was highest.

**Table 8.4:** District-wise spread of SHG-bank linkage in Maharashtra, 2005-06

| *Sl. No.* | *SHGs Linked (Cumulative)* | *Districts* | *Name of Districts* |
|---|---|---|---|
| 1. | Below 1000 | 2 (6) | Hingloi, Sindhudurg |
| 2. | 1001 to 2000 | 5 (15) | Jalna, Nadurbar, Parbhani, Ratnagiri, Thane |
| 3. | 2001 to 3000 | 11 (33) | Ahmednagar, Beed, Buldhana, Dhule, Gondia, Jalgaon, Nagpur, Nasik, Raigad, Wardha, Washim |
| 4. | Above 3000 | 15 (46) | Amravati, Akola, Aurangabad, Bandhara, Chandrapur, Gadchiroli, Kolhapur, Latur, Nanded, Pune, Sangli, Satara, Solapur, Osmanabad, Yeotmal. |

*Note*: Figures in parentheses indicate percentages to total.
*Source*: NABARD, (2006).

**Table 8.5:** Region-wise SHG-linkage in Maharashtra, 2006.

| *Sl. No.* | *Region* | *SHGs Linked* | | *% Share* |
|---|---|---|---|---|
| | | *2005-06* | *As on March 06 (Cumulative)* | |
| 1. | Konkan | 2,253 | 6,397 | 4.86 |
| 2. | Marathwada | 10,862 | 22,484 | 17.11 |
| 3. | Vidharbha | 23,746 | 61,068 | 46.45 |
| 4. | Western Maharashtra | 23,463 | 41,521 | 31.58 |
| | Total | 60,324 | 131,470 | 100 |

*Source*: NABARD (2006).

## *NABARD's Initiatives in SHG-Bank Linkage*

With a view to upscaling the linkage programme in Maharashtra, NABARD has made conscious efforts, and continued to support partner agencies through refinance support, promotion of SHGs,

NGOs, SHPI (Self-Help Promotion Institutes), innovative pilot project, capacity-building and co-ordination of the SHG linkage programme. Apart from extending refinance facility, NABARD supports NGOs in credit linking of SHGs by giving financial assistance. As on 31 March, 2006, 114 NGOs have been sanctioned assistance of Rs. 338 lakhs for promotion and nurturing of 17,539 SHGs. RRBs and DCCBs have also been getting grant for working as SHPI. Eight RRBs and ten DCCBs have been sanctioned grant assistance of Rs. 80.37 lakhs for promotion of SHGs.

Due to non-availability of good NGOs, NABARD has launched Individual Rural Volunteers (IRV) scheme in which, individuals from villages with social commitment, and background in promotion of SHGs are involved in promotion and nurturing of SHGs. As on 31 March, 2006, 170 IRVs involved by five RRBs and a DCCB for promotion of SHGs. Further, "nine farmers' clubs" were also promoted by Solapur Gramin Bank have been included as SHPI. These clubs have promoted 116 SHGs of which, 73 have been credit linked. NABARD has also conducted 464 capacity-building programme covering 19,193 participants from partner agencies (banks, NGOs, government officials, board of directors of DCCBs, farmers' clubs, and SHGs) during 2005-06 (NABARD, 2006). An attempt is made in the following sections to study performance of SHG-bank linkage in selected DCCBs.

## DCCB-Wise, and Age-Wise Classification of SHGs

***Table 8.6*** presents age-wise classification of SHGs across selected DCCBs. Across DCCBs, Chandrapur District Central Cooperative Bank (CDCCB) stood first by forming 11,080 SHGs in a span of five years. At the same time, Latur District Central Cooperative Bank (LDCCB) occupied last place, and formed only 1691 SHGs. On the other hand, 48.37 per cent of total SHGs formed in CDCCB were of 3 years old. Further, it is worth to note that formation of SHGs in CDCCB is steady since inception. Average membership/SHG varied from 13 to 15.

### *SHGs-DCCBs Linkage*

Year-wise breakup of SHGs formed, and percentage of SHGs linked to banks is depicted in ***Table 8.7.*** Selected DCCBs had followed guidelines provided by NABARD in linking of SHGs. These guidelines include (a) SHG should be actively performing for atleast a period of six months, (b) group should have undertaken savings and inter-lending from its own resources, (c) group must have an evident democratic working, (d) group should maintain proper accounts/records, and (e) group should open SB account and deposit its savings regularly in banks (www. nabard.org). During 2004-05, CDCCB achieved highest SHG-bank linkage (67.85 per cent) across selected banks. Table 8.7 also revealed increasing trend in percentage of SHGs formed over the study period.

### *Cost of Formation of SHGs*

DCCBs incurred costs in formation of SHGs in terms of salary and conveyance expenses of staff involved (Table 8.8). Average cost incurred by DCCBs for conducting initial meetings with villagers was Rs. 1578. Across DCCBs, CDCCB had spent more as it hired Sahayoginis from local NGOs. As cost of mobilizing people was less on initial meetings and demonstrations, average amount spent was less (Rs. 785). Looking at performance of initial groups, other villagers took interest on working as a group and approached DCCB's staff. Extensive initial efforts for group formation saved in forming subsequent groups and, hence, cost reduction. Subsequently, DCCB's staff has to monitor working of groups. While monitoring, DCCBs spent on an average, Rs. 1315, and training is imparted on bookkeeping, conduct of meeting, keeping minutes, books of accounts, etc.

### *Mobilisation of Savings*

Total savings mobilized by SHGs, balance in SB account, and balance as percentage to total savings is explained in Table 8.9. Average savings accrued by SHGs in selected DCCBs was Rs. 24.07 lakhs in 2000-01 which rose to Rs. 315.17 lakhs (93%) in 2004-05. Across selected banks, Kolhapur District Central Cooperative Bank (KDCCB) registered highest savings of Rs. 40.94 lakhs and Rs. 856.24 lakhs during 2000-01 and 2004-05 respectively. Percentage of balance to total savings indicates utilization and it ranged from 0.35 per cent in CDCCB to 65.70 per cent in Thane District Central Cooperative Bank (TDCCB) (2000-01). Thus, SHGs of CDCCB utilized majority of their savings for disbursement of internal loans. On the other hand, SHGs of KDCCB registered higher utilization of savings by keeping 0.10 per cent of balance, and the same was 49.62 per cent for CDCCB.

**Table 8.6:** District-wise and Age-wise Distribution of SHGs.

| Age (years) | District | | | | | | | | | | | |
|---|---|---|---|---|---|---|---|---|---|---|---|---|
| | Kolhapur | | | Latur | | | Thane | | | Chandrapur | | |
| | SHGs | % to Total SHGs | Average Members per SHG | SHGs | % to Total SHGs | Average Members per SHG | SHGs | % to Total SHGs | Average Members per SHG | SHGs | % to Total SHGs | Average Members per SHG |
| < One year | 780 | 7.19 | 15 | 756 | 44.70 | 11 | 1340 | 33.23 | 12 | 394 | 3.56 | 15 |
| 1 to 2 years | 986 | 9.09 | 14 | 935 | 55.30 | 12 | 784 | 19.43 | 13 | 421 | 3.80 | 14 |
| 2 to 3 years | 262 | 2.41 | 16 | 0 | 0 | 0 | 557 | 13.81 | 13 | 2201 | 19.86 | 13 |
| 3 to 4 years | 7340 | 67.65 | 12 | 0 | 0 | 0 | 166 | 4.13 | 12 | 5359 | 48.37 | 13 |
| > 4 years | 1482 | 13.66 | 22 | 0 | 0 | 0 | 1186 | 29.40 | 14 | 2705 | 24.41 | 13 |
| Total | 10850 | 100 | 16 | 1691 | 100 | 12 | 4033 | 100 | 13 | 11080 | 100 | 14 |

*Source*: Annual Reports of DCCBs..

**Table 8.7:** District-wise SHGs formed and linked by DCCBs

| Year | District | | | | | | | | | | | | | | | |
|---|---|---|---|---|---|---|---|---|---|---|---|---|---|---|---|---|
| | *Kolhapur* | | | | *Latur* | | | | *Thane* | | | | *Chandrapur* | | | |
| | *Total SHGs* | *Total Members* | *SHGs Lnked* | *% of Linked SHGs* | *Total SHGs* | *Total Members* | *SHGs Linked* | *% of Linked SHGs* | *Total SHGs* | *Total Members* | *SHGs Linked* | *% of Lnked SHGs* | *Total SHGs* | *Total Members* | *SHGs Linked* | *% of Lnked SHGs* |
| 2000-01 | 780 | 11700 | 32 | 4 | 0 | 0 | 0 | 0 | 1186 | 16103 | 25 | 2.10 | 394 | 5761 | 0 | 0 |
| 2001-02 | 986 | 13804 | 153 | 16 | 0 | 0 | 0 | 0 | 166 | 1941 | 44 | 26.50 | 421 | 5933 | 72 | 1.36 |
| 2002-03 | 262 | 4192 | 145 | 55 | 0 | 0 | 0 | 0 | 557 | 7052 | 70 | 12.56 | 2201 | 28842 | 293 | 5.52 |
| 2003-04 | 7340 | 88080 | 343 | 5 | 935 | 11220 | 37 | 4 | 784 | 10049 | 292 | 37.24 | 5359 | 68967 | 1340 | 25.26 |
| 2004-05 | 1482 | 32604 | 174 | 12 | 756 | 8316 | 79 | 10 | 1340 | 16560 | 454 | 33.88 | 2705 | 36520 | 1835 | 67.85 |

*Source*: Annual Reports of DCCBs.

**Table 8.8:** District-wise Cost (Rupees/SHG) of formation of SHGs.

| Particulars | Districts | | | | | | | | Average | |
|---|---|---|---|---|---|---|---|---|---|---|
| | Kolhapur | | Latur | | Thane | | Chandrapur | | | |
| | *Time & days* | *Cost* | *Time & days* | *Cost* | *Time & days* | *Cost* | *Time & days* | *Cost* | *Time & days* | *Cost* |
| Initial meetings with villagers (3 months) | 8 visits of 3 hours duration | 1440 | 7 visits of 4 hours duration | 1120 | 3 visits of 2 and half hours duration | 1650 | 3 visits of 3 hours | 2100 | 5 | 1578 |
| Formation of groups (one month) | 3 visits of 3 hours duration | 540 | 4 visits of 3 hours duration | 600 | 2 visits of 3 hours duration | 1050 | 1 visit of 3 hours | 950 | 2 | 785 |
| Monitoring of groups | 8 visits in a year (1 hours per visit) | 1440 | 7 visits (2 hours per visit) | 1120 | 6 visits in a year (2 hrs. per visit). | 1200 | 8 visits in a year (1 hours per visit) | 1500 | 7 | 1315 |

*Source*: Annual reports of DCCBs

**Table 8.9:** District-wise total savings (Rs. lakhs) and balances in SB accounts of SHGs in DCCBs

| Year | District | | | | | | | | | | | | Average | | |
|---|---|---|---|---|---|---|---|---|---|---|---|---|---|---|---|
| | Kolhapur | | | Latur | | | Thane | | | Chandrapur | | | | | |
| | Total savings mobilized by SHGs | Balance in SB A/C | % of SB balance to total savings | Total savings mobilized by SHGs | Balance in SB A/C | % of SB balance to total savings | Total savings mobilized by SHGs | Balance in SB A/C | % of SB balance to total savings | Total savings mobilized by SHGs | Balance in SB A/C | % of SB balance to total savings | Total savings mobilized by SHGs | Balance in SB A/C | % of SB balance to total savings |
| 2000-01 | 40.94 | 0.79 | 1.93 | 0 | 0 | 0 | 48.03 | 31.56 | 65.70 | 7.33 | 0.93 | 0.35 | 24.07 | 8.32 | 16.99 |
| 2001-02 | 79.06 | 1.74 | 2.45 | 0 | 0 | 0 | 30.15 | 12.11 | 40.16 | 4.07 | 2.18 | 0.82 | 28.32 | 4.01 | 10.86 |
| 2002-03 | 139.84 | 0.45 | 0.32 | 0 | 0 | 0 | 60.70 | 15.32 | 25.23 | 65.76 | 21.87 | 8.22 | 66.58 | 9.41 | 8.44 |
| 2003-04 | 357.42 | 13.97 | 3.91 | 95.72 | 11.36 | 11.86 | 79.04 | 25.58 | 32.36 | 90.59 | 68.80 | 25.86 | 155.69 | 29.93 | 18.50 |
| 2004-05 | 856.24 | 0.85 | 0.10 | 146.53 | 55.24 | 37.69 | 159.65 | 63.06 | 39.49 | 98.26 | 1.32 | 49.62 | 315.17 | 30.12 | 31.72 |
| Average | 294.70 | 3.56 | 1.74 | 58.01 | 17.10 | 30.57 | 75.51 | 29.52 | 40.58 | 53.20 | 19.02 | 16.97 | 118.07 | 17.30 | 22.46 |

*Source*: Annual Reports of DCCBs.

### *Loans Disbursed by DCCBs*

DCCB-wise and year-wise breakup of loans disbursed to SHGs is given in Table 8.10. Amount of loans disbursed by CDCCB was the highest, and ranged from Rs. 5.06 lakhs in 2001-02 to Rs. 548.26 lakhs in 2004-05, and registered a growth of 99 per cent. CDCCB also supported SHGs to enable them to conduct economic activities On the other hand, LDCCB disbursed less amount (Rs. 7.54 lakhs) in 2004-05.

### *Status of Recovery of Loans*

Data on demand, and recovery of loans disbursed are given in Table 8.11. Average recovery of loans was very low (29.1%) during the initial year (2000-01), and the scenario improved (96%) substantially overtime. Across selected banks, TDCCB, CDCCB, and LDCCB achieved 99.8 per cent, 98.7 per cent, and 97.9 per cent of recovery respectively in 2004-05. Thus, recovery position of short-term rural cooperative credit institutions has improved considerably by lending through SHGs, which further reduced NPAs. Leaders of groups played a major role in recovery by insisting their members to repay loans promptly within the time limit.

### *Transaction Cost and Margin of DCCBs*

Table 8.12 provides a comparative picture of transaction costs and margins across selected DCCBs in case loans disbursed to individuals of PACSs as well as to SHGs. Major components of transaction cost are cost of management, and stationary. Average transaction cost incurred by DCCBs through PACSs and SHGs was 1.97 per cent and 0.10 per cent respectively. Thus, results have clearly brought out the advantage of lending through SHGs vis-à-vis individuals. It was low as amount of time spent on maintenance of accounts and recovery costs are low. On the other hand, loans disbursed through PACSs require several mandays in the form of maintenance of accounts, and recovery. Across DCCBs, transaction cost in PACSs ranged from 1.57 per cent in LDCCB to 2.44 per cent in CDCCB, and that of SHGs was 0.10 per cent in TDCCB and 0.20 per cent in LDCCB.

**Table 8.10:** District-wise Status of Advances (Rs. in lakhs) to SHGs

| Year | Districts | | | | | | | | Average | |
|---|---|---|---|---|---|---|---|---|---|---|
| | Kolhapur | | Latur | | Thane | | Chandrapur | | | |
| | Number | Amount | Number | Amount | Number | Amount | Number | Amount | Number | Amount |
| 2000-01 | 32 | 6.72 | 0 | 0 | 25 | 2.10 | 0 | 0 | 14 | 2.20 |
| 2001-02 | 153 | 25.32 | 0 | 0 | 44 | 26.50 | 72 | 5.06 | 67 | 14.22 |
| 2002-03 | 145 | 57.39 | 0 | 0 | 70 | 12.56 | 293 | 53.58 | 127 | 30.88 |
| 2003-04 | 343 | 80.48 | 37 | 3.01 | 292 | 37.24 | 1340 | 180.72 | 503 | 75.36 |
| 2004-05 | 174 | 244.10 | 79 | 7.54 | 454 | 33.88 | 3599 | 548.26 | 1077 | 208.40 |
| Average | 169 | 82.80 | 40 | 3.66 | 177 | 22.45 | 1661 | 157.52 | 358 | 66.21 |

*Source*: Annual Reports of DCCBs.

**Table 8.11:** District-wise Status of Recovery of Loans (Rs. in lakhs) to SHGs.

| Year | Districts | | | | | | | | | | | | Average | | |
|---|---|---|---|---|---|---|---|---|---|---|---|---|---|---|---|
| | Kolhapur | | | Latur | | | Thane | | | Chandrapur | | | | | |
| | Demand | Collection | % of Recovery | Demand | Collection | Recovery | Demand | Collection | % of Recovery | Demand | Collection | % of Recovery | Demand | Collection | % of Recovery |
| 2000-01 | 10.26 | 1.85 | 18.03 | 0 | 0 | 0 | 0.63 | 0.63 | 100 | 0 | 0 | 0 | 2.72 | 0.62 | 29.51 |
| 2001-02 | 20.80 | 6.80 | 32.69 | 0 | 0 | 0 | 3.86 | 3.86 | 100 | 5.06 | 5.06 | 100 | 7.43 | 3.93 | 58.17 |
| 2002-03 | 19.12 | 15.50 | 81.07 | 0 | 0 | 00 | 8.54 | 8.30 | 97.19 | 58.64 | 58.64 | 100 | 21.58 | 20.61 | 69.57 |
| 2003-04 | 29.65 | 23.92 | 80.62 | 0.67 | 0.54 | 80.60 | 25.56 | 25.68 | 99.53 | 205.00 | 198.12 | 96.64 | 65.22 | 62.07 | 89.35 |
| 2004-05 | 31.48 | 28.21 | 89.61 | 2.85 | 2.79 | 97.89 | 52.44 | 52.36 | 99.84 | 580.12 | 572.42 | 98.67 | 166.72 | 163.95 | 96.50 |
| Average | 22.26 | 15.26 | 60.40 | 1.76 | 1.67 | 94.89 | 18.21 | 18.17 | 99.31 | 169.76 | 166.85 | 98.28 | | | |

*Source*: Annual Reports of DCCBs.

**Table 8.12:** District-wise Transaction Costs and Margins (for Rs. 100) to Bank Branch to Individual Borrower and SHGs

| Sl. No. | Particulars | Districts | | | | | | | | Average | |
|---|---|---|---|---|---|---|---|---|---|---|---|
| | | Kolhapur | | Latur | | Thane | | Chandrapur | | | |
| | | Individual Loans | Loans to SHGs | Individual Loans | Loans to SHGs | Individual Loans | Loans to SHGs | Individual Loans | Loans to SHGs | Individual Loans | Loans to SHGs |
| 1. | Cost of Fund | 6.37 | 6.37 | 6.06 | 10.50 | 4.60 | 4.60 | 4.31 | 4.31 | 5.33 | 6.45 |
| 2. | Transaction Cost | 2.00 | 0.10 | 1.57 | 0.20 | 1.88 | 0.10 | 2.44 | 0.00 | 1.97 | 0.10 |
| 3. | Risk Cost* | 0.23 | 0.001 | 2.53 | 0.00 | 0.04 | 0.00 | 0.95 | 0.00 | 0.94 | 0.02 |
| 4. | Total Cost (1+2+3) | 8.60 | 6.47 | 10.16 | 10.70 | 6.52 | 4.7 | 7.70 | 4.31 | 8.25 | 6.55 |
| 5. | Yield from Advance | 8.99 | 10.00 | 10.67 | 12.00 | 7.35 | 12.00 | 7.94 | 7.94 | 8.74 | 10.49 |
| 6. | Margin (5-4) | 0.39 | 3.53 | 0.51 | 1.30 | 0.83 | 7.30 | 0.24 | 3.63 | 0.49 | 3.94 |

*Note*: *It is almost zero in case of SHGs.

*Source*: Annual Reports of DCCBs.

Risk cost is related to management of bad debts (NPAs). As recovery of loans was more than 99 per cent, it was almost zero in SHGs. As of loans disbursed through PACSs, risk cost ranged from 0.04 per cent in TDCCB to 2.53 per cent in LDCCB. It is worthwhile to note that risk cost in TDCCB (loans disbursed through PACSs) is very low (0.04%) as compared to other DCCBs which is mainly due to disbursement of loans to commercial purposes, and therefore, recovery was better. Average margin for DCCBs in case of loans disbursed through PACSs and SHGs were to the tune of 0.49 per cent and 3.94 per cent respectively. The reason for high margins on loans disbursed through SHGs was mainly due to absence of intermediaries between DCCB and SHG. Against this, DCCBs had to share margin with PACSs by giving away some percentage of interest rate in lending through PACSs. Thus, DCCBs can earn more by transacting through SHGs.

### *Status of Training Conducted*

Progress in training programmes conducted for staff of DCCBs and members of SHGs is depicted in Table 8.13. Training programmes such as one-day workshops, exposure visits, training to staff of DCCBs and members of SHGs in bank linkage (concept, philosophy, steps, precautions, etc.) were conducted by NABARD/DCCBs. On an average, 1064 one-day workshops were conducted by each DCCB. CDCCB had conducted highest number of workshops (2946) followed by KDCCB (1140). It was possible for CDCCB to arrange highest number of workshops and bank linkage programmes (2960) as it established own training academy (Mahakali Sahakar Academy), and has own vehicle by which mobile trainings are being conducted throughout the district.

### *Position of Staff in SHG Cells at DCCBs*

In order to undertake smooth administration and monitoring of SHGs formed and linked to credit, DCCBs have created a separate cell for SHGs (Table 8.14). Average number of officers, supporting staff and others (development officers, field officers, and inspectors) employed in SHG cells at DCCBs increased from 1, 2, and 63 in 2001-02 to 4, 3, and 86 respectively in 2004-05. Officers are working at headquarters of respective DCCBs and they conduct regular inspections with other supporting staff. Supporting staff assists officers in monitoring SHGs at district level. Other staff is deployed at various places (branches of DCCBs), and engaged in forming and training of members of SHGs.

**Table 8.13:** District-wise Status of Programmes Conducted for SHGs and staff of DCCBs

| *Name of the Training* | *Districts* | | | | |
|---|---|---|---|---|---|
| | *Kolhapur* | *Latur* | *Thane* | *Chandrapur* | *Average* |
| One day workshop for members of SHGs | 1140 | 25 | 143 | 2946 | 1064 |
| Training for staff members of DCCBs | 50 | 227 | 12 | 130 | 105 |
| Exposure visits for staff of DCCBs | 40 | 72 | 0 | 30 | 36 |
| Bank linkage training for SHGs | 2063 | 2012 | 850 | 2960 | 1971 |

*Source*: Annual Reports of DCCBs.

**Table 8.14:** District-wise-Staff position in SHG Cells at DCCBs

| *Year* | *Districts* | | | | | | | | | | | | *Average* | | |
|---|---|---|---|---|---|---|---|---|---|---|---|---|---|---|---|
| | *Kolhapur* | | | *Latur* | | | *Thane* | | | *Chandrapur* | | | | | |
| | *Officers* | *Supporting Staff* | *Others** | *Officers* | *Supporting Staff* | *Others** | *Officers* | *Supporting Staff* | *Others** | *Officers* | *Supporting Staff* | *Others** | *Officers* | *Supporting Staff* | *Others** |
| 2000-01 | 2 | 6 | 188 | 0 | 0 | 0 | 1 | 1 | 64 | 02 | 0 | 0 | 1 | 2 | 63 |
| 2001-02 | 2 | 6 | 188 | 0 | 0 | 0 | 1 | 1 | 64 | 02 | 0 | 0 | 1 | 2 | 63 |
| 2002-03 | 2 | 6 | 188 | 3 | 5 | 92 | 2 | 1 | 64 | 03 | 0 | 1 | 3 | 3 | 86 |
| 2003-04 | 2 | 6 | 188 | 3 | 5 | 92 | 2 | 1 | 64 | 04 | 0 | 02 | 3 | 3 | 86 |
| 2004-05 | 2 | 6 | 188 | 3 | 5 | 92 | 2 | 1 | 64 | 07 | 0 | 02 | 4 | 3 | 86 |

*Note*: *Others include development officers, field officers, and inspectors.
*Source*: Records of DCCBs.

## Conclusion

Incident of poverty, disguised unemployment, and low level of income in villages prompted NABARD to take steps to provide employment by providing credit through SHG concept. To reduce imbalance in SHG linkage programme, NABARD has started supporting slow progressing states in the scheme of priority sector. Data covered in the study revealed tremendous growth in SHG linkage and loans disbursed through linked banks. Backward region (Vidharbha) has attained significant progress in SHG linkage programme in Maharashtra. The concept of SHG has been encouraging rural people to save small amounts and borrow credit from banks at low rate of interest and within time. Linkage programme helped DCCBs in improving their recovery position with low transaction and risk costs. Chandrapur DCCB established a separate training institute and excelled in organizing variety of programmes to personnel involved in SHGs. Since members have high stakes in SHGs, they don't allow others to default. As a result, margins to DCCBs are high when provided loans through SHGs. Keeping in view of these long-term advantages to financial institutions, policy-makers and administrators should give emphasis in promotion of SHG-bank linkage programme throughout the country.

## END NOTES

1. MRCP, which was sponsored by IFAD (International Fund for Agricultural Development) was implemented in 1995 and covered 400 villages from Chandrapur, Nanded, Yeotmal and Pune districts of Maharashtra. The programme focused on peoples' participation in credit planning and credit administration for poor and non-poor, developing saving habits and credit culture among the ultra poor through medium of SHGs, and procuring support/social services from various agencies and thereby ensuring socio-economic development of the villages [for details on MRCP, see NABARD (1997), and Dond (1999)].
2. On the basis of success of SHG-bank linkage programme, NABARD introduced the concept of priority states, and 13 states were identified. NABARD has been trying to give emphasis on these states to develop SHG-bank linkage programme.

## REFERENCES

CDCCB (various years), *Annual Reports*, CDCCB, Chandrapur.

Erhard, W. K. and B. S. Suran (2002), Linking Banks and (financial) SHGs in India: An assessment, paper presented in a Seminar on SHGs, November 25, NABARD, Mumbai.

KDCCB (various years), *Annual Reports*, KDCCB, Kolhapur.

LDCCB (various years), *Annual Reports*, LDCCB, Latur.

NABARD (1997), MRCP, A saga of peoples' participation, NABARD Regional Office, Pune.

NABARD (various years), *Annual Reports*, NABARD, Mumbai.

NABARD (2006), *SHG-bank linkage programme in Maharashtra*, Regional Office, Pune.

TDCCB (various years), *Annual Reports*, TDCCB, Thane.

# 9

# Innovation in Rural Financial System

GURSHARAN SINGH KAINTH

*Needless to say, inspite of tremendous progress after Independence, both in agriculture and other sectors, much remains to be done in order to improve the condition of farmers. Problems are many. In a vast country like ours, there is bound to be some problem somewhere. At this juncture, it is necessary to identify our priorities with clarity and make all out efforts to ensure effective action. A number of initiatives have been taken. The focus should be to improve the income and welfare of farmer's. This implies not only higher production and productivity but also improving the capabilities of farmers to compete on the market map. The need is to have a holistic approach incorporating rural infrastructure, dissemination of better technology, sustainable use of natural resources and development of the rural non-farm sector.*

One of the serious and unrelenting problems faced by the Indian farmer's households has been indebtedness. While studying the Punjab's peasants, Sir Malcolm Darling (1925) wrote, "*Indian peasant is born in debt, lives in debt and dies in debt*". Though this is written about eight decades back, the problem of indebtedness not only remains true today, but also it has been aggravated further in the recent past, though the goal of doubling farm credit in three years was achieved in two years. Despite substantial improvements in agricultural output and distribution of credit, still majority of the farmers are suffering from this major economic disease called Indebtedness and lack of timely and adequate farm credit. Despite high density of the retail outlets of formal credit institution, the presence of informal agencies for agricultural credit continued to exist although their share has been declining over the years. Informal agencies largely extend credit for consumption and social ceremonies and their interest and other terms of conditions are onerous, yet they coexists with the formal financial institutions mainly due to their proximity, feel-at-ease, timely and quick services, all time access, purpose free credit, flexibility in loan repayments and low transaction costs. To reach the poor, institutional innovations are needed that enable services to be expanded while substantially reducing transactions costs for both the financial institutions and the clients.

**Kisan Credit Cards**

Reserve Bank of India (RBI) setup a one man high level committee of Shri R.V. Gupta in December 1997 to inquire into the reasons for the tail backs of the farm credit and to suggest measure for improving the delivery systems as well as simplification of the procedures for farm credit. Based on the recommendations of the committee, RBI in 1998 directed all Public Sectors Banks (PSBs), Regional Rural Banks (RRBs) and Cooperative Banks (CoBs) to introduce Kisan Credit Cards (KCCs) scheme on the lines of the model scheme formulated by National Bank for Agricultural and Rural Development (NABARD) and in due course of times the KCCs was adopted by all the directed agencies. The basic objective of the KCCs is to extend adequate and timely support to the farmers for meeting their credit needs for farming including input purchases. The credit limit (loans) is sanctioned in proportion to their size of owned land but some flexibility is also provided for the farmers cultivating leased in land in addition to the owned holding. Further borrowing limits are fixed on the basis of proposed cropping pattern. Most of the banks are adhering to the Scale of Finance (SOF) decided by the State Level Bankers Committee (SLBC) but some banks have fixed their own SOF generally higher than the SLBC norms. The nature of credit extended under KCCs is a revolving cash credit, that is, it provide for any number of withdrawals and repayments within the limits. This feature would provide flexibility and reduce the interest burden upon the KCCs beneficiary. Beneficiaries covered under the KCCs are issued with a credit card and a pass book or a credit card-cum-pass book incorporating the name, address and particulars of land, borrowing limit and the validity period. Production credit limits are fixed taking into account the entire production credit needs for a full year plus ancillary activities related to crop production. Till recently, investment credit requirements of farmers remained outside the purview of KCCs, causing additional cost and procedural inconvenience to farmers. To address these deficiencies, NABARD revised the scheme in August 2004 to cover term loans for agriculture and allied activities. Under the KCCs, while the short-term as well as working capital credit is repayable in 12 months, the term loan is to be repaid within a maximum period of five years. Conversion/re-schedulement of loan are permitted in case of damage to crops due to natural calamities.

The major steps involved for the issue of KCCs from banks were:

1. Preliminary interviews;
2. Filling of application forms. It required photographs, no due certificates from credit institutions in the service area and *fard Jamabandhi/fard girdarori*.
3. Pre-sanctioned inspection.
4. Execution of the security documents, which include demand promissory note, continuing security letter, letter of guarantee, letter of declaration and undertaking and mortgage deed.
5. Processing of the application, and
6. Disbursement of the loans.

On the other hand, Cooperative KCCs required fewer documents. No mortgage deed is obtained; only *fard Jamabandhi/fard girdarori* and guarantor are required for the issue of cooperative KCCs.

The scheme is being implemented in all the States and Union Territories through all Commercial Banks, RRBs, State co-operative Banks, Central Co-operative Banks and Primary Agricultural Co-operative Societies. KCCs schemes has made swift progress since its inception with the banking sector issuing more than 6.79 crores cards with cumulative credit of Rs. 2,37,880 crores sanctioned upto August 31, 2007. The implementation has been taken up by all the PSBs; Cooperative Banks and RRBs throughout the country. The cooperative sector banks account for 50 per cent of KCCs issued and 63 per cent of the amount sanctioned. Highest number of KCCs was issued by co-operative banks (327.09 lakhs), followed by commercial banks (255.7 lakhs) and RRBs (82.84 lakhs). The state-wise progress in implementation of KCCs revealed that Andhra Pradesh, Karnataka, Madhya Pradesh, Maharashtra, Orissa, Rajasthan, Tamil Nadu, and Uttar Pradesh were forerunners in implementation of the scheme accounting for 75 per cent of the total cards issued by the banks across the country. The progress was, however, tardy in Goa, Himachal Pradesh, Jammu and Kashmir, Sikkim and the States of NER. Among all the States of Indian Union, Punjab leads the chart with highest KCCs penetration ratio of 118.17 per cent against All India average of 32.44 per cent. Haryana follows Punjab at 85.75 per cent and Andhra Pradesh at 62.23 per cent. More than 100 penetration ratio in case of Punjab implies that some operational holdings have more than one KCCs. NABARD advised banks to identify and cover all farmers including defaulters, oral lessees tenant farmers, share-croppers etc. who might have left outside the fold of KCCs for any reason and also the new farmers.

**Table 9.1:** Progress of Kisan Credit Cards (In lakhs): Agency wise

| Year | Cooperative Banks | Regional Rural Banks | Commercial Banks | Total |
|---|---|---|---|---|
| 2001-02 | 54.36 | 8.34 | 30.71 | 93.41 |
| 2002-03 | 45.79 | 9.64 | 27.00 | 82.43 |
| 2003-04 | 48.78 | 12.74 | 30.94 | 92.46 |
| 2004-05 | 35.56 | 17.29 | 43.95 | 96.80 |
| 2005-06 | 25.98 | 12.49 | 41.65 | 80.12 |
| 2006-07 | 22.97 | 14.06 | 37.67 | 74.70 |
| Total | 327.09 (49.14) | 82.84 (12.45) | 255.7 (38.41) | 665.63 (100.00) |

Growing popularity of KCCs scheme reflects its effectiveness in ensuring hassle-free and timely operations as well as availability of credit with minimum transactions costs and documentations. In order to safeguard the interest of KCCs holders', coverage under Personal Accident Insurance Scheme (PAIS) has been introduced. NABARD has allowed discretion to the banks to opt for any of the insurance company of their choice at competitive rates/terms. Further banks has been advised to ensure that KCCs continue to be renewed in a hassle-free manner and to direct their efforts towards ensuring quality in operations and more importantly crop loans are routed only through KCCs.

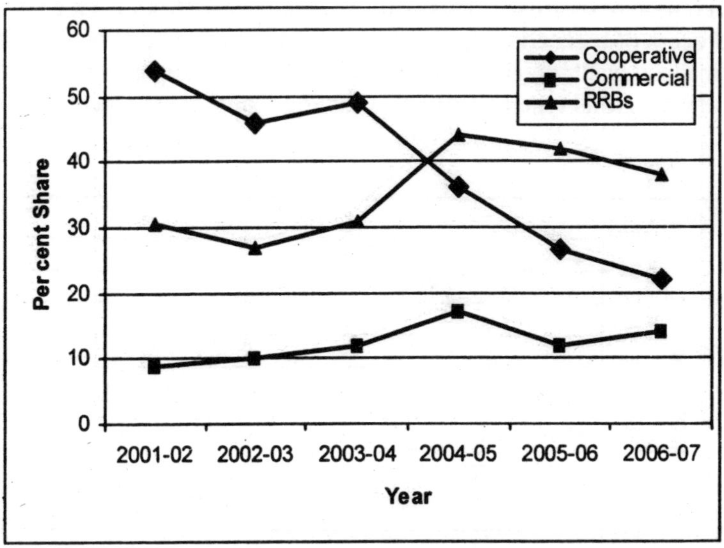


**Fig. 9.1:** Relative Share of Different Agencies in KCCs Issued

Apparently, KCCs was a paradigm shift from the purpose-oriented loaning through a credit product. It has enabled to accelerate production credit compared to investment credit. One of the major feature was the coverage of personal accident benefit with nominal premium for KCCs holders. However, what is disturbing is the fact that inspite of timely sanctions of credit, the beneficiaries were least bothered in making prompt repayment, which eventually threatens the very sustainability of KCCs scheme. Furthermore, no doubt the purchase of cash inputs for farm is spread throughout the agricultural season, yet the farmers restore to lump-sum withdrawals—a peculiar transaction habit of the farmers? Apparently, there seems to be large-scale diversion of credit both for on and off farm investments. However, off farm diversion dominated the diversion scenario. KCCs was not able to flush out multiple financing due to lack of coordination between various sources of institutional credit. Many of the KCCs borrowers are still in the grip of money-lenders. Another major constraint in the working of KCCs was too many intermediaries in obtaining suitable securities and finding guarantor. Therefore, for further simplification of the procedure under KCCs, farmers can be issued a passbook with an authenticated record of land and the borrowings. The banks should accept the same as valid title for the purchase of mortgage. This will save the farmers from cumbersome process of registering the mortgage deed in the name of banks. The financial institutions for the loans against urban property are already following this type of system of getting loans. Hence there should not be any legal complications for its implementation.

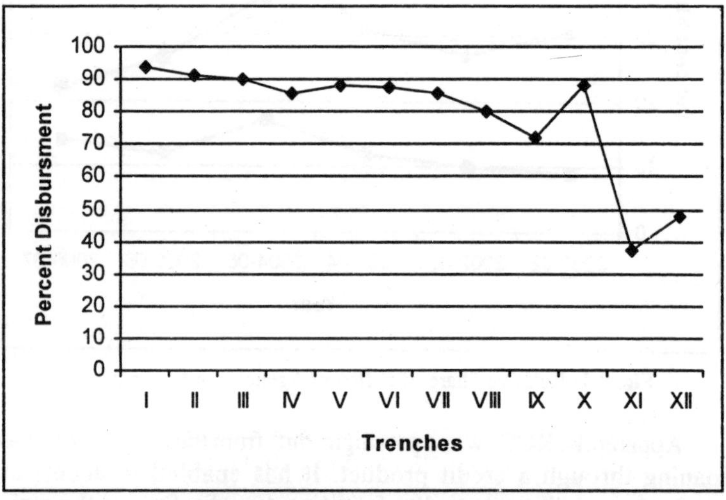


**Fig. 9.2:** Progress of Per cent Disbursment.

National Council of Applied Economic Research (NCAER) at the instance of (RBI) conducted a survey for assessing the impact of KCCs scheme. National Impact Assessment Survey shows that KCCs had augmented flows of credit to agricultural sector, about 6 per cent decrease in the cost of borrowing for farmers after they were given KCCs, cost of the borrowing for KCCs holders from formal sector is about 3 per cent lower than those of non-KCCs holders, significant decline in the number of borrowers depending exclusively on non-formal sources for their short-term credit needs, reduction in cost of borrowing from informal source by about 3 per cent, significant saving in time spent in obtaining short-term agricultural loans and finally decline in cost delivering due to simplified procedure. The survey also had identified certain areas requiring policy initiatives to make the scheme more effective. These relates to restrictions imposed on the issuance of KCCs by banks, restrictions on the use of KCCs only at the card issuing branches, non-availability of incentives for timely repayments, low-credit limits and low awareness regarding the provision of personal accident insurance scheme. RBI has advised the Indian Bankers Association to examine these suggestions and come up with remedial measures. Keeping in view the directives of Government of India for doubling the flow of credit to agriculture, NABARD advised the Cooperative and Regional Rural Banks to identify and bring into their fold such farmers including defaulters, oral lessees, tenant farmers, share-croppers who may have been outside the fold of scheme for any reason as also new farmers. KCCs need to be promoted as a single window for comprehensive rural credit delivery. In the recent past, NABARD has enlarged the scope of KCCs by including even long-term loans for agriculture and allied activities under its purview. In addition to this, KCCs scheme has been extended to long-term borrowers of the cooperative credit structure too.

Theoretically KCCs is well thought of and full of good intentions. To be more successful, education of both the partners—the farmers and the bankers about the scheme is very vital. No doubt, KCCs has significantly improved access of farmers to formal credit, but KCCs programme needs to modify to improve the access to those who cannot sign by making their use through thumb impression. Other measures proposed include new channels of disbursement by means of franchising Village Post Offices to route bank credit. The budget proposed to explore where ever innovations are possible in agricultural credit. For example the issue of allowing banks to accept the agency model by using the infrastructure of civil society organizations, rural kiosks, Village Knowledge Centers, to provide credit support to rural and farm sector; special financial assistance to wipe out the accumulated losses and strengthen the capital base of cooperative credit institutional restructuring to ensure democratic institutions; and to change the legal framework to empower Reserve Bank of India to enforce prudent financial management. What is important is: To put these measures into realities. Few other measures, which have potential to abridge the credit gap are to identify areas such as private market yards, public-private partnership, etc., for integration of farmer's production with domestic and global markets and to promote competitive private and cooperative agricultural markets.

### Rural Infrastructure Development Fund

Rural Infrastructure Development Fund (RIDF) is another innovation in rural financial system. RIDF was setup by the government in 1995-96 for financing on-going rural infrastructure projects. The fund is maintained by the National Bank for Agriculture and Rural Development (NABARD). Domestic commercial banks contribute to the fund to the extent of their shortfall in stipulated priority sector lending to agriculture. The main objective of the fund is to provide loans to State Governments and State-owned Corporations to enable them to complete ongoing rural infrastructure projects. In the Interim Budget for the year 2004-05, an announcement was made regarding setting up of Agriculture Infrastructure and Credit Fund and discontinuation of RIDF mechanism. This decision was reconsidered and the regular Budget presented on July 8, 2004 proposed revival of RIDF with a corpus of Rs. 8000 crores during 2004-05. The total corpus of RIDF (Trenches I to XII) aggregated to Rs. 60,000 crores. So far eleven trenches have been completed and twelfth trench (RIDF-XII) is currently under implementation. A separate window under RIDF-XII for rural roads with a corpus of Rs. 4000 crores was opened. Against this project worth Rs. 2311 crores has been sanctioned in 2006-07, Budget 2007-08 proposes to continue the separate window under RIDF-XIII in 2007-08 with a corpus of Rs. 4000 crores.

In pursuance to the announcement made by the Hon'ble Union Finance Minister that a separate window would be opened under RIDF-XII for funding the rural road component of Bharat Nirman programme with an allocation of Rs. 4000 crores during 2006-07, modalities for sanction and release of funds were finalized. National Rural Roads Development Agency (NRRDA), a society registered under the Society's Act, 1860, working under the Ministry of Rural Development has been identified as a Nodal Agency, which will borrow from NABARD for the purpose. A loan of Rs. 4000 crores was sanctioned for the purpose. For want of suitable amendment to the Central Roads Funds Act, the Tripartite Agreement to be entered into covering the technical, financial and legal aspects of the relationship among NABARD, NRRDA and MoRD is pending for execution.

The cumulative amount sanctioned and disbursed up to 2006-07, was Rs. 61,539.87 crores and Rs. 34,643.87 crores respectively. During 2006-07, 42317 projects involving a loan amount of Rs 10,555.36 crores was sanctioned under RIDF-XII, enhancing cumulative number of projects to 244025 and amount sanctioned to Rs. 615,339.87 crores respectively availed by 28 states governments. It is hoped that NABARD will achieve the target. Of the total amount sanctioned during the year, rural roads and bridge projects accounted for 38.2 per cent, irrigation projects 30.1 per cent, social sector project 18.7 per cent and others 13.0 per cent. The cumulative position of sector-wise sanctions and disbursements is given in Table 9.2. During the year, disbursements were made to the tune of Rs. 6222.58 crores. As per phasing of projects under various trenches (RIDF I to XII) the total amount sanctioned was Rs. 52,579.19 crores against which disbursements aggregated Rs. 37,559.9 crores. Nine states, namely, Andhra Pradesh, Gujarat, Karnataka, Madhya Pradesh, Maharashtra, Rajasthan, Tamil Nadu, Uttar Pradesh and West Bengal, accounted for 71 per cent of total disbursements and 69 per cent of total sanctions as on March 31, 2007. The state-wise analysis of ratio of disbursements to the approved phasing of sanctions reveals that Sikkim topped with 92 per cent, followed by Mizoram (90 per cent), Himachal Pradesh and Jammu & Kashmir (83 per cent), Meghalaya (81 per cent), Gujarat (80 per cent), Maharashtra and Haryana (77 per cent), Punjab (76 per cent), Rajasthan, Uttar Pradesh and Tamil Nadu (75 per cent), Nagaland and Uttrakhand (74 per cent), Karnataka (73 per cent), Chhattisgarh and Kerala (72 per cent) and Madhya Pradesh (71 per cent). Slow pace of utilization of loans under RIDF when compared to the sanctions was mainly due to delay in administrative and technical approval by the state governments, land acquisitions problems, delay in obtaining statutory clearances and tendering process, inadequate budgetary support at state-level, lack of coordination among implementing departments etc. NABARD is in the process of encouraging public-private partnerships and network relation to bring about private sector competence and funds into the realm of rural infrastructure.

The first five trenches of RIDF (I to V) have since been closed by June-2006 and the phasing/period of implementation in respect of various projects under RIDF-VI to IX trenches has been extended up to March 31, 2007. The schedule dates of closure of RIDF-X, XI and XII are March 31, 2007, 2008 and 2009 respectively. In a major thrust-strengthening infrastructure in rural India, government proposed an increase in the corpus of RIDF-XIII to Rs. 12,000 crores during 2007-08 as against Rs. 71301 crores in 2005-06.

The region-wise distribution of cumulative RIDF sanctions and disbursements shows that the southern region accounted for 30 per cent of total sanctions as well as disbursements. On the other hand, the central, eastern and north-eastern regions, which together account for about 58 per cent of farm households, have got just 38 per cent of RIDF project funds sanctioned and 35.4 per cent of the project funds disbursed (Table 9.2). A number of factors including the issues of governance and organisational initiative, population density, and the absorptive capacity of RIDF funds themselves, may have played a role in creating vast regional variations in the use of RIDF funds.

**Table 9.2:** Region-wise Sanction and Disbursement under RIDF

(*As on 31 March, 2006*)

| *State/Region* | *Total (RIDF I to RIDF XI)* | | | | *Disbursement as per cent of Sanction* |
|---|---|---|---|---|---|
| | *Sanction* | *Per cent* | *Disbursement* | *Per cent* | |
| Northern Region | 5620.56 | (10.96) | 3857.16 | (12.31) | 68.6 |
| North-Eastern Region | 2063.24 | (4.02) | 989.97 | (3.16) | 48.0 |
| Eastern Region | 7527.38 | (14.68) | 3746.93 | (11.96) | 49.8 |
| Central Region | 9946.87 | (19.40) | 6365.69 | (20.32) | 64.0 |
| Western Region | 10677.21 | (20.82) | 6953.30 | (22.20) | 65.1 |
| Southern Region | 15447.75 | (30.12) | 9414.21 | (30.05) | 60.9 |
| India | 51283.01 | (100.00) | 31327.26 | (100.00) | 61.1 |

*Note*: RIDF denotes Rural Infrastructure Development Fund. Figures in parentheses denote per cent to total.

*Source*: NABARD.

One of the issues about priority sector lending to agriculture that needs to be highlighted pertains to the shortfall between the priority sector target of 18 per cent for agriculture and the actual amount allocated to RIDF (Table 9.3). For instance, in 2005-06, the amount allocated to RIDF was Rs. 14,000 crores against a shortfall of Rs. 36, 628 crores. There is a need to allocate the additional funds for investment in agriculture either directly by NABARD or through the issue of Rural Development Bonds (RDBs) by the Government of India.

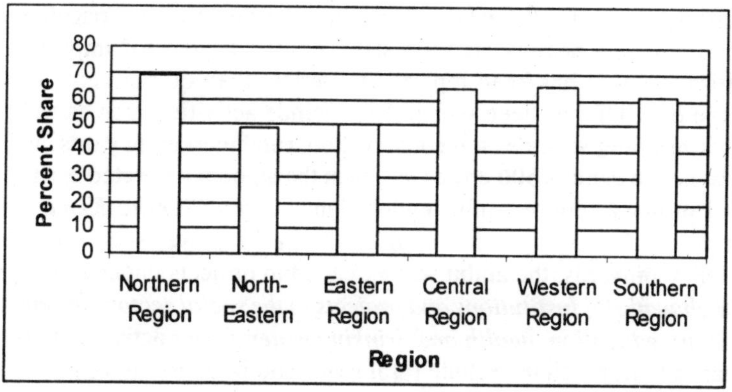


**Fig. 9.3:** Regional Distribution of Disbursement as a Per cent of Sanction.

**Table 9.3:** Measured Gap between Default and RIDF Allocation for all Domestic Scheduled Commercial Banks

| | *2003-04* | *2004-05* | *2005-06* | *2006-07** |
|---|---|---|---|---|
| Number of banks defaulting in respect of achievement of agricultural lending target | 45 | 43 | 44 | NA |
| Amount of agricultural credit defaulted | Rs. 24,585.65 | Rs, 31,759.11 | Rs. 36,627.81 | NA |
| Amount allocated to banks for RIDF under respective trenches as per corpus announced by the Government | Rs. 8,000 crore for RIDF-X (for 2004-05) | Rs, 8,000 crore for RIDF-XI (for 2005-06) | Rs. 14,000** | Rs. 16,000 ** |
| Difference between Amount defaulted and allocations | Rs. 16586 crore | Rs. 23759 crore | Rs. 22628 crore | NA |

Note: * Not yet allocated.

** Rs. 4,000 crore under the separate window for rural roads component of Bharat Nirman Programme under RIDF-XII for 2006-07 and RIDF XIII for 2007-08.

The shortfall in disbursement of RIDF funds as compare to sanctions also continuous to remain a matter of concern in the implementation of RIDF. The government has taken a number of steps to address this problem. Under Accelerated Irrigation Benefit Programme, the allocation of Rs. 7121 is about Rs 500 crores less than the amount projected earlier. The credit of adding six lakhs hectares does not seem encouraging seen against the target of getting additional one crores hectare of land to be brought under irrigation. Though it is a healthy sign, no steps were indicated for improved utilization as it has been reported to be less than 60 per cent. The scope of RIDF has been widened to include activities such as rural drinking water scheme, soil conservation, rural marketing yards, and rural health centers 500 crores less than the amount projected earlier. And primary schools, mini hydel plants, *Sishu Shiksha Kendras, Angan wadis*, and system improvement in the power sector. From RIDF-V onwards, the ambit was extended to projects undertaken by *Panchayati Raj Institutions and projects in the social sector covering primary education, health and drinking water*. Other activities to be financed under RIDF include rural roads and bridges, minor/micro/

**Table 9.4:** Cumulative Sanctions and Disbursements under different Trenches (As on 31 March, 2007)

*(Rs. in Crores)*

| RIDF Trenches | Corpus | No of Projects | Amount Sanctioned | Amount Phased | Amount Disbursed | Percentage of Disbursement@ |
|---|---|---|---|---|---|---|
| I | 2000 | 4168 | 1906.21 | 1906.21 | 1760.87 | 92.4 |
| II | 2500 | 8193 | 2636.08 | 2636.08 | 2397.95 | 91.0 |
| III | 2500 | 14345 | 2732.69 | 2732.69 | 2453.50 | 89.8 |
| IV | 3000 | 6171 | 2902.55 | 2902.55 | 2482.00 | 85.5 |
| V | 3500 | 12234 | 3472.40 | 3472.40 | 3054.96 | 88.0 |
| Vi | 4500 | 43925 | 4503.53 | 4503.53 | 3956.95 | 87.9 |
| VII | 5000 | 24781 | 4624.72 | 4624.72 | 3947.28 | 85.4 |
| VIII | 5500 | 20968 | 5987.26 | 5987.26 | 4770.28 | 79.7 |
| IX | 5500 | 19595 | 5592.96 | 5592.96 | 4007.75 | 71.7 |
| X | 8000 | 17524** | 8117.03 | 8117.03 | 4732.10 | 58.3 |
| XI | 8000 | 30434 | 8509.08 | 6820.92 | 2455.59 | 36.0 |
| XII | 10000 | 42317 | 10555.36 | 3282.84 | 1540.69 | 46.9 |
| Total | 60000 | 244025 | 61359.87 | 52579.19 | 37559.92 | 71.4 |
| Irrigation | | 118931 | 20431.95 | 17522.46 | 12752.13 | 72.6 |
| Rural roads & bridges | | 66313 | 27139.68 | 23783.14 | 18011.44 | 75.7 |
| Social Sector | | 38660 | 6987.60 | 5431.91 | 3039.05 | 55.9 |
| Power | | 727 | 1433.60 | 1380.80 | 931.86 | 67.5 |
| Others | | 19394 | 5547.04 | 4430.88 | 2825.44 | 63.8 |

*Note:* * One lakh STWs sanctioned to Assam Government treated a single project, @ with phased amount, ** 42616 Construction of Primary School structures to Madhya Pradesh Government converted to 213 projects.

medium/major irrigation projects, flood protection; water shed development, reclamation of waterlogged areas, drainage, forest development, market yard, godown, *apni mandi, rural haats and other marketing infrastructure, cold-storage (public or joint sector at various exit points, seed/agriculture/horticulture* farms, plantation and horticulture, grading and testing/certifying laboratories, etc., community irrigation wells for irrigation purposes for the village as a whole, fishing harbours/jetties, riverine fisheries, animal husbandry and modern abattoir, drinking water supply, infrastructure for rural education and public health institutions including mobile health clinic, construction of toilet blocks in existing schools and pay and use toilets rural areas, village knowledge centers, desalination plants in coastal areas, infrastructure for information technology in rural areas and construction of aganwadi centers.

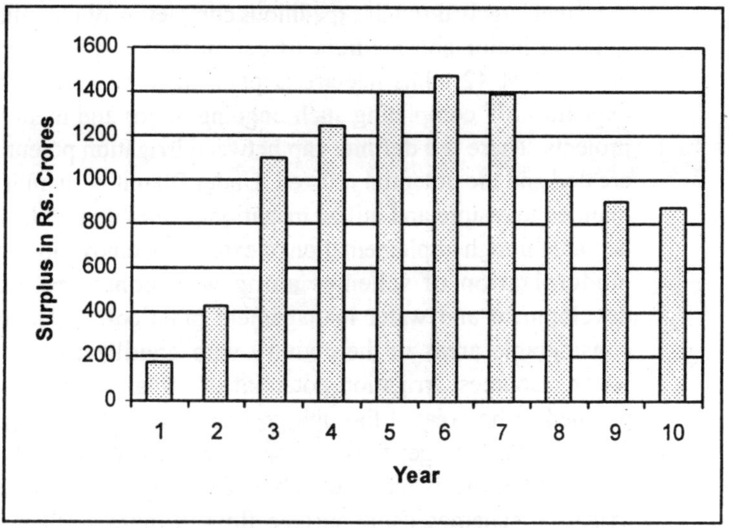


**Fig. 9.4:** Surplus in Rs. Crores

## Bharat Nirman

Dr. A.P.J. Abdul Kalam, then President of India, in his address to the Parliament outlined an overreaching vision to build India known as *Bharat Nirman.* Bharat Nirman has been conceived as a business plan to be implemented over a period of four years (2005-09) for building infrastructure, especially in rural India with a total estimated investment of Rs. 1,74,000 crores. It will have six components, namely, *Irrigation* (to bring an additional one crore hectares under assured irrigation), *Roads* (to connect all villages having a population of 1000 or 500 in hilly/tribal areas with a road, *Water supply* (to provide drinking water to the remaining 74,000 habitations that are uncovered), *Housing* (to construct 60 lakhs additional houses for the poor), *Rural electrification* (to reach electricity to the remaining 1,25,000 villages and offer electricity connection to 2.3 crores households), and *Rural telecom connectivity* (to give telephony connectivity to the remaining 66,822 villages) in each of these areas. The progress during the current financial year is as follows:

- *Irrigation:* Under the Irrigation Component of Bharat Nirman, the target of creation of additional irrigation potential of 1 crore hectare in 4 years (2005-06 to 2008-09) is planned to be met largely through expeditious completion of identified ongoing major and medium irrigation projects. Irrigation potential of 42 lakhs hectare is planned to be created by expeditiously completing such ongoing major and medium projects. There is a definite gap between irrigation potential created and the potential utilized. Under Bharat Nirman it is planned to restore and utilize irrigation potential of 10 lakhs hectare through implementation of extension, renovation and modernization of schemes along with command area development and water management practices. There are considerable areas in the country with unutilized ground water resources. Irrigation potential of 28 lakhs hectare is planned to be created through ground water development. The remaining target for creation of irrigation potential of 10 lakhs hectare is planned to be created by way of minor irrigation schemes using surface flow.10 lakhs hectare of irrigation potential is also planned by way of repair, renovation and restoration of water bodies and extension, renovation and modernization of minor irrigation schemes.

  Under the Accelerated Irrigation Benefit Programme, Rs. 19,437.88 crores has been released so far as CLA/grant for 200 major/medium irrigation projects and 5562 surface minor irrigation scheme up to March 2006. As against an outlay of Rs. 7121 crores in 2006-07, the outlays of 2007-08 will be increased to Rs. 11,000 crores. Of this, the grant release component to State Governments will be Rs. 3580 crores against Rs 2350 crores of previous fiscal.

- *Water supply:* Under the Accelerated Rural Water Supply Project (ARWSP), against the physical target of 55,067 habitations, 31,633 uncovered habitations, 213901 slipped back habitations and 93896 quality affected habitations have been addressed. Moreover 16,1731 schools have also been provided with safe drinking water facility. National Rural Drinking Water Quality Monitoring and Surveillance Programme has been launched in 2005-06 under which 5 persons from each village Panachayats are being trained for testing their own drinking water sources by using simple test kits provided. Further government has planned to achieve total sanitation coverage by 2012. During 2005-08, more than 3 crores toilets for individual households have been constructed, besides constructing 3.9 lakhs school toilets. Progress of *Nirmal Gram Puraskar* scheme, which was launched from 2005, reveals that the campaign is getting the desired momentum. The achievements in this sector are being appreciated by various international agencies. In order to meet the challenge of supplying drinking water, the priority is to tackle arsenic and fluoride contamination. During 2007-08, 1.55 lakhs habitations are planned to be covered under the programme. During the first six months of the current fiscal, 2,982 uncovered, 23,645 habitations that had slipped back and 3,283 quality-affected habitations have been covered. In 2007-08, the allocation for rural drinking water supply is Rs 6,500 crores, out of which Rs 2,991 crores has been spent.
- *Roads*: So far, over, 20,000 habitations have been connected and project for connecting over 16,000 habitations are at different stages of construction. The projects are yet to be approved for about 23,000habitations. So far, 55,684 km. of new roads has been constructed and 78,418 km. existing rural roads have been upgraded/renewed. Up to February 2008, Rs. 29,681.82 crores has been utilized. All State Governments have been advised to arrange joint inspection of on-going as

well as completed works by MPs/MLAs/MLCs/functionaries of *Panchayati Raj Institutions* and implementing agencies. Three-tier quality monitoring is fully functional. So far over 45,000 roads work have been inspected by National Level Quality Monitors.

- *Housing:* A total of 51.77 lakhs houses have been taken up for construction, out of which over 49 lakhs have been completed. Over 21 lakhs houses shall be taken up in 2008-09. The budgetary allocation has been substantially enhanced from Rs. 2900 crores in 2004-05 to Rs. 5400 crores in 2008-09. For ensuing transparency in selection of beneficiaries, selection of permanent IAY waitlist has been introduced. So far, 14 states have completed preparation of permanent Indra Awas Yojana (IAY) waitlist and displayed it at conspicuous places in the Panachayats. Moreover, unit cost of IAY houses sanctioned on or after 1 April 2008 has been enhanced from Rs. 25,000 to Rs. 35,000 in the plains areas and from Rs. 27,500 to Rs. 38,500 in the hilly areas. Similarly for upgradation of an existing *kutcha* houses, the financial assistance has been enhanced from Rs. 12,500 to Rs. 15,000 per unit. Further Department of Financial Services have advised the Reserved Bank of India to include IAY houses under the Differential Rate of Interest (DRI) and to lend up to Rs. 20,000 per unit at an interest rate of 4 per cent.
- *Rural Electrification:* Under the Rajiv Gandhi *Grameen Vidyutikaran Yojana,* 28241 villages have been electrified and 504141 connections to BPL households have been released until February 9, 2007. The budgetary support has been increased from Rs. 3000 crores in 2006-07 to Rs. 3983 crores in 2007-08.
- *Rural Telecom Connectivity:* Telecom connectivity constitutes an important part of the effort to upgrade the rural infrastructure. Under the Bharat Nirman Programme, it will be ensured that 66,822 revenue villages in the country, which have not yet been provided with a Village Public Telephone (VPT), shall be covered by November, 2007. Out of the above villages, connectivity in 14,183 remote and far- flung villages will be provided through digital satellite phone terminals.

Assistance for both capital as well as operational expenditure for these VPTs will be met out of the Universal Services Obligation Fund (USOF).15054 villages have been provided with telephone connectivity against the target of 20 thousand villages. The balance is expected to be covered by the end of current fiscal.

- *Bharat Nirman* epitomizes the UPAs approach to governance. It is *paradigm shift* that will enable us to see the resources thrown up by the engine of growth for building infrastructure and bringing basic amenities to rural India. Since the implementation of Bharat Nirman has gathered pace, budgetary support to the programme is increased to Rs. 18,696 crores—an increase of 54 per cent. We must dare to be bold and set for ourselves high targets to be achieved by the year 2009. Though Bharat Nirman require huge resources, government believes that Bharat Nirman is an achievable project and wanted to give rural India a new deals fully involving *Panchayati Raj Institutions* in the planning and implementation.

**National Commission on Farmers**

No sooner did the new government assume office, then the Prime Minister set up a *National Commission on Farmers (NCF)* under the chairmanship of Dr. M.S. Swaminathan, to prescribe the exigency measures and has submitted five reports between December 2005 and October 2006. Key Recommendations of the NCF is incorporated in the *Revised Draft National Policy for Farmers*. These include: asset reforms covering land, water, livestock and bio-resources; farmers friendly support services covering extension, training and knowledge, connectivity, credit and insurance; assured and remunerative marketing; inputs and delivery services; and curriculum reforms in agriculture universities. Other major initiatives recommended include: bringing agriculture in the *Concurrent List of the Constitution*; setting up of a National Food Security and Sovereignty Board, universalization of PDS; setting up of an Indian Trade Organization; making the Commission on agricultural Cost and Prices into an autonomous statutory organization with MSP with atleast 50 per cent more than the cost of production and launch of a

*Rural Non-farm Livelihood Initiative (RNFLI)* to absorb higher number of people when implemented. Various recommendations of NCF are already implemented and or active consideration of the government.

National Commission on Farmers has recommended the establishment of Village Knowledge Centers (VKCs) all over the country using modern Information and Communication Technology (ICT). A National Alliance comprising of over 230 organizations representing IT corporate, government, academics and civil society organizations power Mission—2007 launched in 2004, it aims to facilitate setting up a center in each of India's 60,000 villages by 2007—the 60th anniversary of country's Independence. These would be the knowledge windows to the world of knowledge for our villages and also reap the benefits of our e-governance, tele-education, tele-medicine, e-commerce and e-judiciary initiatives. Inspite of all pervasive nature of computers, they would still be far away from being truly friendly access device for our villagers.

We need in such cases a human intermediary who would act as the Village Information Officer. He will be the extended eyes and ears of the villagers to the world of knowledge. ICT do not by themselves create transformations in the society. But they are the facilitators of change and have a powerful multiplier effect on the overall economy. Farmers require a proactive advice on various aspects. Computerized data can be transmitted to the farming community through VKCs. Village school can also play a notable role in this regard. The mission objective is to facilitate and accelerate through multi-stakeholder collaborations the provision of knowledge centers in each village. Each of these would be a center for knowledge based live-hoods and income generation's opportunities for poor women and men farming communities and all disadvantaged people. Government supports the goal and joined the alliance and routed its support through NABARD by providing 100 crores out of RIDF as initial investment. It is easy to put a computer in the village knowledge center but a lot more difficult to make it work for the betterment of the Indian farmers. This is a question one must ponder, especially against the background of Rs. 100 crores has been set apart from the RIDF for this purpose. Indian planners, bureaucrats and scientist turned administrators need to do some honest soul searching here, lest the tax payer's money keep going down the drain all the time, and the farmers are left in the lurch as has been the case for decades now in the country. The recommendations of National Commission on Farmer have resulted into first ever *National Policy for Farmers.* The policy focuses on the farmer and aims to improve the economic viability of farming. The policy *inter alia* aims at sustainability and conservation of resources, development of affordable support services, strengthening of bio-security market safeguards and risk management, furthering reforms and enhancing competitiveness for holistic development of our agrarian economy. The broad areas of its coverage include:

1. Focus will be on the *economic well-beings* of the farmers in addition to production and productivity.
2. *Asset Reforms:* To ensure that a farmer household in villages either possesses or has access to a productive asset or marketable skill.
3. *Water Use Efficiency*: The concept of maximizing yield and income per unit of irrigation water in all the crop production programmes would be accorded priority with stress on awareness and efficiency on water use.
4. *New Technologies* like biotechnology, Information and Communication technology (ICT), renewable energy technology, space applications and nano Technology would be encouraged for improving productivity per unit of land and water.
5. *National Agricultural Bio-Security System* should be established to organize a coordinated agricultural bio-security programme.
6. *Seed and Soil Health*: Quality seeds, disease-free planting material and soil health enhancement hold the key to raising farm productivity. Every farmer is to be issued with a soil health passbook containing integrated information on farm soils with corresponding advisories.
7. *Support Services for Women*: Appropriate support services like crèches, child care centers and adequate nutrition needed by women working in the fields would be funded.
8. *Credit and Insurance*: The financial services would be galvanized for timely, adequate and easy reach to the farmers at reasonable interest rates.

9. *Gyan Chaupals* at village level with the help of ICT and farm schools in the field of outstanding farmers to promote farmer to farmer learning would be set up through state governments for strengthening the extension services.
10. Necessary steps would be taken to put in place an appropriate *Social Security Scheme* for farmers.
11. *Minimum Support Price* mechanism to be implemented effectively to ensure remunerative prices for agricultural produce across the country.
12. *Food Security Basket* to be enlarged to include nutritious millets such as jowar, bajra, millets, ragi mostly grown in the dryland farming areas.

In recent days, there has been greater focus on the agricultural sector. It is for the first time after independence that a special meeting of National Development Council (NDC) was conveyed in May 2000 to discuss the matter relating to agriculture. Following NDC meeting, the government launched within the shortest possible time, two mega schemes namely, *Rashtriya Krishi Vikas Yojana (RKVY)* and *National Food Security Mission (NFSM)* for which the central government would spend nearly Rs. 30,000 crores during the11th Plan Period (2007-12):

**National Food Security Mission**

The Department of Agriculture and Cooperation, Ministry of Agriculture has launched a centrally sponsored scheme on NFSM in pursuance of the resolution of National Development Council (NDC) to increase the production of rice, wheat and pulses by 18, 8 and 2 million tonnes respectively over the benchmark levels of production by the end of Eleventh Plan Period with a plan outlay of Rs. 4882.5 crores. The mission aim at increasing foodgrain production of the above crops through area expansion and productivity enhancement; restoring soil fertility and productivity; creating employment opportunities and enhancing farm level economy to restore confidence of the farmers of targeted districts.

Various activities of NFSM relate to demonstration of improved production technology, distribution of quality seeds of HYVs and hybrids, popularization of newly released varieties, support for micronutrients, and training and mass-media campaign including awards for best performing districts. The identified districts are given flexibility to adopt any local area specific interventions as are included in the Strategic Research and Extension Plan (SREP) prepared on the district. Rs. 2 crores each will be provided during the Eleventh Five Year Plan period to those districts which have a programme for two or more crops of the NFSM and Rs. 1 crore to the districts having a programme for any one crops. NFSM is being implemented in 305 districts of the 16 States of the country. An amount of Rs. 149.4 crores has been released to various states to plan and implement various interventions during 2007-08.

**Rashtriya Krishi Vikas Yojana**

The NDC in its 53rd meeting also decided to launch a programme to incentivise the States to increase the share of investment in agriculture in their state Plans. Accordingly on August 16, 2007 the Government approved RKVY with an allocation of Rs. 25,000 crores for the Eleventh Five Year Plan. RKVY aims at achieving 4 per cent annual growth in the agricultural sector by ensuing holistic development of agriculture and allied sectors. It will be a state plan scheme and the eligibility for assistance would depend upon the amount provided in the state budget for agriculture and allied sector over and above the baselines percentage expenditure incurred on agriculture and allied sector. The funds under the scheme would be provided to states as 100 per cent grant by the central government. The main objectives of the scheme are:

1. To incentivise the States to increase public investment in agriculture and allied sector.
2. To provide flexibility and autonomy to the states in planning and executing a griculture and allied sector schemes.
3. To ensure the preparation of plans for the districts and the sates based on agro-climatic conditions, availability of technology and natural resources.
4. To ensure that the local need/crops/priorities are better reflected.
5. To achieve the goal of reducing the yield gaps in important crops through focused interventions.
6. To maximize returns to the farmers.

A number of initiatives have been taken to provide wider choice and greater options to farmers to sell their produce. As a safety net for formers, the system of MSP is in existence for many years. There has been unprecedented increase in MSP for important crops such as cereals, pulses and oilseeds in order to ensure remunerative prices to farmers and protect their interests. Marketing infrastructure is important to reduce price risks. A number of initiatives have been taken. The objective of the ongoing process of reforms in agricultural marketing is to provide wider choice and greater options to farmers to sell their produce. Government of India has circulated a Model Act and also a set of Model Rules to the states to facilitate the process of reform. A law has also been enacted to make storage/godown receipts negotiable so that farmers are able to get loans from banks based on the produce stored by them in warehouses.

Needless to say, inspite of tremendous progress after independence, both in agriculture and other sectors, much remains to be done in order to improve the condition of farmers. Problems are many. In a vast country like ours, there is bound to be some problem somewhere. At this juncture, it is necessary to identify our priorities with clarity and make all out efforts to ensure effective action. The focus should be to improve the income and welfare of farmers. This implies not only higher production and productivity but also improving the capabilities of farmers to compete on the market map. It appears that the government expenditure in rural areas is getting somewhat more welfare oriented than providing growth impetus. Investment in Agricultural Research and Development have the highest rate of return in terms of agricultural growth, but the situation is that India has hardly 0.5 per cent of agriculture GDP into agricultural research. Agriculture research needs more resources and commensurate institutional reform if it has to be a catalyst for making our agriculture globally competitive. The need is to have a holistic approach incorporating rural infrastructure, dissemination of better technology, sustainable use of natural resources and development of the rural non-farm sector.

10

# Role of Commission Agents in Rural Finance

MANMOHAN SINGH GILL

---

*Agriculture plays an important role in the economic development of countries like India. The cost of production is increasing with the demand of inputs and declining soil fertility due to extensive cultivation and following the same cropping pattern. At the same time, the size of the farmland is decreasing with division and mushrooming of nuclear family norm. There has been a rise in the demand for capital to sustain agricultural production system. The institutional credit advancing agencies is largely serving the interest of the rich farmers leaving the small and marginal farmers at the mercy of money-lenders and commission agents/arhtiyas. Based on secondary sources of information, this article explores the role of commission agents/arhtiyas and other moneylenders to meet the aspirations and needs of the vast farming community. The analysis provides that the institutional agencies are withdrawing from their social responsibility of catering the demands of the rural society and making way for the moneylenders and other non-institutional agencies to lend in a big way in cash and kind. The system of their dependency has elements of exploitation because of the vulnerability of the farming community and lack of their borrowing power. Further, the populist policies of the respective governments are responsible for the unhealthy economic structure of the rural credit that has encouraged high level of institutional advance.*

Adoption of farm technology is capital intensive and its application requires sufficient supply of credit to meet input demands. The development of infrastructure in the form of cooperatives societies especially credit cooperatives and Gramin Banks have supported the needs of the farming community. The financial and technical support provided by the cooperatives to the farmers have helped tremendously in achieving higher production of various crops and saved the farmers from the exploitative structure of the moneylenders (Singh, 1998). The credit cooperatives besides helping the farmers in achieving higher production, it was expected that it may save the farming community from the exploitative structure of moneylenders and bring lenders and borrowers close to each other (Singh, 2003). Moreover, cash requirement for cultivation with new agrarian technologies is eleven times higher than the traditional methods (Prasad, 1991) and it is much higher at the present level of technological adoption and use of other inputs. In addition, so as to diversify the cereal oriented production pattern towards allied activities, lot of financial assistance is needed by the farmers because their own sources are not sufficient to meet the expenses of diversified production programme (Brar, 2001). With such an increase in the demand for capital, a question arises: Can a farmer have access to the financial resources that are prerequisite for the present farming needs? Studies (Kaushal, 1971; Gulati, 1996; Lekshmi *et al.*, 1998; Chahal, 2005) reveal that there exist a big gap between what a farmer owns and what he requires in terms of finance. The cost of different inputs has increased enormously as compared to the increase in the farm output prices. Cooperative credit societies and other formal institutions of finance have been made functional to meet the rising demand of farming community but the credit advanced by these institutional agencies is inadequate to match the demand and so the farmers are made to depend upon non-institutional sources of credit (Patel, 1963; Thingalaya, 1978; Bell, 1990; Gill, 2001). This paper addresses to one of the important non-institutional source of rural finance. With the help of secondary sources of information supported by the primary data provided by different studies, this paper analyzes the importance and the shortcoming of such source of farm credit. Also it highlights the circumstantial forces that keep this non-institutional source in vogue despite its adverse effect on the socio-economic life of the rural farming community.

Among the non-institutional agencies, commission agents/ *arhtiyas* have emerged as an important financier of the rural society. A great proportion of the funds and inputs requirements of the farming community for diverse agricultural needs come from the *arhtiyas* who have been able to appreciate the multifarious demands of farmers and lend them in all seasons and for all purposes. Studies by Khan and Tripathi (1972), Desai (1990), Jodka (1995), Gill (2003) have concurred similar inferences. In Andhra Pradesh, as against 20 crores advance by banks and credit societies, Rs. 90 crores of credit is being advanced by the *arhtiyas* in the form of inputs (Parthasarthy, 1993). Another report on the situation in Punjab states that 61.3 per cent of the farmers' needs are met by 63.85 per cent of the credit advanced by *arhtiyas*. Further, small and marginal farmers due to their inability to finance high cost inputs are forced to cultivate low value crops and if their credit needs are fulfilled only then they will shift to high value crops. On the other hand, large farmers have large resources and manage to avail credit from the institutional sources to their advantage to reap the scale of agricultural development. In the process, the small and marginal farmers are at the disadvantageous position in terms of operation and management of credit needs. Thus, there is difference with regard to credit availability among various classes of cultivators. Likewise, Mehta and Prasad (1988) have reported that cultivators in the more advanced States like Punjab, Gujarat, Tamil Nadu and other have more access to credit from institutional agencies and there is uneven flow of credit among the farming communities of different states. Epstein (1978) finds that cooperatives particularly credit societies are serving the wealthy farmers due to which they are able to make use of advanced agricultural technology to raise production and productivity of the farm. Under such situations, the poor farmers have to depend upon the non-institutional sources of credit. The data in Table 10.1 reveals that out of the 83.9 per cent households with landholding up to 2 hectare, 79.9 per cent are under debt and 49.7 per cent have taken loan from the non-institutional agencies. Secondly, the households possessing more than 10 hectare of landholding have their outstanding loan more from the institutional agencies as compared to that of the non-institutional agencies. This amply justifies that the outstanding loan of the large farm households is from the institutional credit agencies rather than the non-institutional ones.

**Table 10.1:** Total and Indebted Farm Households According to Landholding Size, 2003

| *Size of Land possed (hectare)* | *Per cent Total Households* | *Per cent Indebted Household* | *Per cent Loan from Institutional Agencies* | *Per cent Loan from Non-institutional Agencies* |
|---|---|---|---|---|
| < 0.01 | 1.4 | 1.3 | 22.6 | 77.4 |
| 0.01 – 0.40 | 32.8 | 30.0 | 43.3 | 56.7 |
| 0.41 – 1.00 | 31.7 | 29.8 | 52.8 | 47.2 |
| 1.01 – 2.00 | 18.0 | 18.9 | 57.6 | 42.3 |
| Up to 2.00 | 79.9 | 79.9 | 51.3 | 49.7 |
| 2.01 – 4.00 | 10.5 | 12.5 | 65.1 | 35.0 |
| 4.01 – 10.00 | 4.8 | 6.4 | 68.8 | 31.1 |
| 10.00+ | 0.9 | 1.2 | 67.6 | 32.4 |
| All sizes | 100.0 | 100.0 | 57.7 | 42.4 |

*Source*: *Economic and Political Weekly* Research Foundation, 2008.

An analysis of non-institutional sources of credit requires having an overview of the situation with regard to agricultural credit advanced by institutional agencies like cooperative credit societies, banks and the like. Going through the data regarding loan advanced and recovered of the agricultural cooperative societies of Punjab, it is found that the loan advanced and loan recovered varies considerably. In 1970-71, the outstanding amount of loan advanced was 90.76 per cent and it increased to 139.07 per cent in 1990-91 (Table 10.2). With reforms setting in 1990's, banks profitability increased but their availability for rural credit and for backward regions has been adversely affected (Shah, Rao and Shankar, 2007). In other words, the rural sector was left at the mercy of moneylenders and the banks priority shifted from agricultural sector to industrial one. It may be because of the lack of collateral as security with the vast majority of small and marginal farmers. This indicates at the same time that farming community is under heavy debt as they either have not paid the outstanding advance or have not been able to get remunerative returns on the farm. This is amply evident from 2001-02 onwards trends of loan advanced. Equally, there has been a trend of decreasing outstanding loans; the outstanding amount has not increased more than 70 per cent.

**Table 10.2:** Progress of Primary Agricultural Credit Societies in Punjab

| *Year* | *Number* | *Loan Advanced* | *Loan Outstanding* | *Societies Showing Loss* |
|---|---|---|---|---|
| 1970-71 | 10,932 | 5,726.59 | 5,197.32 (90.76) | 2001 (18.30) |
| 1980-81 | 4,266 | 19,920.65 | 14,625.88 (73.42) | 1022 (23.96) |
| 1990-91 | 4,633 | 34,630.66 | 48,161.63 (139.07) | 962 (20.76) |
| 2000-01 | 4,084 | 2,13,899.47 | 1,53,029.93 (71.54) | 808 (19.78) |
| 2003-04 | 3,996 | 3,32,817.83 | 2,31,948.64 (69.69) | 1203 (30.11) |
| 2004-05 | 3,985 | 3,78,947.69 | 2,66,475.56 (70.32) | 1272 (31.92) |
| 2005-06 | 3978 | 4,55,191.12 | 3,03,515.18 (66.68) | 1171 (29.44) |
| 2006-07 | 3981 | 5,106,17.43 | 3,612,48.39 (70.75) | 1183 (29.72) |

*Source*: *Statistical Abstract of Punjab*, Various Issues.

Moreover, the data provides that the number of societies going under loss has increased from 18.30 per cent in 1970-71 to 31.92 per cent in 2004-05 and it is 29.72 per cent in 2006-07. It amounts to the level of non-payment of debts by the farming community in Punjab; considered as the food basket of India. The amount of loss increased from Rs. 36.44 lakhs in 1970-71 to Rs. 2334.50 lakhs in 2004-05. This amply depicts the plight of farming community. Since data pertaining to class structure of agrarian society is not available, it cannot be generalized that the outstanding amount is with the rich and influential farmers or the small and marginal farmers. The analysis of EPW Research Foundation finds that with increase in size of holding, non-institutional loan decreases and that of institutional loan increases (2008). According to another estimate (Shergill, 1998 cited from *Human Development Report*, 2004), per acre indebtedness of the small and marginal farmers is the highest (Rs. 10,105) followed by that of the farmers with landholding between 5 to 10 acres (Rs. 7941) and those between 10 to 15 acres (Rs. 4230). Keeping the size of land holding into consideration, it is very clear that the upper strata of landholders have greater outstanding amount as compared to that of the lower strata. Even the study (Epstein, 1978) points out these credit societies are serving the wealthy farmers as against the poor one and the outstanding amount is largely with the rich class of the farming community. Bardhan (1984), Gill (2001), Kaur (2003) find that landless and small farmers remain dependent on informal sources for most of their credit requirements, thus supporting the above inference that the outstanding loan is invariably of the farmers above the category of small ones. Not only this, there is growing interference of governmental officials and these cooperatives have not been able to fulfil the aspirations in terms of new technology and cash requirements (Singh, 2003). Under such circumstances, the small and marginal farmers stand at the disadvantageous position if Government waive off the debt as the debt waiver specifically for the institutional outstanding credit. In other term, the debt waiver is in the interest of the already 'have' class. It is also the political compulsion of the so called farmer's oriented parties to justify the waiver of farm credit so as to bail out themselves of the covert economic rhetoric of dwindling position of the farm sector in the light of globalization. It is the expectation of the borrowers that the loan will be waived off, has eroded the repayment behaviour of the farmers (Chaudhary and Makhija, 1999). Secondly, looking at the distribution of landholding, the small and marginal farmers account for 78.2 per cent of the agricultural holdings in the country (*Human Development Report*, 2004). The share of marginal and small holding increased to 77.65 per cent between 1970-71 and 1990-91. Consequentially, the small and marginal farmers will lag behind in the process of debt waiver and their dependency on the non-institutional sources of credit further deteriorate their position in the agrarian society. Equally, the rural elite dominates the cooperative structure as they used to during the colonial rule and hence, keep control of the credit advanced in their favour as against those without political or economic power.

Moreover, another institutional source of farm credit is commercial banks that advance agricultural credit and it has increased from Rs 165.27 crores in 1984-85 to 245.59 crores in 1986-87 and after that there was drastic fall in the credit advanced by the commercial banks (Sekhon and Kaur, 2003) due to low returns and high transaction costs and overdue. At the same time, the cost of production increased, degradation of soil and water resources continued and farmers carried out their wheat-paddy rotation that resulted in increase demand of the credit. Since, the commercial bank continue to withdraw from agricultural advance and cooperatives standing advance continued to soar and many cooperatives come under losses, the non-institutional sources became important source of finance to fill the gap. Mukherjee and Bandyopadhyay (1993) narrate that with the cooperative structure going in disarray and the institutional finance from the commercial banks is in a state of destitute, the poor farmers have no option except to non-institutional credit sources and for this reason, money-lenders continue to hold ubiquitous position in the rural India. Even the Regional Rural Banks with their domain being confined to weaker sections of the rural areas (Misra, 2006) are finding it difficult to curb loan default and so treading a safe path by cutting advances to the rural poor. Such trends amplify the need and existence of non-institutional sources of credit. The observation (Kaur *et al*, 2001) that formal agricultural credit agencies shall have to review their lending policies in order to cater to the credit needs of the farmers to reduce the presence of informal agencies in the agricultural credit markets, justifies the hold of non-institutional agencies over the credit market in the agricultural sector.

The inadequate supply of institutional credit has increased the dependency of farming community in particular the small and marginal farmers on the non-institutional sources of credit. Also, their inability to provide sufficient collateral as security debars them to avail the institutional credit. Shah, Rao and Shankar (2007) have in their observation regarding rural credit point out that the reforms have made the return of moneylenders especially to meet the needs of the peasantry. Reddy (2006) states that it is distressing that government is considering to bring in moneylenders to solve the problem of rural credit. The fact is that the main source of credit for the pure tenants and mixed tenants are the traders (Kaur, 2003). Singh (2003) finds that majority of the farmers take loan from the cooperative societies and the private moneylenders. Nearly 21 per cent of the farmers have taken loan from the private moneylenders in their study of 150 respondents of four blocks of Muktsar district. Another study of a Ludhiana village reveals that majority of the respondents have taken advance from the commission agents for inputs like insecticides, pesticides, fertilizers, seeds and even to run the diesel pump for irrigation (Gill and Kaur, 2003). Parthasarthy (1997) finds that 90 crores of credit is advanced by the *arhtiyas* in the form of inputs as against 20 crores advance by banks and credit societies in Andhra Pradesh. Sengupta (2008) in his analysis of Vidharbha region finds that moneylenders have considerable hold on the farmer's entire life cycle. The farmer borrows for diversification without realizing its prospects and borrows money for tapping ground water sources and application of fertilizers. The downward global trends of cash crops many a time leave farmer indebted to moneylenders and other institutional credit sources. According to Chahal (2005), it is not easy for the farmers to get requisite amount of credit from cooperative banks and credit societies. They still have to depend on the moneylenders and commission agents to get loan for their investments.

He further holds that the bulk of the loans have been arranged from the commission agents and moneylenders, which is estimated to be about Rs.5500 crores. Even the study by the Punjab Cooperative Department reveals that commission agents provided 61.31 per cent of the credit during the two major farm operations in 1997 (cited from Kaur *et al.*, 2000). According to Singh (2008), 43 per cent of the farmers' needs are met by the commission agents/ *arhtiyas* who have a business of Rs.43 thousands crores in Punjab only (cited from *Dhanik Bhaskar*, 2008). If this is the situation in Punjab, the Indian scenario cannot be at variance from that of Punjab. In other words, commission agents and moneylenders are the powerful groups that support Indian agriculture in its road to agrarian development and plight of the farming community.

The credit advanced by the commission agents or *arhtiyas* is mostly for the purchase of farm inputs like fertilizers, insecticides etc. besides their non-productive purposes. Reddy (2007) finds that over the last 20 years, there is decline in the borrowing for consumption purpose and increase in that of for production purpose. The moneylender lends in kind to the tune of 77.71 per cent for seed and fertilizers. On the other hand, Jeromi (2007) finds that 66 per cent of the loan is utilized for non-productive uses. In Punjab, majority of the farmers take loan from the *arhtiyas* for meeting their non-productive purposes, such as socio-religious ceremonies, housing and the like (Gill and Kaur, 2003; Kaur, 2003; Singh and Kaur, 2003). Secondly, the rate of interest charged for the advance extended by the *arhtiyas* or moneylenders is quite exorbitant ranging from 24 to 36 per cent. Ahlawat (2002) has reported 30 per cent rate of interest charged for the loan advanced by the traders whereas Gill and Kaur (2003) and Reddy (2007) have reported 14 to 21 per cent as rate of interest on the credit advanced by the commission agents. Irrespective of the high rate on interest, the easy availability of loan is another factor conducive to their hold over the credit market in the agricultural sector. The cumbersome procedure and file work makes it difficult for the farming community to procure loan. Getting advance from the banks requires sureties as well as collateral as security, which is often difficult for the small and marginal farmers. Many a time, farmers take loan from the *arhtiyas* to repay their loan installment of the banks to keep their account in continuity. Gill and Kaur (2003) have come out with this observation in their study besides pointing out the ease of securing loan from these non-institutional sources.

Further, *arhtiyas* extend loan depending upon the credit worthiness of the loaners and their social relations with the commission agents. Also, the *arhtiyas* make sure that the sale deeds are processed through them which act as collateral for the advance made to the borrower. Darling (1925) has long time back observed that traders and moneylenders used to purchase the produce of the borrowers at much cheaper rates. The situation has changed with the emergence of markets and procurements made by government agencies and the debtor is not under compulsion to sell his produce at the prearranged price. But the *arhtiyas* still rule the roast especially in the case of farmers where they have lent the credit for one or the other purpose. According to Ghuman (2008), 52 per cent of the debt is from non-institutional agencies. In this way, the borrowing farmers are under compulsion to maintain continuity of the economic ties through the services of their lenders. Not only this, they participate in their social ceremonies to strengthen the economic relationship. Gill and Kaur (2003) have found that *arhtiyas* lend helping hand in all odd situation and their mutual trust and keeping parity of the accounts consolidate their economic relations. Such bondage gets further strengthened with their participation in socio-religious ceremonies and offering gifts on such occasions. The vulnerability and weak bargaining position of the borrower define his subordination to the lender and for this, the scale remains in favour of the lender not borrower. This relationship is of exploitative type in which the lender position gets strengthened with poverty of the borrower and his vulnerability for credit needs for non-productive purposes. In this way, the *arhtiyas*, moneylenders and other informal institutions of rural credit play positive role of providing credit under distress situations where institutional agencies fail to address the demand and needs of the farming community. They also play a negative role as exploiters and are largely responsible for rural indebtedness. They are charging exorbitant rate of interest and defining their buying and selling domains.

## Conclusion

The above analysis based on secondary sources of information depicts the exploitative and volatile situation of the rural society. The institutions meant to serve the needs and demands of the rural community have not been able to appreciate the non-productive needs of the farming community. Secondly, the greater outstanding advances have made the institutional agencies to think twice before lending in the rural sector for agricultural development. The cumbersome procedures and collateral as security for loan are the major hurdles in realization of the needs and aspirations of the farming community. This inference is corroborated by a study undertaken by the EPW Research Foundation in 2008. With the result, these institutions are giving way to informal credit agencies to operate on a large scale. Moneylenders or commission agents are of course lending at a high rate of interest but are able to cut their costs of lending because they are better informed about the borrower and the borrower keep their economic relations with the bonding of social ones. For this reason, they are ought to survive in the rural setting and continue to fill the credit gap created with the resultant no advance for the consumption and distress need of the farming community. The government may exonerate the farming community by writing off their outstanding in the institutional credit agencies but what about the outstanding credit farmers have with the non-institutional agencies. Small and marginal farmers have more than 75 per cent of their outstanding loan from the non-institutional sources. Secondly, the process of waiving off the loan will encourage the farming community to get advances from the institutional agencies on a large scale and then wait till the government again waive off the loans. Meanwhile, they will take the support of the non-institutional agencies to meet their credit needs and consolidate the position of the moneylenders or commission agents. How long will the government continue to waive off loans rather the public continue to pay for none of their fault? Did ever the planners or farmers oriented political parties realize the consequences of such a waiver? Why not to help those who regularly pay installments of their outstanding farm credit? All these questions have to be answered if farming community has to bring back to the path of development and set the economic structure of the society. In whole scenario despite the exploitative nature of the informal credit agencies, these are a social and economic reality.

## REFERENCES

Ahlawat, S.R. (2002). "Political Economy and Peasant Suicide", *Guru Nanak Journal of Sociology*, Vol. 23, No. 1.

Bardhan, P.K. (1984). *Land, Labour and Rural Poverty: Essays in Development Economics*, Oxford University Press, Delhi.

Bell, C. (1990). "Interaction between Institutional and Informal Credit Agencies in Rural India", *The World Bank Economic Review*, Vol. 4, No. 3.

Brar, S.S. (2001). "Capital Requirements for Diversified Production Programme in Punjab", *Indian Economic Panorama*, Vol. 11, no. 2.

Chaudhary, R.L. and Makhija, (1999). "Repayment Performance of Crop Loan", *Indian Economic Panorama*, Vol. 9, No. 3.

Chahal, T.S. (2005). *Forced Fall: A Case of Punjab Farmers*, Institute of Development Planning, Amritsar.

Darling, Malcolm (1925). *The Punjab Peasantry in Prosperity and Debt*, South Asia Book, Columbia.

Desai, S.M. (1990). *Agriculture and Rural Banking in India*, Himalaya Publishing House, Bombay.

Epstein, T. (1978). *South India: Yesterday, Today and Tomorrow*, Macmillan, London.

EPW Research Foundation, (2008). "The Loan Waiver Scheme", *Economic and Political Weekly*, Vol. XLIII, No. 11.

Gill, Anita (2001). *Rural Credit Markets*, Deep and Deep Publications, New Delhi.

Gill, M.S. (2003). *Punjab Society: Perspectives and Challenges*, Concept Publishing Company, New Delhi.

Gill, M.S. and R. Kaur (2003). "Commission Agents in Rural Setting" in Gill (ed.) *Punjab Society: Perspectives and Challenges*, Concept Publishing Company, New Delhi.

Ghuman, R.S. (2008). "Socio-Economic Crisis of Rural Punjab", *Economic and Political Weekly*, Vol. XLIII, No. 7.

Gulati, A. (1996). "New Economic Policy and Agriculture", *Indian Journal of Economics*, Jan-June.

*Human Development Report*, Government of Punjab, 2004.

Jeromi, P.D. (2007). "Farmers' Indebtedness and Suicides", *Economic and Political Weekly*, Vol. XLII, No. 31.

Jodka, S.S. (1995). "Changing Structure of Informal Credit in Rural Haryana", *Economic and Political Weekly*, Vol. XXX.

Kaur, Gian (2003). "Tenancy and Demand for Agricultural Credit" in Gill (ed.) *Punjab Society: Perspectives and Challenges*, Concept Publishing Company, New Delhi.

Kaur, P. *et al.* (2000). "Role of Cooperative Credit Institutions in Agricultural Development of Punjab", *Indian Economic Panorama*, Vol. 11, No. 2, 2001.

Kaur, Milkho et al, "Institutional Agricultural Credit in Punjab: An Overview", *Indian Economic Panorama*, Vol. 10, No. 2.

Kausal, G. (1971). *Economic History of India*, Kalyani Publication, Ludhiana.

Khan, W. and R.N. Tripathi (1972). *Intensive Agriculture and Modern Inputs*, National Institute of Community Development, New Delhi.

Lekshmi, R. *et al.* (1998). "Characteristics of Defaulters in Agricultural Credit Use", *Indian Journal of Agricultural Economics*, Vol. 53, No. 4.

Mehta and Prasad (1998). *Agrarian Relations and Rural Exploitation*, Ashish Publishing House, New Delhi.

Misra, B.S. (2007). "The Performance of Regional Rural Banks in India", cited from *Economic and Political Weekly*, Vol. XLII, No. 15.

Mukherjee, N. and D. Bandyopadhyay, (1993). "New Horizon for West Bengal Panachayats", *Indian Journal of Agricultural Economics*, Vol.48, No.4, September-October.

Parthasarthy, V. P. (1997). "Supply of Short-Term Credit and Estimation of Credit Gaps", *Indian Cooperative Review*.

Patel, M.L. (1963). "Direction of Cooperative Review", *Indian Cooperative Review*.

Prasad, K.N. (1991). *India's Rural Problems*, Concept Publishing Company, New Delhi.

Reddy S.T.S. (2007). "Diary of a Moneylender", *Economic and Political Weekly*, Vol. XLII, No. 29.

Reddy, Y.U. (2006). *Rural Banking: Review and Prospects*, Centre for Economic and Social Studies, Hyderabad.

Sekhon, M.K. and Parminder Kaur (2003). "Role of Institutional Finance and Government Investments in Capital Formation of Punjab Agriculture", in Gill (ed) *Punjab Society: Perspectives and Challenges*, Concept Publishing Company, New Delhi.

Sengupta, J. (2008). "Why Farmers Commit Suicides", *The Tribune*, Feb. 16.

Shah, M. *et al.* (2007). "Rural Credit in 20th Century India", *Economic and Political Weekly*, Vol. XLII, No. 15.

Singh, Sukhdev (1998). "The Lot of Small, Marginal Farmers Remains Same", *The Tribune,* May 8.

Singh, S. and Mandeep, Kaur (2003). "Socio- economic Adversities of Farmers" in Gill (ed.) *Punjab Society: Perspectives and Challenges,* Concept Publishing Company, New Delhi.

*Statistical Abstract of Punjab*, Economic and Statistical Organization Government of Punjab, Chandigarh (various issues)

——— (2008). "Siyasat ke Pale me kisano ka Bhagya", *Dainik Bhaskar*, July 9.

Thingalaya, N.K. (1978). "Report of Rural Credit Structure and Flaws", *Indian Journal of Agricultural Economics*, Vol. 33.

11

# Indebtedness among Agricultural Labour Households in West Bengal

RATHINDRA NATH PRAMANIK

*Agricultural labourers are the poorest of the poor and deprived section of the rural society in our country. Low wages, unemployment, assetlessness and social backwardness constitute the poverty syndrome among agricultural labourers, which again compels them to borrow for consumption, house construction and repairs, health care, marriage and other social ceremony purposes. Our objective is to discuss the incidence and extent of indebtedness among agricultural labourers households, sources of debt, purposes of debt and, terms and conditions of debt taken by agricultural labourers households in West Bengal as well as in Uttar Dinajpur District. The incidence and extent of indebtedness of Uttar Dinajpur District at the village level is higher than the state level figures. The main cause of indebtedness is the borrowing for marriage and social ceremonies followed by medical purposes and household consumptions at the village level of Uttar Dinajpur District. But at the state level, the main cause of indebtedness is the borrowing for household consumption followed by purchase of land and construction of building and productive purposes. However, as these loans are not only economically productive in that they do not help in the creation of additional incomes. They are bound to borrow money from non-institutional as well as institutional sources years after years. At the state level, the main source of rural credit is friends and relatives followed by shopkeepers and moneylenders. But at the village level, the share of subsidized loans provided by the Government under different anti-poverty programmes in total borrowing is higher than the shares of friends and relatives and moneylenders. Out of non-institutional sources, friends and relatives emerged as the main source of rural credit at the village level of Uttar Dinajpur District. The role of financial institutions is not sufficient in supplying rural credit. In this context, the role of the Bangladesh Grameen Bank Model of micro-financing turned out to be an extremely effective tool in supplying rural credit. This innovation of Self-Help Groups and the micro-credit has helped the poor, especially women to gain better access to credit facilities. But the progress of formation of SHGs is not expected rate in this district. As a result poor people of this district deprived from the institutional finance. Agricultural labourers mainly get institutional finance from the Government under different anti-poverty programmes.*

Agricultural labourers are the poorest of the poor and deprived section of the rural society in our country. Low wages, unemployment, asset less ness and social backwardness constitute the poverty syndrome among agricultural labourers, which again compels them to borrow for consumption, house construction and repairs, health care, marriage and other social ceremony purposes. However, as these loans are not economically productive in that they do not help in the creation of additional incomes. They are bound to borrow money from non-institutional as well as institutional sources years after years. The indebtedness may be defined as the amount of outstanding debt principal as well as interest accrued thereon as on the date of enquiry (R.L.E—1987-88). The average amount of outstanding borrowing comprises the previous outstanding plus current year's borrowing minous repayment made during the current year by the same household. Our objective is to discuss the incidence and extent of indebtedness among agricultural labourers households, sources of debt, purposes of debt and, terms and conditions of debt taken by agricultural labourers households in West Bengal as well as in Uttar Dinajpur District.

This study is based on intensive field investigation personally done by the author in three sets of diverse villages (highly developed, moderately developed and least developed villages). The analysis is mainly based on 180 agricultural labour households from the categories of landless agricultural labourers and marginal farmers-cum-agricultural labourers. The data have been collected by personal interview method through suitable designed questionnaires and informal discussion with many employers and labour households in the sample areas during the course of fieldwork.

## Incidence and Extent of Indebtedness in West Bengal

The different rounds of Rural Labour Enquiry Reports show that the incidence of indebtedness among agricultural labour households though fluctuates over the years but declined in 1999-2000 in West Bengal. In 1977-78, 40.2 per cent of agricultural labour households were in debt and in 1999-2000, it declined to 36.40 per cent in West Bengal (Table 11.1). The rapid spread of new techniques (HYV seeds, fertilizers and pesticides) of production and multi-copping system in agriculture reduce the seasonal variation of employment in agriculture to some extent as compared to earlier periods in West Bengal. Availability of employment in agriculture in most of the part of the year will increase the income of labourers, which will in turn reduce the incidence of indebtedness in West Bengal.

**Table 11.1:** Incidence and Extent of Indebtedness of Agricultural Labourers in West Bengal

| | *1977-78* | *1983* | *1987-88* | *1993-94* | *1999-00* |
|---|---|---|---|---|---|
| Percentage Number of Indebted Agricultural Labour Household | 40.2 | 49.01 | 39.40 | 43.20 | 36.40 |
| Average debt Per Indebted Agricultural Labour Household (In Rs.) | 244 | 679 | 1725 | 1410 | 1527 |

*Source*: Rural Labour Enquiry Reports on Indebtedness for the years 1977-78, 1983, 1987-88, 1993-94 and 1999-00.

The average debt per indebted agricultural labour household in West Bengal has increased over the years except 1993-94. The average debt per indebted household in 1977-78 was Rs. 244 which increased to Rs. 1527 per household in 1999-2000 (Table 11.1) in West Bengal.

This is due to better access to credit in rural areas as compared to earlier periods. Absence of repayment culture is also contributing to the increase in the size of indebtedness.

At the village level, the situation is worse. The incidence of indebtedness in all villages of Uttar Dinajpur District is 71.11 per cent which is higher than the state level (Table 10.2). From table it is clear that the incidence of indebtedness is highest (83.33%) at Jagatagaon—a village under least developed blocks followed by Tilna (80%)—a village under moderately developed blocks and Malan (76.67%)—a village under highly developed blocks. The average debt per agricultural labourer in all villages of Uttar Dinajpur District was Rs. 3614.79 which was more than double of the state level figure in 1999-2000. The average debt per agricultural labour household was highest at Dharampur (Rs. 5345) a village under least developed blocks followed by Nakol (Rs. 3889.46)—a village under moderately developed blocks.

**Table 11.2:** Incidence of Indebtedness among Agricultural Labour Households across the Villages of Uttar Dinajpur District

| *Particulars* | *Delwalpur* | *Malan* | *Tilna* | *Nakol* | *Dharampur* | *Jagatagaon* | *All Villages/ Uttar Dinajpur District* |
|---|---|---|---|---|---|---|---|
| Families With Debt | 17 (56.67) | 23 (76.67) | 24 (80.00) | 19 (63.33) | 20 (66.67) | 25 (83.33) | 128 (71.11) |
| Families without Debt | 13 (43.33) | 67 (23.33) | 6 (20.00) | 11 (36.67) | 10 (33.33) | 5 (16.67) | 52 (28.89) |
| Total | 30 (100.00) | 30 (100.00) | 30 (100.00) | 30 (100.00) | 30 (100.00) | 30 (100.00) | 180 (100.00) |

*Source*: Own Field Survey.

The question of indebtedness among agricultural labour households has always been viewed as a problem rather than a harbinger of prosperity. This has been so primarily due to the preponderance of the deficit nature of their family budgets due to low wages, low employment availability and seasonal variations of employment opportunities in agriculture. As indebtedness among agricultural labour households is incurred only to meet the deficit in family budget rather than to create additional productive facilities. The quantum of indebtedness will go on accumulating beyond one's repaying capacity.

## Sources of Debt

The sources of debt may be broadly classified into two categories—institutional and non-institutional sources. Institutional sources include government, banking institutions and co-operative societies. Non-institutional sources include moneylenders, employers, shopkeepers, and friends and relatives. From the table 11.4, it is clear that the share of institutional sources in supplying rural credit increases over the years in West Bengal. In 1977-78 the share of institutional sources was 16.81 per cent, which increased to 27.28 per cent in 1999-2000. On the other hand, the share of non-institutional sources decreased from 83.19 to 72.72 per cent in 1999-00 in West Bengal. During 1999-2000, out of different sources, the share of friends and relatives was highest (30.45%) followed by shopkeepers (23.90%). But the share of moneylenders in supplying rural credit declined from 26.64 per cent in 1977-78 to 13.49 per cent in 1999-2000.

**Table 11.3:** Percentage of Indebted Agricultural Labour Households according to Sources Across the Villages of Uttar Dinajpur District

| *Sources* | *Delwal-pur* | *Malan* | *Tilna* | *Nakol* | *Dharampur* | *Jagatagaon* | All Villages/ District |
|---|---|---|---|---|---|---|---|
| Government | 36.00 | 38.89 | 28.57 | 25.00 | 21.43 | 28.13 | 30.16 |
| Bank | — | — | — | — | — | 3.12 | .58 |
| Co-operative Society | — | — | 7.14 | — | — | — | 1.16 |
| Moneylender | 8.00 | 16.67 | 14.29 | 20.83 | 46.43 | 25.00 | 21.97 |
| Employers | 12.00 | 5.56 | 7.14 | 8.33 | 7.14 | 9.38 | 8.09 |
| Friends and Relatives | 32.00 | 25.00 | 32.14 | 37.5 | 14.29 | 28.12 | 27.74 |
| Shop Keepers | 12.00 | 13.89 | 10.71 | 8.33 | 10.71 | 6.25 | 10.40 |
| Total | 100.00 | 100.00 | 100.00 | 100.00 | 100.00 | 100.00 | 100.00 |

*Source*: Own Field Survey.

At the village level, the source-wise distribution of indebted agricultural labour households is sown in Table 11.3. The data have been presented separately for each type of sources to bring out their relative positions in indebtedness. It is a matter of concern that 68.2 per cent of the indebted households of Uttar Dinajpur District had borrowed money from Non-institutional sources like part time money lenders, landlords, friends and relatives, and shop-keepers as against a mere 31.80 per cent households which went to institutional agencies like government, banks and co-operatives.

**Table 11.4:** Average Amount of Debt Per Indebted Agricultural Labour Household by sources of Debt in West Bengal

| *Sources* | *1977-78* | *1983* | *1987-88* | *1993-94* | *1999-00* |
|---|---|---|---|---|---|
| Government | 13 | 50 | 106 | 313 | 146 |
| | (5.33) | (8.50) | (6.14) | (22.20) | (9.56) |
| Co-operatives | 21 | 44 | 151 | 43 | 68 |
| | (8.61) | (7.48) | (8.75) | (3.05) | (4.45) |
| Banks | 7 | 88 | 313 | 207 | 203 |
| | (2.87) | (14.97) | (18.13) | (14.68) | (13.29) |
| Employers | 25 | 131 | 146 | 78 | 36 |
| | (10.25) | (22.28) | (8.46) | (5.53) | (2.36) |
| Moneylenders | 65 | 90 | 221 | 267 | 206 |
| | (26.64) | (15.31) | (12.80) | (18.94) | (13.49) |
| Shopkeepers | 32 | 42 | 191 | 219 | 365 |
| | (13.11) | (7.14) | (11.07) | (15.53) | (23.90) |
| Friends and Relatives | 61 | 111 | 236 | 242 | 465 |
| | (25) | (18.88) | (13.67) | (17.16) | (30.45) |
| Others | 19 | 33 | 362 | 41 | 38 |
| | (7.79) | (5.61) | (20.97) | (2.91) | (2.49) |
| Total | 244 | 588 | 1726 | 1410 | 1527 |
| | (100.00) | (100.00) | (100.00) | (100.00) | (100.00) |

*Source*: Rural Labour Enquiry Reports on Indebtedness for the years of 1977-78, 1983, 1987-88, 1993-94 and 1999-00.

At highly developed villages of Uttar Dinajpur, the higher proportion of indebted agricultural labour households depend on institutional sources as compared to villages under moderately developed and least developed blocks. From the Table 11.4 it is clear that out of non-institutional sources, friends and relatives emerged as a major source of rural credit in Uttar Dinajpur District. It may be noted that 27.74 per cent households depend on friends and relatives for their borrowing. The next important sources is part-time money-lenders. Except Dharampur—a village under least developed blocks, in all villages, friends and relatives played an important role in supplying rural credit in Uttar Dinajpur District. At Dharampur, 46.63 per cent households depend on money lenders. The role of money lenders is more important in villages under least developed blocks. These money lenders are not professional money lenders. They are rich cultivators or serviceman in rural areas. They lend money to agricultural labourers or other rural people on part-Time basis. Apart from maintaining agricultural activities or other activities, they provide money to the poor people on the basis of mortgage of land or other valuable articles.

**Table 11.5:** Average Amount of Debt Per Indebted Agricultural Labour Households Acoording to Sources Across the Villages of Uttar Dinajpur District

| *Sources* | *Delwalpur* | *Malan* | *Tilna* | *Nakol* | *Dharampur* | *Jagatagaon* | *All Villages/Uttar Dinajpur District* |
|---|---|---|---|---|---|---|---|
| Government | 1376.47<br>(51.80) | 1747.39<br>(53.81) | 1062.50<br>(38.94) | 1421.05<br>(36.45) | 775<br>(14.10) | 1128<br>(29.97) | 1268.40<br>(35.09) |
| Bank | — | — | — | — | — | 100<br>(2.65) | 16.66<br>(.46) |
| Co-operative Society | — | — | 75<br>(2.69) | — | — | — | 12.5<br>(.35) |
| Moneylender | 138.24<br>(5.20) | 452.17<br>(13.92) | 270.83<br>(9.72) | 836.84<br>(21.52) | 1625<br>(30.40) | 1108<br>(29.44) | 738.51<br>(20.43) |
| Employers | 36.40<br>(1.37) | 37.48<br>(1.07) | 187<br>(6.73) | 57.89<br>(1.49) | 350<br>(6.55) | 20<br>(.53) | 114.44<br>(3.17) |
| Relatives | 1041.18<br>(39.19) | 739.13<br>(22.73) | 985.83<br>(35.39) | 1205.26<br>(30.99) | 2250<br>(42.10) | 1280<br>(34.01) | 1250.24<br>(34.59) |
| Shop-keepers | 64.71<br>(2.44) | 273.91<br>(8.43) | 204.17<br>(7.33) | 368.42<br>(9.47) | 345<br>(6.45) | 128<br>(3.40) | 238.70<br>(6.38) |
| Total | 2657.07<br>(100.00) | 3247.38<br>(100.00) | 2785.83<br>(100.00) | 3889.46<br>(100.00) | 5345<br>(100.00) | 3764<br>(100.00) | 3614.79<br>(100.00) |

*Source*: Field Survey.

Table 11.5 gives the average amount of debt per indebted agricultural labour households by source of debt across the villages of Uttar Dinajpur District. Observation shows that the shares of institutional sources was found to be considerably low at 35.44 per cent of total borrowing in Uttar Dinajpur District. Out of institutional sources, the share of government is highest (35.09%) and the share of co-operative (.35%) and banks (.46%) were very negligible. Out of non-institutional sources, the friends and relatives emerged as the major sources of credit for the agricultural labour households at the district level. It is a matter of concern that friends and part-time money-lenders jointly contributed more than half of the total rural borrowings. But it is true that these two sources provide loans to the villagers (sometimes without bothering much about security of loans) during their hard times—ill health, natural calamities, death, accidents etc.

When we discuss the sources of credit according to the development of villages, we found the considerably the high share of institutional sources at highly developed villages as compared to moderately developed and least developed villages. The institutional sources at highly developed villages supplied more than 50 per cent of their total borrowings. This is due to the fact that the number of beneficiaries under anti-poverty programmes at the highly developed villages were higher as compared to moderately developed and least developed villages. Subsidized loans under anti-poverty programmes since 20 years increased the shares of institutional sources at highly developed villages. Out of non-institutional sources, friends and relatives is the important source of credit providing 39.19 per cent of total borrowings at Delwalpur and 22.76 per cent of total borrowing at Malan followed by moneylenders, shopkeepers and employers. In contrast, for the moderately developed and least developed blocks, the shares of institutional sources was found to be considerably low as compared to non-institutional sources. Villages under these blocks, friends and relatives emerged as the major source of credit followed by moneylenders, shopkeepers and employers.

## Purposes of Debt

Agricultural labourers takes loans for both productive and unproductive purposes. The productive purposes include buying or improvement of iand, draught animals, improved seeds, fertilizers, agricultural implements, digging of wells, construction of minor canals for irrigation, fencing and banking of fields; or setting up of small business like dairy farming through milch animals, rearing of live stock, development of horticulture, cultivation of cash crops i.e. vegetables and fruits, poultry farming, bee-keeping, basket or rope making etc. Loans taken and utilized for these purposes usually generate additional income there by enhancing the repaying capacity to a large extent. The share of productive purposes in total borrowing was very much marginal in West Bengal. During 1977-78, only 15.57 per cent borrowing were for productive purposes. But in 1999-2000. the share of productive purpose loan in total borrowing increased to 33.4 per cent, while 66.60 per cent (Table 11.6) loans were used for unproductive purposes. The loans taken for unproductive purposes result in debt burden as they do not generate income and are raised generally to fulfill household consumption needs, performance of religious or/and social functions like marriages, births and deaths, meeting the need of obligations like litigation or settling the disputes, buying of jewellary etc. As these loans generally do not help in creating economic assets, it, therefore, becomes very difficult for the borrowers to repay such loans. It is basically this form of debt which perpetuates the miseries of a sizable population of agricultural and rural labour household (RLE Indebtedness, 1983).

The field-level study shows that sample agricultural labour households on an average of Rs. 2584.97 were indebted for unproductive purposes and this constituted about 71.51 per cent of the total indebtedness in all villages of Uttar Dinajpur District. Marriages and other ceremonies is evidently the main cause of largest amount of borrowing, as it constitutes 19.98 per cent of their total borrowing (Table 11.7). The marriage of a daughter is now much more expensive than the marriage of a son because large portion of expenditure for marriage is incurred for paying dowry and money also used for entertaining with neighbours. The marriage of a daughter of an agricultural labourer might have cost of Rs. 20,000 to Rs. 35,000. The other important cause of indebtedness is expenditure on medical purpose, as it constitutes 19.55 per cent of their total borrowing followed by household consumption (18.67%) and business activities (13.90%). Agricultural labourers suffers from malnutrition, ill health and poverty. Poverty forces them to borrow money for medical purposes and consumption purposes from moneylenders and friends and relatives at high rate of interest rate. A part of borrowing under consumption purposes was taken by them in the form of paddy known as 'dehri loans' and genuine borrowing to keep going over the difficult days before the harvest. This indebtedness is confined to a small number of individuals. Out of 180 families, only 15 families (8.33%) borrowed 32 maunds odd of paddy in the year of 2004-05 stipulating to repay 52 maunds paddy after six months. The month of borrowing was Asharh and Sraban, Magh and Phalgun were the months of repayment. The normal stipulation is that 1.25 maunds should be repaid for every maund borrowed after six months.

Only 28.49 per cent of debt was incurred for productive purposes in Uttar Dinajpur District. Here productive purpose include a debt for agricultural production, small business and purchase of milch animals. The share of debt for productive purpose was highest (61.54%) at Delwalpur—a village under highly developed blocks. At Delwalpur, we find that more than 50 per cent of their debt were supplied by the Government under different anti-poverty programmes for running small business, agricultural production and for purchasing milch cow. In this village, most of the labourers engaged in the business of paddy husking apart from hiring out labour. They purchase paddy from the market and converted into rice, and sell into market and earn some money. But all labourers of this district are not able to utilize these subsidized loans properly for business purposes or purchasing milch animals, they also used some part of subsidized loans for consumption purposes or other unproductive purposes. This will reduce their repaying capacity. At Jagatagaon—a village under least developed blocks, labourers get loans for bamboo basket making or for small shopping under various anti-poverty programmes. But 50 per cent (Table 11.9) of the agricultural labourers beneficiaries in this village reported that they are not able to utilize this loan properly. As a whole of this district, 30 per cent (Table 11.9) of agricultural labourers beneficiaries under different anti-poverty programmes, reported that they are not able to utilize their subsidized loans due to acute poverty.

On the other hand, the amount of debt for productive purpose was lowest (15.43%) at Dharampur a village under least developed blocks. So with the development of villages, the amount of debt incurred for productive purposes declined. Out of unproductive purposes, the average amount of debt for household consumption was highest (29.38 per cent and 30%) at Delwalpur and Malan—villages under highly developed blocks followed by house construction (2.66%) at Delwalpur and, marriage and social ceremonies (20.22%) at Malan. At moderately developed villages, out of unproductive purposes, the amount of debt for household consumption was highest (20.66%) at Tilna followed by debt medical expenditure (16.38%). But at Nakol, the amount of debt for medical purposes formed 34.24 per cent followed by house construction (18.94%). At Dharampur—a village under least developed blocks, the amount of debt per household was highest (34.61%) for medical purposes followed by marriage and other ceremonies (29.65%). The amount of debt incurred for medical purposes was highest at Nakol and Dharmpur because most of them reported that they generally go outside the state for doing work in various industries in Delhi, Haryana and Punjab for few months when there is scarcity of work in their villages. Due to excessive pressure of work and unhealthy and unhygienic conditions of living in the slum areas of industries, they fell into ill and return home. After returning home, they take loans for treatment from relatives, money lenders at high rate of interest. On the other hand, at Jagatagaon, the average amount of debt per household was highest (44.85%) for marriage and other ceremonies followed by household consumption (17.75%). At Jagatagaon, the amount of debt per household was highest for marriage and other ceremonies because of prevalence of dowry system at a higher rate as compared to other villages of this district.

**Table 11.6:** Average amount of Debt per Indebted Agricultural Labour Household by Purpose of Debt in West Bengal

| *Purposes* | *1977-78* | *1983* | *1987-88* | *1993-94* | *1999-00* |
|---|---|---|---|---|---|
| Household Consumption | 162 (66.39) | 312 (53.15) | 799 (46.32) | 507 (35.93) | 741 (48.53) |
| Marriage and other Social Ceremonial Occasions | 21 (8.61) | 42 (7.16) | 32 (1.86) | 174 (12.33) | 96 (6.23) |
| Productive Purposes | 38 (15.57) | 174 (29.64) | 469 (27.19) | 101 (7.16) | 169 (11.07) |
| Purchase of Land and Construction of Buildings | — | 33 (5.62) | 40 (2.32) | 347 (24.59) | 341 (22.33) |
| Repayment of Old Debt | — | — | 2 (.12) | 2 (.14) | 8 (.52) |
| Others | 23 (9.43) | 26 (4.43) | 383 (22.20) | 280 (19.84) | 172 (11.26) |
| Total | 244 (100.00) | 588 (100.00) | 1725 (100.00) | 1410 (100.00) | 1527 (100.00) |

*Source*: Rural Labour Enquiry Reports on Indebtedness for the years of 1977-78, 1983, 1987-88, 19993-94 and 1999-2000.

**Table 11.7:** Average Amount of Debt Per Agricultural Labour Households According to Purposes.

| *Purposes* | *Delwalpur* | *Malan* | *Tilna* | *Nakol* | *Dharampur* | *Jagatagaon* | *All Villages/District* |
|---|---|---|---|---|---|---|---|
| Household Consumption | 780.59 (29.38) | 991.30 (30.53) | 575.42 (20.66) | 600 (15.43) | 435 (8.14) | 668 (17.75) | 675.05 (18.67) |
| Medical | 58.82 (2.21) | 334.78 (10.31) | 456.25 (16.38) | 1331.58 (34.24) | 1850 (34.61) | 208 (5.53) | 706.57 (19.55) |
| Marriage and other Ceremonies | 47.06 (1.27) | 656.52 (20.22) | 241.67 (8.67) | 115.79 (2.98) | 1585 (29.65) | 1688 (44.85) | 722.34 (19.98) |
| Production Activities | 676.47 (25.46) | 56.09 (1.73) | 208.33 (7.48) | 315.79 (8.12) | 100 (1.87) | 120 (3.19) | 246.11 (6.81) |
| House Construction | 70.59 (2.66) | 195.65 (6.02) | 429.17 (15.41) | 736.84 (18.94) | 650 (12.16) | 380 (10.10) | 410.38 (11.35) |
| Business Activities | 594.12 (22.36) | 878.26 (27.05) | 375 (13.46) | 142.11 (3.65) | 525 (9.82) | 500 (13.28) | 502.41 (13.90) |
| Purchase of Milch Animal or Cow | 364.71 (13.73) | 65.21 (2.01) | 500 (17.95) | 357.89 (9.20) | 200 (3.74) | 200 (5.31) | 281.30 (7.78) |
| Repayment of Old Debt | 64.71 (2.43) | 69.57 (2.14) | — | 289.47 (7.44) | — | — | 70.63 (1.95) |
| Total | 2657.07 (100.00) | 3247.38 (100.00) | 2785.83 (100.00) | 3889.46 (100.00) | 5345 (100.00) | 3764 | 3614.79 (100.00) |

*Source*: Own Field Survey.

## Outstanding Loans according to Terms and Conditions

Access to institutional credit of agricultural labour households is very much limited due to lack of adequate and proper assets, illiteracy and ignorance of agricultural labourers, and unwillingness to go through the complex procedure of borrowing from the commercial banks and other financial institutions. As a result, they are forced to go non-institutional agencies like money lenders, friends and relatives, employers and shopkeepers for getting credit against unfavourable terms and conditions like mortgaging of land, gold, silver and other valuable assets, hand notes etc. On the basis of available data in the study area, the term and conditions under which credit is available by the sample agricultural labour households are grouped under two broad categories: (i) favourable/normal terms and conditions with nominal or zero interest rate; (ii) unfavourable/abnormal terms and conditions with abnormal rate of interest.

Borrowing under favourable/normal terms and conditions refers to the loan available by the sample households at a very low rate of interest from the institutional agencies and from the very close friends and relatives, and employers. It includes financial assistance received under different anti-poverty programmes and also loans obtained from close relative and employers at zero interest rates. The beneficiaries of such Govt. loans pay nominal rate of interest and security received here includes third party guarantee over and above personal loans. The agricultural labour households are given loans by the government with a maximum of 4 per cent rate of interest. These loans are given to agricultural labour households for their economic development after deducting subsidy and no security is needed for sanctioning this loan. Some times agricultural labourers also get loans from very close friends and relatives without any security with zero interest to meet productive and unproductive purposes. Employers also provide loans or wage advances to the labourers against their labour with zero interest rate. They provide loans to the labourers to secure labour service during peak agricultural seasons at prevailing wage rates due to scarcity of labour. But this percentage is negligible.

The loans under unfavourable/abnormal terms and conditions includes loans obtained from money lenders, friends and relatives who charge exorbitant/arbitrary rate of interest and provide loans against mortgage of land, gold and silver etc. The abnormal terms and conditions are further classified into three subheads like (i) loans against mortgage of land with abnormal rate of interest known as 'sudvarna'; (ii) loans against mortgage of gold, silver with interest rate of Rs. 24 to 60 per annum; (iii) loans without mortgaging any assets with high rate of interest of Rs. 60 to 180 per annum.

It is observed that 66.66 per cent (Table 11.8) of the total outstanding debt incurred by the agricultural labourers have been borrowed at high rate of interest under abnormal terms and conditions and the share of borrowing under normal term and conditions is only 33.33 per cent in the study area of Uttar Dinajpur District. But it is true that most of the agricultural labourers have no proper assets/or property for borrowing. As a result they are bound to take loans without mortgaging any assets from non-institutional sources. Loans without mortgaging any assets entails higher interest rate (Rs. 60 to 180 per annum) as compared to the interest rate (Rs. 24 to 60 per annum) charged for loans against mortgaging gold, silver. Agricultural labourers have borrowed 36.27 per cent of their total borrowing without mortgaging any assets at high rate of interest. Loans against mortgaging land constitute 22.32 per cent of the total borrowing. Some agricultural labourers have some cultivable land. They borrow money against mortgaging land from money-lenders or friends and relatives. The all crops of mortgaging land is taken away by money lenders as interest rate years after years until the agricultural labourers is able to repay the principal amount. This system is known as 'Sudvarna'. Another exploitative practices is prevailed in this district in the form of 'Khaikhalasi'. Under this system, borrowers are taken loans against mortgaging land from money lenders for certain periods. In this case, there is no need to repay loans in cash to money lenders. In exchange, the crops of this land is consumed by money lenders for that stipulated periods. Land will be returned by money lenders after this stipulated periods. This system is rarely found in this district. Loan against mortgaging silver, gold constitute 8.07 per cent of the total borrowing. Sometimes, labourers get loans without any interest rate. This type of loans is provided by very close relatives and employers. This will constitute 3.19 per cent of the total borrowing.

The share of loans under normal terms and conditions is higher in the highly developed villages as compared to moderately developed and least developed villages. The share of loans against mortgaging of land is highest at Dharampur (32.74%)—a village under least developed blocks followed by Nakol (27.06%)—a village under moderately developed villages of Uttar Dinajpur District.

**Table 11.8:** Average Outstanding Loans per Agricultural Labourers according to Terms and Conditions Across the Villages of Uttar Dinajpur District

| *Term and Conditions of Loans* | *Delwalpur* | *Malan* | *Tilna* | *Nakol* | *Dharampur* | *Jagatagaon* | *All Villages/District* |
|---|---|---|---|---|---|---|---|
| A. *Loans Under Normal Terms and Conditions* | | | | | | | |
| 1. Loans Under Zero Interest Rate | 147.06<br>(5.53) | 252.17<br>(7.77) | 83.33<br>(2.99) | 78.94<br>(2.03) | 50<br>(.94) | 80<br>(2.13) | 115.25<br>(3.19) |
| 2. Loans Under Nominal Rate of Interest (4 per cent per Annum) | 1376.47<br>(51.80) | 1608.25<br>(49.52) | 645.84<br>(23.18) | 1026.32<br>(26.39) | 975<br>(18.24) | 908<br>(24.12) | 1089.98<br>(30.15) |
| B. *Loans Under Abnormal Terms and Conditions* | | | | | | | |
| 1. Loans against Mortgage of Land with Abnormal Rate of Interest (Known as Sudvarna). | 570.59<br>(21.47) | 573.91<br>(17.67) | 472.92<br>(16.98) | 052.63<br>(27.06) | 1750<br>(32.74) | 420<br>(11.16) | 806.68<br>(22.32) |
| 2. Loans against Mortgage of Gold, Silver with Abnormal Rate of Interest (Rs. 24 to Rs. 60 per annum) | 200<br>(7.52) | 125<br>(3.85) | 195<br>(7.00) | 263.16<br>(6.77) | 475<br>(8.89) | 492<br>(13.07) | 291.69<br>(8.07) |
| 3. Loans without Mortgaging of any Assets with Abnormal Rate of Interest (Rs. 60 to Rs. 180 per annum) | 362.95<br>(13.66) | 688.05<br>(21.91) | 1388.74<br>(49.85) | 1468.41<br>(37.75) | 2095<br>(39.20) | 1864<br>(49.52) | 1311.19<br>(36.27) |
| Total | 2657.07<br>(100.00) | 3247.38<br>(100.00) | 2785.83<br>(100.00) | 3889.46<br>(100.00) | 5345 | 3764 | 3614.79<br>(100.00) |

*Source*: Own Field Survey.

**Table 11.9:** Utilization of Loans by Indebted Agricultural Labour Households under different Anti-Poverty Programmes Across the Villages of Uttar Dinajpur District

| *Villages* | *Number of Indebted Agricultural Labour Households (Beneficiaries) taken Loan for Small Business or for Purchasing Milch Cow under Different Anti-poverty Programmes* | *Number of Indebted Agricultural Labour Households (Beneficiaries) not utilized Properly Loans taken under Different Anti-Poverty Programmes for the Said Purposes* | *Number of Indebted Agricultural Labour Households (Beneficiaries) utilized Properly Loans taken under different Anti-Poverty Programmes for the said Purposes* |
|---|---|---|---|
| Delwalpur | 9 (100.00) | 3 (33.33) | 6 (66.67) |
| Malan | 14 (100.00) | 3 (21.43) | 11 (78.57) |
| Tilna | 8 (100.00) | 2 (25.00) | 6 (75.00) |
| Nakol | 6 (100.00) | 2 (33.33) | 4 (66.67) |
| Dharampur | 6 (100.00) | 1 (16.67) | 5 (83.33) |
| Jagatagaon | 10 (100.00) | 5 (50.00) | 5 (50.00) |
| All Villages | 53 (100.00) | 16 (30.19) | 37 (69.81) |

*Source*: Own Field Survey.

## Conclusion

The incidence and extent of indebtedness of Uttar Dinajpur District at the village level is higher than the state level figures. The main cause of indebtedness is the borrowing for marriage and social ceremonies followed by medical purposes and household consumptions at the village level of Uttar Dinajpur District. But at the state level, the main cause of indebtedness is the borrowing for household consumption followed by purchase of land and construction of building and productive purposes. At the state level, the main source of rural credit is friends and relatives followed by shopkeepers and money lenders. But at the village level, the share of subsidized loans provided by the Government under different anti-poverty programmes in total borrowing is higher than the shares of friends and relatives and money lenders. Out of non-institutional sources, friends and relatives emerged as the main source of rural credit at the village level of Uttar Dinajpur District. The role of financial institutions is not sufficient in supplying rural credit. As a result agricultural labourers are bound to depend on non-institutional sources. Most of the agricultural labourers did not have sufficient assets, security to take loans from financial institutions. But banks and co-operatives provide loans to the people against security of assets. Asset less ness and landlessness of agricultural labourers deprived them from credit facilities from the institutional finance. In this context, the role of the Bangladesh Grameen Bank Model of micro-financing turned out to be an extremely effective tool in supplying rural credit. This innovation of Self-Help Groups and the micro-credit has helped the poor, especially women to gain better access to credit facilities. But the progress of formation of SHGs is not expected rate in this district. As a result poor people of this district deprived from the institutional finance. Agricultural labourers mainly get institutional finance from the Government under different anti-poverty programmes.

## REFERENCES

Ananda, Jaya (2000). 'Micro Finance in Kerala', *Kurukshetra*, August.

Hooda, R. P. and Turan, M.S. (1993). '*Rural Indebtedness, Problems, Policy Measures and Solutions—A Study in Caste—Occupational Dimensions*' Deep and Deep Publications, F-159, Rajouri Garden, New Delhi.

Mohanty, Pratap Chandra (2001). 'Income and Living Condition of Scheduled Caste Households in Orissa', Unpublished Ph. D. Thesis.

Panda, R.K. (1985). '*Agricultural Indebtedness and Institutional Finance*' Ashis Publishing House, 8/81 Punjabi Bagh, New Delhi.

Pandit, Byomkesh (2003). '*The Story of the Kishan Agrarian Labour in Bengal* (1885.1952)', Corpus Research Institute, 26, Jodhpur Gardens, Kolkata.

Purkayastha, Gautam (2001), 'Rural Indebtedness in Assam—Changing Scenario' *Economic and Political Weekly*, June 23.

Sajjad, Haroon (1998). '*Employment of Landless Labourers*' B. R. Publishing Corporation (A Division of BRPC India Ltd.) Delhi.

Sengupta, Jatindra Chandra (1964). 'West Bengal District Gazetteers—West Dinajpur' Editor, West Bengal District Gazetteers, Government of West Bengal, at 23 Rajendra Nath Mukherjee Road, Calcutta-1.

12

# Management of Rural Finance and Inequality in Short-Term Credit Flow in Maharashtra

K.L. JADHAV

---

*Using secondary data, the study examines the financial management, magnitude and direction of inequality in the flow of short-term credit amongst the different regions of Maharashtra and factors influencing the inequality in short-term credit disbursement of District Central Cooperative Banks. Western Maharashtra region maintained the highest position in terms of disbursements of loans and advances. Over 80 per cent of the total loans and advances issued were in the form of short-term loans and the remaining being medium terms and other terms indicating focused emphasis on short-term loans by DCCBs. The total loans advanced by DCCB increased by 12.6 per cent per annum. However the increase was highest in Western Maharashtra (14.77%) as compared to Vidarbha region (13.69%) and Marathwada (12.85%). The inter-regional inequality showed subsequent reduction in inequality in Western Maharashtra and Konkan regions as compared to Marathwada region having a slight non-significant increase. Gross rope, area under commercial crops, deposit with banks and average rainfall appeared as important factors influencing regional inequality in per hectare credit. Due importance needs to be given to borrower members which will lead to increased disbursement. Official machinery of DCCBs should make all out efforts to minimize the inequality.*

**Introduction**

Production credit plays an important role in enhancing production and productivity of agricultural commodities. Financial system. co-operatives, commercial banks and regional rural banks are the pillars of the institutional credit. The co-operative credit system in India is comprised of the Short-Term (ST) production credit structure and the long-term or investment credit structure. The Short-Term Cooperative Credit Structure has its base with the Primary Agricultural Credit Societies (PACS) that are affiliated to District Central Co-operative Banks (DCCBs) at the district level, which are affiliated to State Co-operative Bank (SCB) at the State level.

The DCCBs in the Maharashtra had played a pivotal role in the development of agriculture by providing a regular flow of short-term and medium term credit to the agriculturists through the PACS in rural areas. The sickness of DCCBs is mainly due to the low recovery and mounting overdues. Improvement in recovery and thereby reducing the burden of overdues of the DCCBs called for concerted efforts on the part of official machinery. The Indian banking system is passing through a metamorphosis due to the impact of the revolutionary financial sector reforms. A major element of the financial sector reforms in India has been the introduction of prudential norms and regulations. These prudential norms and regulations are basically aimed at ensuring the safety and soundness of the financial system imparting greater transparency and accountability in operations and restoring creditability and confidence of the...

It is said that the performance of co-operative agricultural credit advanced is uneven among districts/regions with respect to the amount of credit advanced for various purposes. Further, the gain of credit development is said to have been flown mostly to large farmers, though it was expected to reach primarily to small and marginal farmers. Under this pretext, the present study was undertaken to examine the financial management, magnitude and direction of inequality in the flow of short-term credit amongst the different regions of the State and factors influencing the disparity in short-term credit disbursement of District Central Co-operative Banks (DCCBs) in Maharashtra.

## Methodology

The study is based on secondary data obtained from the annual reports of 30 DCCBs in Maharashtra for the period of 16 years i.e. from 1985-86 to 2000-01. The region-wise and period-wise performance in respect of growth in loans and advances was estimated with the help of Compound Growth Rates (CGRs) The annual rates of compound growth were estimated for three different periods viz; Period I i.e. 1985-86 to 1993-94, Period II i.e. 1994-95 to 2000-01 and Period III covered the entire study period (1985-86 to 2000-01). The region-wise and period-wise average loans advanced per DCCB and its composition were estimated for the base year (1985-86) and the terminal year (2000-01) with the help of ratios, averages and percentages.

### *(i) Coefficient of Variation*

To examine the inequality in flow of short-term credit, the region-wise Coefficient of Variation (CV) was calculated for each of the 16 years (1985-86 to 2000-01) by using the formula,

$$CV = \frac{SD}{Mean} \times 100$$

Where,

CV = Coefficient of Variation
SD = Standard Deviation
Mean = $\Sigma dx/n$
$\Sigma x$ = Per Hectare Credit
$n$ = Number of Districts

Then, taking CV as dependent variable and time as independent variable, a linear equation viz.; $CV = a + bt + u$ was fitted to examine the trend of region-wise variation.

### *(ii) Theils Entropy*

Theil (1967) evolved the measure of inequality to assess the income inequality, which was given by Zeratsion (2001),

$$H(Yi) = \sum_{i=1}^{N} Y_i \left[ \frac{1}{(\log(Y_i))} \right]$$

Where,

H (Y*i*) = Theils Entropy.

Y*i* = Proportion of ith district in the total credit flow from DCCBs in the State

H (Y*i*) = has been modified and is given by

I (Y*i*) = log N-H (Y*i*)

Where,

I (Y*i*) = Theils Entropy coefficient which ranges from 0 to log N

N = Number of districts

Taking I (Y*i*) as dependent variable, linear trend equation was fitted to examine the region-wise inequality over the period of 16 years (1985-86 to 2000-01).

$$I(Yi) = a + bt + u$$

***(iii) Gini Concentration Ratio***

Gini concentration ratio was used to measure the inter-region and intra-region inequality of short-term credit flow by the DCCBs.

The Gini ratio (L) is estimated as follows:

$$L = 1 - \frac{\sum_{i=1}^{N} (P_i - P_i - 1)(Q_i + Q_i - 1)}{10{,}000}$$

Where,

P*i* = Cumulative percentage of number of DCCBs upto and including i[th] class.

Q*i* = Cumulative percentage of credit flow per hectare of gross cropped area by DCCBs up to and including i[th] class.

N = Number of DCCBs.

Higher the value of Gini ratio (L), more is the inequality in distribution of credit and *vice versa* (0 < L < 1).

***(iv) Lorenz Curve Analysis***

It is the graphical representation of cumulative proportion of number of DCCBs in Maharashtra on horizontal X-axis and cumulative proportion of agricultural credit flow of gross cropped area by DCCBs on per hectare on vertical Y-axis. The line of equal distribution is the straight line at $45^0$ angle joining (0,0) and (100,100) points. The degree by which Lorenz Curve deviates from the line of equal distribution is a measure of the inequality of disbursement of loan. As the curve moves away from the equality line, the greater is the inequality. Both Gini Ratios and Lorenz Curves were obtained for the base year (1985-86), average year (1993-94) and terminal year (2000-01) of the study.

In order to study the factors influencing per hectare short-term credit flow by DCCBs, a multiple linear regression analysis was attempted for all the regions and State as a whole, separately covering the period from 1985-86 to 2000-01.

The form of the equation used for analysis is given below:

$$Y = a + b_1 X_1 + b_2 X_2 + b_3 X_3 + b_4 X_4 + b_5 X_5 + b_6 X_6 + u$$

Where,

$Y$ = Per hectare short-term agricultural credit (Rs.)

$X_1$ = Gross cropped area (lakh hectares)

$X_2$ = Proportion of area under commercial crops to GCA (%)

$X_3$ = Proportion of area under horticultural (fruit) crops to GCA (%)

$X_4$ = Average rainfall (mm)

$X_5$ = Total deposits (Rs. in crores)

$X_6$ = Short-term agricultural loan recovery (%)

## Results and Discussion

### *1. Average Total Loan Disbursed and Its Composition*

It can be revealed from Table 12.1 that total amount of loan disbursed per DCCB to its members in Maharashtra state had increased from Rs. 74.84 crores in 1985-86 to Rs. 515.25 crores in 2000-01.

**Table 12.1:** Average Loans and Advances Disbursed by DCCBs in Maharashtra.

*(Rs. in Crores)*

| Region and Period | Short-Term Loans | | | Medium- Term Loans | | | Other Loans and Advances | Total Loans and Advances |
|---|---|---|---|---|---|---|---|---|
| | Agricultural | Non Agricultural | Total Short Term | Agricultural | Non Agricultural | Total Medium Term | | |
| *Western Maharashtra* | | | | | | | | |
| 1985-86 | 25.91 (19.82) | 86.52 (67.47) | 113.93 (87.29) | 8.19 (6.38) | 2.59 (2.02) | 10.78 (8.41) | 5.52 (4.30) | 128.23 (100.00) |
| 2000-01 | 219.60 (19.58) | 731.91 (65.25) | 951.51 (84.83) | 48.48 (4.32) | 17.57 (1.57) | 66.05 (5.89) | 104.06 (9.28) | 1121.62 (100.00) |
| *Konkan* | | | | | | | | |
| 1985-86 | 1.02 (0.93) | 84.71 (77.52) | 85.73 (78.45) | 1.30 (1.19) | 0.39 (0.36) | 1.69 (1.55) | 21.86 (20.00) | 109.28 (100.00) |
| 2000-01 | 17.06 (5.16) | 239.22 (72.40) | 256.28 (77.56) | 3.04 (0.92) | 36.03 (10.90) | 39.07 (11.82) | 35.09 (10.62) | 330.44 (100.00) |
| *Marathwada* | | | | | | | | |
| 1985-86 | 9.18 (20.16) | 28.51 (62.61) | 37.69 (82.76) | 1.21 (2.66) | 0.30 (0.68) | 1.52 (3.34) | 6.33 (13.90) | 45.54 (100.00) |
| 2000-01 | 116.41 (42.24) | 139.61 (50.65) | 256.02 (92.89) | 10.45 (3.79) | 3.86 (1.40) | 14.32 (5.19) | 5.29 (1.92) | 275.63 (100.00) |
| *Vidarbha* | | | | | | | | |
| 1985-86 | 6.17 (24.58) | 14.73 (58.67) | 20.90 (83.23) | 0.52 (2.05) | 0.27 (1.10) | 0.79 (3.15) | 3.42 (13.62) | 25.11 (100.00) |
| 2000-01 | 39.86 (20.14) | 59.22 (29.92) | 99.08 (50.06) | 10.64 (5.37) | 12.15 (6.14) | 22.79 (11.51) | 76.07 (38.43) | 197.94 (100.00) |
| *Maharashtra* | | | | | | | | |
| 1985-86 | 11.79 (15.75) | 51.14 (68.34) | 62.93 (84.09) | 3.11 (4.16) | 1.00 (1.33) | 4.11 (5.49) | 7.80 (10.42) | 74.84 (100.00) |
| 2000-01 | 107.85 (20.93) | 309.78 (60.12) | 417.63 (81.05) | 20.68 (4.01) | 15.82 (3.07) | 36.50 (7.08) | 61.12 (11.87) | 515.25 (100.00) |

Figures in the parentheses are the percentages to the respective total..

In the year 1985-86, the total loan disbursed per DCCB was relatively more in Western Maharashtra region (Rs. 128.23 crores) followed by Konkan (Rs. 109.28 crores), Marathwada (Rs. 45.54 crores) and Vidarbha (Rs. 25.11 crores) regions. In the terminal year of the study (2000-01), the DCCBs from Western Maharashtra region had maintained top position by disbursing total loans of Rs. 1121.62 crores per DCCB followed by Konkan (Rs. 330.44 crores), Marathwada (Rs. 275.63 crores) and Vidarbha (Rs. 197.94 crores) regions.

Over 80 per cent of total loans and advances issued were in the form of short-term loans and remaining being medium-term and other loans and advances indicating focused emphasis on short-term loans by the DCCBs in Maharashtra. In region-wise study, it can be revealed that, the share of short- term loans was the highest in Western Maharashtra region (87.29%) followed by Vidarbha (83.23%), Marathwada (82.76%) and Konkan regions (78.45%) in 1985-86. In the terminal year of the study, the share of short-term loan was the highest in Marathwada (92.89%) followed by Western Maharashtra (84.83%), Konkan (77.56%) and Vidarbha (50.06%) regions. The percentage shares of medium-term loan and other loans were 5.49 and 10.42 per cent in 1985-86, which had marginally increased to 7.08 and 11.87 per cent in 2000-01, respectively. The proportion of total agricultural loans (both ST and MT) in the total loans was above 20 per cent in the base year, which increased to about 25 per cent during the terminal year. Regionwise analysis indicated that the per cent share of agricultural loans showed an increase in Marathwada and Konkan regions, while it showed a slight decline in Western Maharashtra and Vidarbha regions.

## 2. Growth in Loan Disbursement

The total loan advanced by the DCCBs in Maharashtra State had increased by 12.76 per cent per annum for the entire period (Table 12.2).

The regionwise results revealed that the magnitude of compound growth of total loans disbursed in the Western Maharashtra region was high (14.77%) as compared to Vidarbha (13.69%) and Marathwada (12.85%) regions. The non-significant growth in the total loans disbursed was recorded in the Konkan region over a period of time.

**Table 12.2:** Growth of Loans Disbursement by the DCCBs in Maharashtra (%)

| Region and Period | Short-Term | | | Medium -Term | | | Other Loans and Advances | Total Loans and Advances |
|---|---|---|---|---|---|---|---|---|
| | Agricultural | Non Agricultural | Total | Agricultural | Non Agricul-tural | Total | | |
| *Western Maharashtra* | | | | | | | | |
| I | 11.43*** | 21.86*** | 19.92*** | 6.58** | 27.43*** | 12.96*** | 27.31** | 20.36*** |
| II | 3.21$^{NS}$ | 5.35*** | 4.72** | 25.09*** | 4.92$^{NS}$ | 17.24*** | -1.13$^{NS}$ | 4.70* |
| III | 14.00*** | 14.28*** | 14.22*** | 13.68*** | 15.95*** | 14.21*** | 23.04*** | 14.77*** |
| *Konkan* | | | | | | | | |
| I | 5.11$^{NS}$ | 13.78$^{NS}$ | 13.70$^{NS}$ | -11.79$^{NS}$ | 61.16*** | 39.33** | 6.13*** | 14.07$^{NS}$ |
| II | 34.89*** | 15.74*** | 16.40*** | 0.84$^{NS}$ | 5.50$^{NS}$ | 4.08$^{NS}$ | 8.34$^{NS}$ | 13.56** |
| III | 15.24*** | 3.68$^{NS}$ | 3.92$^{NS}$ | 6.37$^{NS}$ | 32.86*** | 25.05*** | 6.94*** | 5.26$^{NS}$ |
| *Marathwada* | | | | | | | | |
| I | 14.11** | 23.02** | 21.14** | 15.77$^{NS}$ | 36.47*** | 20.57** | 17.36$^{NS}$ | 21.84*** |
| II | 20.96*** | 7.09$^{NS}$ | 11.80** | 32.62*** | 20.76** | 29.88*** | -16.83$^{NS}$ | 11.31** |
| III | 16.64*** | 12.97** | 14.31*** | 7.05* | 11.27** | 7.78** | 1.18$^{NS}$ | 12.85*** |
| *Vidarbha* | | | | | | | | |
| I | 5.32$^{NS}$ | 2.43$^{NS}$ | 3.44$^{NS}$ | 13.89$^{NS}$ | 27.94*** | 19.31** | 17.64** | 8.19* |
| II | 12.26*** | 16.84** | 15.15** | 20.94* | 23.13*** | 22.11** | 31.00*** | 20.09*** |
| III | 13.51*** | 11.99*** | 12.51*** | 14.70*** | 23.38*** | 18.16*** | 16.43*** | 13.69*** |
| *Maharashtra* | | | | | | | | |
| I | 11.13*** | 20.89*** | 19.28*** | 8.12* | 34.61*** | 17.83*** | 18.76*** | 19.28*** |
| II | 7.78$^{NS}$ | 6.92*** | 7.00*** | 23.73*** | 9.00$^{NS}$ | 16.05*** | 6.49$^{NS}$ | 7.45** |
| III | 14.58*** | 11.86*** | 12.36*** | 12.19*** | 20.13*** | 14.84*** | 14.71*** | 12.76*** |

*Note*: ***, **, * Significant at 1, 5 and 10 per cent level, NS—Non-Significant..

Increase in the medium-term loans advanced was relatively more than the short-term loans by the DCCBs in all the regions and also at the State level with the exception of DCCBs in Konkan region during the entire period. The increase in the short-term loans disbursed was mainly attributed to the increase in the loans issued for agricultural purposes, while the increase in medium-term loans was largely attributed by the loans advanced to non-agricultural sector. The growth in other loans disbursed was significant during Period I and later on, it turned out to be non-significant in Period II due to which the growth in total advances in Period II was relatively low in all the regions and at the State-level, except in the Vidarbha region, where it was high.

### *3. Inequality in Short-Term Credit Flow by DCCBs*

The inter-regional and intra-regional inequality in credit flow by DCCBs over the years was assessed by using different measures.

#### *(i) Coefficient of Variation*

In order to examine whether the DCCBs have disbursed the short-term credit uniformly across the regions and state, coefficient of variation was computed for each year and the trend equations are fitted as follows,

*Trend equations in regional inequality*

Western Maharashtra $CV = 75.37 - 1.63^{NS}$
(1.29)

Konkan $CV = 106.52 - 4.04^{***}$
(1.14)

Marathwada $CV = 42.99 + 0.66^{NS}$
(0.55)

Vidarbha $CV = 39.92 - 0.022^{NS}$
(0.92)

Maharashtra $CV = 96.48 - 1.26^{NS}$
(1.31)

*Note*: ***, Significant at 1 per cent level.
NS = Non-significant.
(Figures in the parentheses are the standard errors of respective coefficients).

The coefficients of trend equations were negative and non-significant in Western Maharashtra, Vidarbha and at the state level, which indicated not much variation in the short-term credit flow over the study period. The regression coefficient for Konkan region is observed to be negative and highly significant indicating decline in variation of short-term credit during the study period. Importantly, there was non-significant increase in variation of short-term credit disbursement in Marathwada region.

*(ii) Theil's Entropy Coefficient*

*Trend equations of regional inequality*

| | | |
|---|---|---|
| Western Maharashtra | $I(Y_i)$ | $= 0.80 - 0.0014^{NS}$ (0.0027) |
| Konkan | $I(Y_i)$ | $= 0.10 - 0.0041^{**}$ (0.0017) |
| Marathwada | $I(Y_i)$ | $= 0.35 + 0.0012^{NS}$ (0.0010) |
| Vidarbha | $I(Y_i)$ | $= 0.04 - 0.0006^{NS}$ (0.0013) |
| Maharashtra | $I(Y_i)$ | $= 0.16 - 0.0012^{NS}$ (0.0034) |

*Note*: ** Significant at –5 per cent level and NS = Non-Significant
Figures in the parentheses are the standard errors of respective coefficients.

The analysis of Theil's Entropy coefficient showed that the regression coefficients of trend equations were negative and non-significant in the case of Western Maharashtra, Vidarbha and at the State level, which indicated a non-significant decline in inequality. There was a significant decline in inequality of short-term credit flow in the DCCBs of Konkan region during the period under study. In Marathwada region, the coefficient of trend equation indicated a non-significant increase in inequality of short-term credit flow.

*(iii) Gini Concentration Ratio and Lorenz Curve Analysis*

The results of the Gini Ratio (Table 12.3) and Lorenz Curve (Fig, 12.1) showed increase in inequality in the average year and subsequent reduction in inequality in the terminal year in Vidarbha region. The reverse trend was noticed for the Marathwada region, where inequality showed a declining trend in the average year and then increase in the terminal year. The declining rate of inter-regional inequality in respective years was observed in Western Maharashtra and Konkan regions. The inequality at the State level showed an increase in the average year and subsequently got reduced in the terminal year.

**Table 12.3:** Gini Coefficient Ratio in Short-term Credit Flow by DCCBs in Maharashtra.

| Year | Western Maharashtra | Konkan | Marathwada | Vidarbha | Maharashtra |
|---|---|---|---|---|---|
| Base Year (1985-86) | 0.30 | 0.38 | 0.24 | 0.19 | 0.43 |
| Av. Year (1993-94) | 0.25 | 0.28 | 0.11 | 0.23 | 0.45 |
| Terminal Year (2000-01) | 0.24 | 0.23 | 0.25 | 0.21 | 0.40 |

It can be observed that the Gini Ratio were 0.43, 0.45 and 0.40 for the base year, average year and terminal year, respectively, indicating moderate intra-regional inequality in short-term credit flow by DCCBs in Maharashtra. The Lorenz Curve (Fig. 12.2) for short term credit flow showed an increase in intra-regional inequality in the average year and subsequently reduction in inequality in the terminal year.

## 4. Factors Influencing Inequality

From Table 12.4, it can be observed that at the state level, the per hectare short-term credit flow was significantly influenced by the factors like gross cropped area ($X_1$), area under commercial crops ($X_2$), average rainfall ($X_4$) and deposits ($X_5$). The results of multiple regression analysis showed a positive influence on short-term credit flow by all these variables except area under horticultural crops ($X_3$), which was positive but non-significant. The $R^2$ indicates that the six independent variables have jointly explained 85 per cent of the variation in the disbursement of ST credit in Maharashtra

In Western Maharashtra, the coefficients of gross cropped area ($X_1$), deposits ($X_5$), proportion of area under commercial crops ($X_2$) to GCA and average rainfall ($X_4$) were found to be significant.

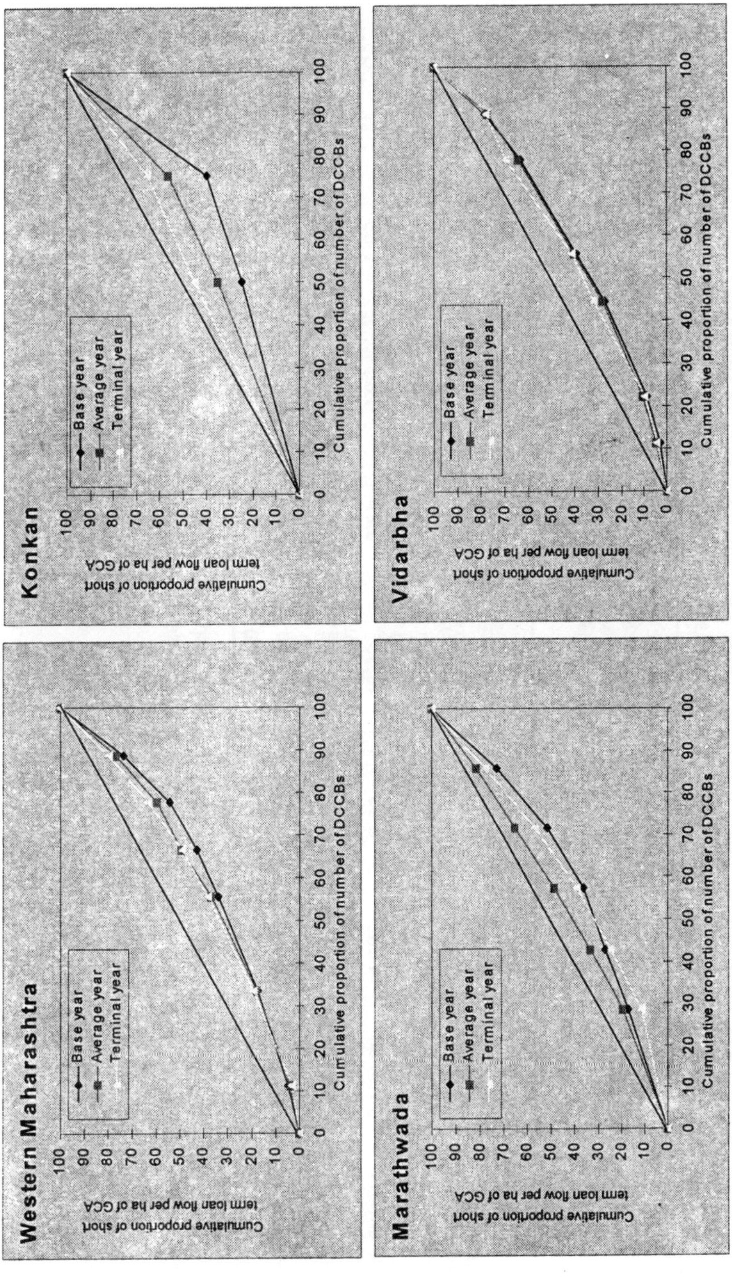


**Fig. 12.1:** Region-wise Lorenz Curves for Short-term Credit Flow by DCCBs in Maharashtra

**Table 12.4:** Factors Influencing Regional Inequality in Disbursement of per Hectare Short-term Agricultural Loans in Maharashtra.

| Variables | Constant | Gross Cropped Area (lakh ha) | Proportion of Area under Commercial Crops to GCA (%) | Proportion of Area under Horticultural Crops to GCA (%) | Average Rainfall (mm) | Deposits (Rs. Crores) | Recovery of ST. Agril loan (%) | $R^2$ | F-value |
|---|---|---|---|---|---|---|---|---|---|
| Regions | 0 | $X_1$ | $X_2$ | $X_3$ | $X_4$ | $X_5$ | $X_6$ | | |
| Western Maharashtra | 550.84<br>(127.78) | 18.36**<br>(7.78) | 9.13*<br>(4.81) | 42.95 NS<br>(49.12) | 1.14*<br>(0.58) | 0.09**<br>(0.04) | 1.46 NS<br>(20.51) | 0.83 | 7.32*** |
| Konkan | 471.45<br>(22.78) | 9.30*<br>(4.52) | -103.20**<br>(39.61) | 7.20**<br>(2.44) | 0.04**<br>(0.018) | 0.06***<br>(0.012) | 0.17 NS<br>(0.52) | 0.87 | 10.04*** |
| Marathwada | -238.88<br>(57.16) | 14.99 NS<br>(10.82) | 8.53 NS<br>(10.07) | 18.53 NS<br>(35.15) | 0.27*<br>(0.13) | 0.60***<br>(0.11) | 2.85 NS<br>(2.35) | 0.86 | 9.21*** |
| Vidarbha | 471.35<br>(49.98) | 9.45*<br>(6.95) | 4.43*<br>(2.34) | 4.29 NS<br>(8.74) | 0.08*<br>(0.04) | 0.18**<br>(0.04) | -3.07*<br>(1.67) | 0.83 | 7.32*** |
| Maharashtra | 363.20<br>(104.22) | 14.82*<br>(6.64) | 8.44*<br>(4.52) | 9.46 NS<br>(12.49) | 0.98*<br>(0.51) | 0.098**<br>(0.04) | -8.74 NS<br>(10.26) | 0.85 | 8.5*** |

*Note*: *, **and *** are Significant at 1, 5 and 10 per cent level, respectively NS=Non-significant.
Figures in parentheses indicate standard errors of respective regression coefficients.

The coefficients of proportion of horticultural crops to GCA ($X_3$) and recovery percentage of S.T. loans ($X_6$) were found to be positive but turned out to be non-significant. This has therefore indicated that the factor viz; the gross cropped area, deposits, proportion of area under commercial crops to GCA and average rainfall play an important role in determining the disbursement of short-term credit in Western Maharashtra. It must be indicated that these six regressors jointly explained 83 per cent variation in the disbursement of ST credit in Western Maharashtra.

In Konkan region, regression coefficient of deposits ($X_5$), proportion of area under horticultural crops to GCA ($X_3$), average rainfall ($X_4$), gross cropped area ($X_1$) were found to be positive and significant. The regression coefficient of proportion of area under commercial crops to GCA ($X_2$) was (-103.20), which is found to be significant at five per cent level. This has indicated that if the proportion of area under commercial crops to GCA is increased by one per cent, the ST credit flow per hectare would diminish by Rs. 103.20 in Konkan region. This is acceptable in view of the low scales of finance for commercial crops viz; sugarcane and summer groundnut as compared to fruit crops in Konkan region. The $R^2$ was 0.87, has indicated that the six regressors indicated in the model have jointly explained 87 per cent of the variation in disbursement of ST credit in Konkan region.

In Marathwada region it is noted that the coefficient of the factor viz; GCA ($X_1$), proportionate area under commercial crops to GCA ($X_2$), proportionate area under horticultural crops to GCA ($X_3$) and recovery per cent of ST loans ($X_6$) were observed to be positive but turned out to be non-significant. Importantly, the coefficient of the variables viz; rainfall ($X_4$) and deposits ($X_5$) were positive and significant indicating their influence on disbursement of ST credit by the DCCBs in Marathwada region. It is seen that these factors together have explained 86 per cent of the total variation in the disbursement of ST credit in Marathwada region.

As regards Vidarbha region, it is noted that the coefficient of variables viz; GCA ($X_1$), proportionate area under commercial crops ($X_2$), average rainfall ($X_4$) and deposits ($X_5$) were observed to be positive and significant. This means that these variables have the significant role in increasing the disbursement of ST credit in the Vidarbha region. Importantly the coefficient of recovery of ST loans i.e. ($X_6$) was (–3.07) which is significant at 10 per cent level, this

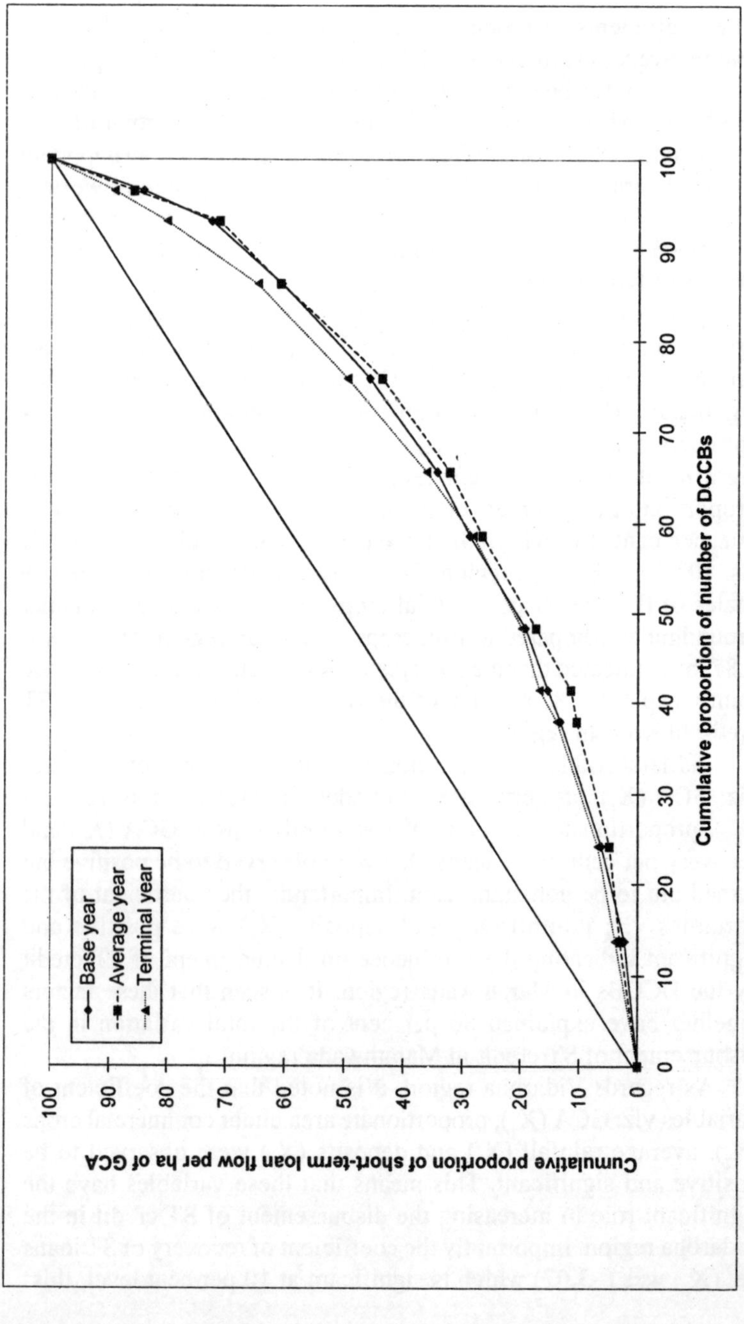


**Fig. 12.2:** Lorenz Curve for Short-term Credit Flow by DCCBs in Maharashtra

means that increase in recovery of ST credit by one per cent ceteris paribus, the disbursement of ST credit would significantly diminish by Rs. 3.07. It is noted that even though, the recovery per cent was low, the DCCBs made the disbursement of ST credit in Vidarbha region. This is a reason, why such a contrary relationship between recovery and ST credit disbursement in Vidarbha region is observed. $R^2$ suggested that 83 per cent variation in ST loan have been explained six independent variables selected in the model.

## Conclusion

In the base year (1985-86) and terminal year (2000-01), the DCCBs from Western Maharashtra region had maintained top position by highest disbursement of loans and advances. Over 80 per cent of total loans and advances issued were in the form of short-term loans indicating focused emphasis on short-term loans by the DCCBs in Maharashtra. The trend analysis of Theil's Entropy coefficient and coefficient of variation showed that there was a significant decline in inequality in short-term credit flow in the Konkan region during the entire period. In Marathwada region, the coefficient of trend equation indicated a slight increase in inequality. The results of Gini Ratio and Lorenz Curve for short-term credit flow showed that there existed inter and intra-regional inequality in the short-term credit flow by the DCCBs in Maharashtra, which needs to be minimized through appropriate corrective measures. It looks that the GCA, average rainfall and deposits with the DCCBs are the most important factors influencing the regional inequality in the disbursement of per hectare ST credit in all the regions as well as State as a whole. It is suggested that the due importance is required to be given to borrower members, which will lead to increase in loan disbursement. It is also suggested that the official machinery of DCCBs should make efforts to minimize the inequality in disbursement of loans.

## REFERENCES

Arora, V.P.S. and S.K. Tewari (1978). Inter and intra-state disparities in the flow of co-operative credit in India. *Indian Co-operative Review*, 7(3): 221-230.

Barik, B.B. and Puyalavannaan (2©001). Management of Funds in Central Co-Operative Banks. *National Seminar on Co-operative Reforms* at VAMNICOM, Pune.: 55-66.

Borude, S.S. (1993). Co-operative Movement in Maharashtra vis-à-vis Konkan Region. M.Sc. (Agri.) Thesis (Unpublished), KKV, Despoil, Maharashtra.

Deobhankar, S.G. (1984). Working of DCCBs in Gujarat—Some issues. *Indian Co-operative Review*, 22 (2): 208-210.

Haque, T. and Sunita Verma (1988). Regional and Class Disparities in the Flow of Agricultural Credit in India. *Indian Journal of Agricultural Economics*, 43 (3): 356-363.

Jairath, M.S. (1990). Regional Disparities in Co-operative Credit Services in Himachal Pradesh. *Indian Co-operative Review*, 27 (3): 240-249.

Narayanaswami and S. Ramchandran (1987). Indicators of Development—A Case Study of District Central Co-operative Banks. *Indian Co-operative Review*, 24 (4): 335-344.

Zeratsion, F, S. Suryaprakash, and B.M. Shashidhar (2001). Performance Analysis of PACS in Karnataka. *National Seminar on Co-operative Reforms*, at VAMNICOM, Pune,: 37.

13

# Role of Rural Bank in Economic Development: A Micro-Analysis

R.P. SINGH

---

*The study seeks to examine role of Ranchi Kshetriya Gramin Bank in economic development of farmers. Hundred beneficiaries farmers consisting marginal (55), small farmers (37) and medium (8) were selected randomly from four villages where agricultural loans were given by Kanke branch of Ranchi Kshetriya Gramin Bank. The data were collected for the crop year 2001-02 and tabular analysis technique was used. The analysis revealed that the R.K.G.B. is providing maximum loan to marginal farmers and weaker section of the society. The average growth rate of agricultural loan was about 26 per cent per annum. The bank provided maximum production loan to marginal farmers while investment loan to medium and small farmers. The agricultural loan changed cropping pattern in favour of cash crops i.e. vegetables and wheat and pulses crops which increased cropping intensity, employment and income of farmers. The farmers were able to meet their annual expenditure from own resources and also made further investment of their net saving in agricultural development and resource generation. This process creates additional revenue of the farmers in particular and the state in general.*

## Introduction

Gunner Myrdal has termed credit as an accelerator of development. Insuring the provision of timely and sufficient credit to a large segment of rural population as possible has been one of the major policy initiatives, which has guided the formation of public policy in the country. The rural credit in India has evolved through different phases as a result of these initiatives, there has been a substantial broadening of the infrastructure for credit delivery resulting in increased out reach and reduction in the influence of informal agencies as evidence by the increase in the share of institutional sources of the cash debts of rural households from 7.3 per cent in the early 1950 to 64 per cent in 1991 as per All-India Debt and Investment Survey.

Inspite of phenomenal increase in overall agricultural advance (from Rs. 242.30 million in 1950-51 to Rs. 33891.60 in 1980-81), which further increased to 96176.90 million in 1990-91, the total credit flow to agriculture in IXth plan (1997-2002) amounted to Rs. 229956 crores and substantial jump in XIth plan (2002-07) is envisaged which is projected at Rs. 736570 crores almost three times the IX plan achievement. *Ranchi Kshetriya Gramin Bank (R.K.G.B.)* was established on 21st June 1980 and covers all blocks of Ranchi, Gumla and Lohardaga district. The bank has been providing loan since inception to labours, rural artisans and all categories of farmers. There has been good progress in loan advancement through branches of R.K.G.B. in rural areas and by the end of 2001-02 distributed Rs. 326.10 lakhs. Keeping long service of Gramin Bank, it is expected that rural economy might have changed. The present study seeks to examine role of R.K.G.B. in economic development of farmers.

The specific objectives are:

(1). To study growth of agricultural credit in various categories of farmers.

(2). To find out the extent of loan advance, loan repayment and outstanding in different categories of agricultural loans on selected farmers.

(3). Examine impact of loan on cropping pattern and cropping intensity, expenditure, income and net saving of farmers.

## Methodology

Finally 100 borrowers consisting marginal farmers (55) small farmers (37) and medium farmers (8) were selected from four villages where agricultural loans were given by Kanke branch of Ranchi, Kshetriya Gramin Bank. The data were collected for the crop year 2001-02 through survey method. Tabular analysis technique was used to achieve objectives.

## Result and Discussion

### *1. Flow and Growth Rate of Agricultural Loan*

The agricultural loan, through Ranchi Kshetriya Gramin Bank, Kanke, distributed from 1996 to 2001 among marginal, small, scheduled tribe farmers, and others including medium farmers is presented in Table 13.1. The analysis shows that out of the total loan distributed in 1996, marginal farmers got maximum loan (51 per cent) followed by small and scheduled tribe farmers 20 per cent each and other including medium farmers 9 per cent. During 1999 the total agricultural loan was distributed Rs. 774350, which was 23.6 per cent higher over 1996. The share of marginal farmers, small farmers, scheduled tribe and others was to the tune of 73 per cent, 7 per cent, 14 per cent and 6 per cent respectively in total loan given.

**Table 13.1:** Flow and Growth Rate of Agricultural Loan through R.R.B. Kanke on Different Categories of Farms.

| *Sl. No.* | *Category* | *1996* | *1997* | *1998* | *1999* | *2000* | *2001* | *Average Growth Rate (%)* |
|---|---|---|---|---|---|---|---|---|
| 1. | Marginal | 118590 (51.00) | 103010 (35.67) | 219860 (44.53) | 567900 (73.00) | 217980 (23.81) | 278020 (53.0) | 23.80 |
| 2. | Small | 46270 (20.0) | 40530 (14.03) | 91930 (18.63) | 51930 (7.0) | 116670 (12.74) | 96870 (19.0) | 19.40 |
| 3. | S.T. | 47000 (20.0) | 120310 (41.66) | 152100 (30.80) | 106620 (14.0) | 543795 (59.39) | 96820 (19.00) | 25.22 |
| 4. | Others | 18500 (9.00) | 24900 (8.64) | 29800 (6.04) | 47900 (6.0) | 37110 (4.06) | 49650 (9.0) | 33.35 |
| 5. | Total | 230360 (100) | 288750 (100) | 493690 (100) | 774350 (100) | 915555 (100) | 521360 (100) | 26.00 |

Figures in parentheses indicate percentage and share of loan.

The positive trend of agricultural loan was not maintained throughout the period and during 2001-02 the total amount of loan was Rs. 521360, which was less than 33 per cent of the total amount given during 1999. The share of marginal farmers was again found to be maximum (53 per cent) followed by small farmers and scheduled tribe farmers (each 19 per cent). The other farmers/household got 9 per cent of total loan given during the year. The analysis further indicates that the R.K.G.B is ful filling the objectives by providing maximum loan to marginal farmers and other weaker sections of the society.

The average growth rate analysis indicates that the agricultural loan for marginal farmers increased about 24.00 per cent per annum during 1996-2001. The average growth rate of agricultural loan for small farmers was observed to be 19.40 per cent per annum during the same period. Agricultural loan for scheduled tribe farmers also increased at the rate of 25.22 per cent per annum during 1996-2001. The positive growth rate was also observed for other farmers' loan during the same period.

### *2. Average Amount of Loan on the Selected Farmers*

Kanke branch of Ranchi Kshetriya Gramin Bank provided two types of loans to the selected farmers i.e., production loan (crop loan) and investment loan. The average amount of loan per farm and per hectare is present in Table 13.2. It revealed from the Table 13.2 that per farm total amount of loan increased as size of holding increased while per hectare loan was just opposite i.e., increased as size of holding decreased. This was mainly due to variation in size of farm holding. The average amount of loan per farm and per hectare was Rs 6869.88 and Rs 4872.25 respectively.

The analysis further indicates that share of production loan and investment loan in total loan per farm varied with the size of farm holding. The share of production loan was nearly 61 per cent of total loan on the marginal farm while on small and medium farm its share was 43 and 34 per cent respectively. The amount of production loan per farm was also observed to be high on marginal farm and decreased as size of holding decreased. The investment loan per-farm further revealed that amount increased as size of holding increased. The proportion of investment loan in total loan was 39 per cent, 57 per cent and 56 per cent on marginal, small and medium farms respectively. The investment loan was more on small and medium farm mainly due to loan for tubewell and pump set. It is concluded that Gramin Bank played significant role in capital formation of small and medium farmers through investment loan.

**Table 13.2:** Average Amount of Production and Investment Loans of the Selected Farmers

*(In Rupees)*

| Sl. No. | Category | Crop Loan (Production Loan) | % | Investment Loan | % | Total Amount of Loan (Per farm) | Per ha. Loan |
|---|---|---|---|---|---|---|---|
| 1. | Marginal | 3608.91 | 60.85 | 2321.09 | 39.15 | 5930.00 (100.00) | 8984.85 |
| 2. | Small | 2935.95 | 42.82 | 3920.68 | 57.18 | 6856.63 (100.00) | 5116.85 |
| 3. | Medium | 2666.75 | 34.09 | 5156.25 | 65.91 | 7823.00 (100.00) | 3476.8 |
| 4. | Average | 3070.54 | 44.70 | 3799.34 | 55.30 | 6869.88 (100.00) | 4872.95 |

Figures in parenthesis indicate percentage.

### *3. Status of Outstanding, Overdue and Loan Payment*

The average amount of loan taken, amount of loan paid and outstanding loan of the selected farmers are present in Table 13.3. The analysis revealed that about 58 per cent of actual amount of loan taken was repaid by the sample borrower farmers. The medium farmers were very prompt at initial stage in repayment of loan. About 97 per cent of taken amount of loan was repaid by the medium farmers. The repayment performance was very low on marginal and small farmers nearly 30 per cent and 39 per cent. The recovery was better on medium farms, which may be due to higher income from agriculture and other source in comparison to marginal and small farms. The outstanding loan figure of the selected farmers was about Rs. 6515.10 per farm, which increased with size of holding decline. The amount of outstanding loan was Rs. 8711.84 and Rs. 6647.92 on marginal and small farmers. Against this the amount of outstanding loan on medium farm was Rs. 4185.63 which was 53.5 per cent of total loan taken. In case of small farmers the outstanding loan per farm was amounted to be Rs. 6647.92 which was 97 per cent of loan taken. The overdue of loan per farm further shows that nearly 96 per cent outstanding of loan was inform of overdue on the selected farms. The findings of overdues and recovery was accordance with the finding of Balishter and Singh (1994), Patel and Paramar (1994), Mansur (1995) and Veerashekharappa (1996) respectively.

**Table 13.3:** Average Amount of Loan Taken, Amount of Loan Paid, Outstanding and Overdue of the Selected Farmers.

*(In Rupees)*

| Sl. No. | Category | No. of Loanee | Average Amount of Loan Taken | Average Amount of Loan Paid | Outstanding Amount | Overdue Amount |
|---|---|---|---|---|---|---|
| 1. | Marginal | 55 | 5930.00 | 1770.00 (30.00)* | 8711.84 | 8565.25 (98.32)** |
| 2. | Small | 37 | 6856.62 | 2685.10 (39.00)* | 6647.92 | 6304.78 (94.84)** |
| 3. | Medium | 8 | 7823.00 | 7567.5 (96.73)* | 4185.63 | 4185.63 (100.00)** |
| 4. | Average | 100 | 6869.88 | 4007.53 (58.34)* | 6515.10 | 6268.16 (96.20)** |

Figures in parenthesis indicate percentage.

*Per cent to actual amount taken.

**Per cent to total outstanding loan amount.

The category-wise analysis further explained that there was no much variation in extent of loan overdue on the farm. The small farmers performed slightly better than marginal and medium farmers. The magnitude of overdue of outstanding loan was about 98.32 per cent, 94.84 per cent and about 100 per cent on marginal, small and medium farms respectively.

### *4. Cropping Pattern and Cropping Intensity*

The area occupied by different crops on the sample farms is presented in Table 13.4. The results indicated that cereals crops were dominated in cropping pattern sharing 67 per cent of total cropped area on the farm. The percentage of cereal area on marginal and small farmers was more than that of medium farmers. This shows that small and marginal farmers were producing those crops, which were required for home consumption. The next important crop in cropping pattern was vegetable crops on all categories of farms indicating nearly 19.31 per cent of total cropped area, which varied from 18.95 to 23.64 per cent on the farms. The area under vegetable crops showed increasing trend with size of farms. The average area occupied by pulse crop was 11.39 per cent of total was cropped area. On different categories of farms, further indicated that area under pulses crop increased with farm size. The average cropping intensity was about 143.25 per cent on sample farms indicating that small and marginal farmers were more efficient in increasing cropping intensity on the farm as compared to medium farmers. This analysis shows that investment in tubewells/pump sets on borrowers farms through loan from Ranchi Kshetriya Gramin Bank has certainly increased cropping intensity on the farm resulted more production and more income from crop cultivation. Similar findings were reported by Srivastava *et al.* (1981), Reddy and Kumar (1982) and Balishter and Singh (1986).

**Table 13.4:** Cropping Pattern and Cropping Intensity

*(Area in ha)*

| Sl. No. | Category | Cereals | Pulses | Vegetables | Others | Total Cropped Area | Cropping Intensity (%) |
|---|---|---|---|---|---|---|---|
| 1. | Marginal | 0.67 (70.53) | 0.06 (6.32) | 0.18 (18.95) | 0.04 (4.2) | 0.95 | 141.97 |
| 2. | Small | 1.41 (71.57) | 0.29 (14.72) | 0.25 (12.7) | 0.02 (1.02) | 1.97 | 144.75 |
| 3. | Medium | 2.00 (63.90) | 0.34 (10.86) | 0.74 (23.64) | 0.05 (1.60) | 3.13 | 139.00 |
| 4. | Average | 1.36 (67.33) | 0.23 (11.39) | 0.39 (19.31) | 0.03 (1.49) | 2.02 | 143.25 |

Figures in parenthesis indicates percentage.

### 5. *Average Annual Expenditure*

The average annual expenditure includes expenditure on food consumption, expenditure on crop production, expenditure on non-food items, and old loans to be paid during the year. Table 13.5 shows that expenditure on food items was 46.53 per cent of total expenditure. Average expenditure on crop production was about 40.47 per cent. The average expenditure on non-food items was very low and it was only 11.94 per cent of total expenditure. Old loan contributed 1.07 per cent of the total expenditure. The average expenditure per year was about Rs. 63,882.21, which increased as size of holding increased. Category-wise analysis further revealed that share of expenditure on consumption decreased as size of farm holding increased, which was maximum (55.17%) on marginal farms and minimum (40.33%) on medium farms. The expenditure on crop production increased as size of holding increased, which was expected so. The analysis further revealed that expenditure on old debt to be paid increased as size of holding increased. The total expenditure per farm per year varied from Rs. 38060.58 to Rs. 92519.20. This showed that total farm expenditure increased as size of holding increased.

**Table 13.5:** Average Annual Expenditure on Crop Production, Family Maintenance etc. of the Selected Farmers

*(In Rupees)*

| Sl. No. | Category | Expenditure on Food Consumption | Expenditure on Crop Production | Expenditure on non food Items | Old Loans during the Year | Total Expenditure Per Year |
|---|---|---|---|---|---|---|
| 1. | Marginal | 20998.45 (55.17) | 11760.59 (30.89) | 4789.09 (12.58) | 512.45 (1.35) | 38060.58 (100.00) |
| 2. | Small | 30842.4 (50.51) | 22042.38 (36.10) | 7527.04 (12.32) | 655.00 (107.00) | 61066.82 (100.00) |
| 3. | Medium | 37324.90 (40.35) | 43756.75 (47.30) | 10562.55 (11.42) | 875.00 (0.95) | 92519.20 (100.00) |
| 4. | Average | 29721.92 (46.53) | 25853.24 (40.47) | 7626.23 (11.94) | 680.81 (1.07) | 63882.21 (100.00) |

Figures in parenthesis indicates percentage.

## *6. Saving Capacity*

The loan amount may be productive enough to generate additional income to the borrower but, it may not be productive enough to repay the loan. Hence, the necessary condition here is that the loan should not only be profitable but also have potential for effective repayment. Then only the farmers have a favourable point on his side. The above condition emerges out of the fact that saving capacity not only depends upon return but also several other factors as given below.

$$Y = f(x_1, x_2, x_3, x_4)$$

Where,

$Y$ = Saving capacity (in Rs.).
$X_1$ (+) = Gross return from crop production during year + other sources of income during the year.
$X_2$ (-) = Total expenditure on crop production during the year.
$X_3$ (-) = Total expenditure on family maintenance during the year.
$X_4$ (-) = Expenditure on old loan to be paid during the year.

In other way the saving capacity is also expressed as.

Saving capacity = Gross income (includes crop production income + income from other sources)—(Total expenditure on crop production + family maintenance cost per year + old debt to be paid).

The saving capacity of marginal, small and medium farmers was estimated and is exhibited in Table 13.6. It may be observed that an average farmer had Rs. 4287.01 as net saving capacity. The net saving capacity of medium farmers was maximum Rs. 14173.35. This was mainly due to higher income from crop production as well as other source of income as compared to small and marginal farmers. The saving capacity of marginal farmers was poor because gross income could just only meet total expenditure of the farmer during year. The net saving was merely Rs. 63.36. The gross income of small farmers could also meet the total expenditure of the farmer during year. The positive saving on beneficiaries farms was probably due to increase in production which enables farmers to meet their expenditure and further invested in developmental work.

## Conclusion

It is clear from the analysis that Ranchi Kshetriya Gramin Bank has played important role in providing both types of agricultural loan i.e. production loan and Investment loan to rural farmers. The agricultural loan changed cropping pattern in favour of cash crops i.e. vegetables crops and wheat crop in *rabi* season which ultimately increased cropping intensity and income of farmers. The beneficiary farmers were able to meet their annual expenditure (Crop production + family expenditure) and also made further investment of their net saving in agricultural development and resource generation. This process creates additional revenue of the farmers particularly and the state in general.

**Table 13.6:** Average Saving Capacity of the Selected Farmers (Per annum)

*(In Rupees)*

| Sl. No. | Category | Average Gross Income from Agriculture | Average Income from Other Sources | Average Total Income | Average Expenditure on Crop Production | Average Total Expenditure on Family Maintenance | Average Old Loan Paid during Year | Average Total expenditure | Average Net Saving (Repayment Capacity) |
|---|---|---|---|---|---|---|---|---|---|
| 1. | Marginal | 22591.31 | 15532.63 | 38123.94 | 11760.59 | 25787.54 | 512.45 | 38060.58 | 63.36 |
| 2. | Small | 45007.46 | 16683.78 | 61691.24 | 22042.38 | 38369.54 | 655.00 | 61066.82 | 624.42 |
| 3. | Medium | 82942.5 | 23750 | 1,06,692.5 | 43756.75 | 47887.4 | 875.00 | 92519.15 | 14173.35 |
| 4. | Average | 50180.42 | 17988.80 | 68835.89 | 25853.24 | 37348.16 | 680.81 | 63882.21 | 4953.68 |

Figures in parenthesis indicate percentage.

## REFERENCES

Balishter, A.K. and Singh Viswajit (1994). A study of overdues of loan in Agriculture, *Indian Co-operative Review*, XXXI (4): 377-383.

Balishter and Singh, Rosan (1986). A study of institutional finance in agriculture. *Agriculture Situation in India*, XV (11): 979-986.

Mansur, M.A. (1995). A study on methods of finance and recovery of agricultural credit: A case study of some rural bank branches of Bangladesh. *Economic Affairs*, XXXX (3): 146-153.

Patel, A.R., and Paramar, T. (1994). Recovery of priority sector advances by Commercial Banks, *Agricu*ltural Banker. XVII (1): 1-5.

Pathak, B.S (1995). Agricultural loan recovery can, Non-legal measure help? *Financing Agricultural*, XXV (4): 19-23.

Reddy, C.R. and Kumar, D.V.S. (1982). The impact of RRBs credit on farm economy. *Rural India*, XXXXV (405).

Shrivastava, R.N., Singh, D.K. and Singh, R.P. (1981). "Impact of Champaran Kshetriya Gramin Bank on Rural Economy". *Economic Affairs* XXIV (4): 266-272.

Singh, R.P. (1997). Analysis of opinion regarding, non-payment of loan case study of tribal farmers. *Banking Finance* X (7): 12-13.

Singh, R.P. (1999). Rural indebtness in Tribal Villages of Kanke, Ranchi. *Banking Finance.* XII (2): 9-12.

Singh, R.P., Pandey, A.K. and Singh, S.K. (2001). Rural credit and participation of credit agencies-an analysis. *Banking Finance* XV (II): 10-18.

Veerashekharappa (1996). Rural credit in VIP district. A study in U.P. *Economic and Political Weekly* XXX (39): 123-130 Sept. 1-6.

14

# Sustainable Competitive Advantage to India in Terms of Export and Agriculture

VAIDEHI PANDURENGAN and HEMANTKUMAR P. BULSARA

*Globalization of business means that the structure of modern industry is based increasingly around competitive advantage, and that these competitive advantages are more and more based on knowledge, intellectual capital, and the management of information. Companies that compete by selling similar products (or even substitutes) to the same group of customers constitute an industry. A company that is more profitable than its rivals is exploiting some form of advantage. The benchmark for profitability is the company's cost of capital. To consistently make profits in excess of its cost of capital-economic rent—the company must posess some form of Sustainable Competitive Advantage (SCA). A key difference between CA and SCA is that the processes and positions a firm may hold are non-duplicable and inimitable when a firm possesses A SCA. Hence a sustainable competitive advantage is one that can be maintained for a significant amount of time even in the presence of competition. This brings us to the question what is a "significant amount of time". A CA becomes a SCA when all duplication and imitation efforts have ceased and the rival firms have not been able to create the same value that the said firm is creating. In this paper we have made an attempt to understand three factors relating it to India and stress on two areas where India could take competitive advantage.*

*Firstly we have tried to understand our export market, its present situation and how this could be improved to get compititive advantage for India. Secondly we have tried to study the agicultural sector and see this could bring competitive advantage for India because every country must adopt a growth strategy tailored to its country advantages, population needs and resource availability keeping this point in mind we feel that agriculture although not contributing greatly in NI it certainly has a major role to play in its future development. The era of nationalism may be over, but national images are still powerful influences on our imaginations. Thus it has to be kept in mind is that India to create Sustainable Competitive Advantage cannot happen only bringing reforms and development in the sectors mentioned above but the effort has to be matched to meet the global standards which would help build its brand image. Like brand images, country images dynamically change over time. Rather than leaving it for chance, governments, trade organizations and companies should join forces in forging promoting and maintaining country images that yield competitive advantage. All this is possible only if there is a sincere and focused effort on the part of the government with full support of the public in general. Thus it is important for government to make policies taking public in confidence. Public needs to understand that the whole effort is made to improve their quality of life, which is directly related to the development of the country.*

## Introduction

Globalizations of business means that the structure of modern industry is based increasingly around competitive advantage, and that these competitive advantages are more and more based on knowledge, intellectual capital, and the management of information. Companies that compete by selling similar products (or even substitutes) to the same group of customers constitute an industry. A company that is more profitable than its rivals is exploiting some form of advantage. The benchmark for profitability is the company's cost of capital. To consistently make profits in excess of its cost of capital—economic rent—the company must possess some form of Sustainable Competitive Advantage (SCA). A firm possesses a SCA when it has value creating processes and positions that cannot be duplicated or imitated by other firms. A SCA is different from a Competitive Advantage (CA). A CA is a position a firm attains that lead to above normal rents or a superior financial performance. The processes and positions that engender such a position (CA) are not necessarily non-duplicable or inimitable. It is possible for some companies to, temporarily, make profits above the cost of capital without sustainable competitive advantage.

A key difference between CA and SCA is that the processes and positions a firm may hold are non-duplicable and inimitable when a firm possesses a SCA. Hence a sustainable competitive advantage is one that can be maintained for a significant amount of time even in the presence of competition. This brings us to the question what is a "significant amount of time". A CA becomes SCA when all duplication and imitation efforts have ceased and the rival firms have not been able to create the same value that the said firm is creating.

There are basically three types of assets that help build an SCA.

**Organization and Managerial Process**

(a) *Coordination and integration*: Coordination among teams in organization is key to organizational success. Interdepartmental coordination and resource sharing to reach a common goal is fundamental to creating "value". Integrating resources is key to the success of firms. Firms that are able to integrate resources see synergistic effects of resources coming together.

(b) *Learning*: Organizational learning is key to the success of a firm. It determines how a firm collects, distributes, interprets and responds to market-based information collection and changes in the environment. Firms have to develop robust market sensing and spanning capabilities to effectively collect information. Once they collect info they have embed this knowledge in the products they produce.

(c) *Reconfiguring and Transformation*: The environment for firms is constantly changing and constant reconfiguring and transformation is key to forming SCA. A double loop learning and transformation is key to producing innovative products. Innovative capacity of a firm determines how it reacts and learns from market information.

**Positions**

Market positions are the assets of a company. Most of them are self explanatory. (a). Technological assets (b). Financial assets (c). Reputational assets (d). Structural assets: The structure of a company can determine how it performs. The hierarchy of a company can influence its culture, procedure and routines.

***Path Dependencies***

The birth of a company is usually accompanied with certain orientations. The progenitor brings certain orientations and attributes that stay with the company for a long time. The path the company takes then determines the development of its competencies. Technological development at a time can determine how a firm can exploit opportunities to form SCA. Very often we see the advent of several technological factors converging into a capability that forms a SCA. An example would the rise of companies such as Genentech at the turn of the previous century with the advent of gene mapping, significant developments in target selection and databases of previous studies and gene pools.

***Four Forces***

The bargaining power of customers, the bargaining power of suppliers, the threat of new entrants, and the threat of substitute products—combine with other variables to influence a fifth force, the level of competition in an industry. Each of these forces has several determinants:

**Sustainable Competitive Advantage and India**

In this paper an attempt has been made to understand three factors relating to India and stress on two areas where India could take competitive advantage.

## Building Sustainable Competetive Advantage through Building Exports

Exports have been one of the largest drivers of India's economic growth, contributing over 25 per cent of GDP growth in the last decade. Exports is now 10 per cent of India's GDP, and has grown by 11 per cent in dollar terms per annum over the last 10 years—more than twice the rate of the domestic sector.

India has always focused on exports largely to manage Balance of Payments, but not any more in today's global economy, exports need to become one of the cornerstones of India's economic planning and growth.

If we aspire a export growth of 20 per cent per annum over the next decade—nearly double the current target of 12 per cent in our 10th Plan. This will take exports to over US$ 100 billion in five years, and add 2 per cent to GDP growth every year. It will double the current employment growth rate in the organized private sector, creating 70 million new jobs over 10 years. This vision could fundamentally reshape India's economic growth with its multiplier effects.

## The Potential for Manufactured Exports

India clearly has the potential to become a global sourcing centre for services. 72 per cent of global trade worth US$ 6 trillion is of manufactured goods so it is important that we focus on manufactured exports too.

Korea, Mexico, Thailand and China are all examples, where the power of manufactured exports has been leveraged to drive economic growth and raise per capita incomes. India, with roughly similar intrinsic strengths, is a poor comparison in both absolute and relative terms—our manufactured exports are less than a third of those of Mexico, Korea or China.

## The Global Opportunity for Sourcing

A substantial part of manufactured exports comes from global companies outsourcing manufacturing activities from low-cost locations. Reasons for outsourcing is fragmenting of value chains to manage

- Economic cycles.

- Market.
- Competitive pressures.

It is estimated that a large portion of manufacturing across a broad category of industries would grow because of outsourcing in the coming years. Several countries have successfully used outsourcing to build their economies.

- Taiwan is the world's leading source for semi-conductor manufacturing.
- China today produces 30 per cent of all air conditioners, 24 per cent of all washing machines and 16 per cent of all refrigerators sold in the US. 60 per cent of the US$ FDI into China was to build capacity for outsourcing.

**Sectors where India could take Advantage:**

- In Auto Components, the global market is US$ 750 billion with most of its manufacturing in high-cost countries. The Indian auto components industry is a mere US$ 3 billion, with exports of US$ 375 million. Given Indian engineering and design skills as well as lower costs, there is a big opportunity to increase sourcing of auto components for global companies.
- In Apparel, although a fair amount of manufacturing has already moved out of the developed world, the US still produces US$ 47 billion of apparel, Italy US$ 27 billion and Germany US$ 21 billion. Indian exports in comparison are approximately US$ 5 billion. This could be another window of opportunity for us. Even if some countries limit our exports through quotas, we can emulate China and grow our share in non-quota countries.
- In the FMCG sector, the top 20 companies generate sales of over US$ 450 billion. As consumption is largely driven by the developed economies, most of the manufacturing is still located in high-cost regions. HLL is one company, which is taking advantage of this sector to take advantage of outsourcing opportunities.

**Advantages of driving exports by sourcing:**

- It attracts FDI into India.
- It also avoids the large marketing investments required to gain foreign consumer and market access with its associated risks.

Sourcing thus offers a powerful and sustainable driver for India's economic growth.

**HLL as an Example to Cost Advantage:**

1. Conversion cost of saving from sourcing toothpaste from Europe is 15 per cent.
2. In the sourcing of tea bags, for instance, HLL's conversion costs are 25 per cent of the US.

**According to HLL Report They have taken Advantage of,**

1. Superior Indian skills in engineering design and manufacturing have helped substitute imported capital goods at a fraction of the international cost.
2. In-house project management gives considerable benefit, as does higher asset utilization.
3. HLL has also leveraged domestic business to derive scale benefits and institute best practices to reduce costs and wastages.

If HLL can do it other firms can do it too. Than why is India uncompetitive in comparison to China?

**Factors which Effect Cost Competitiveness**

Producing a shirt in China today costs 20 per cent less than what it does in India. Labour costs account for half of this differential, with infrastructure costs and taxes making up the rest. World Development Indicators show that India's labour productivity in manufacturing is 70 per cent lower than China, and over 80 per cent lower than the US. This differential is seen only in manufacturing, while India's labour productivity in both the agriculture and services sectors being higher than that of China.

*Labour reform will be a very important enabler and it is critical* : that we move with resolve and speed.

- Good port infrastructure is critical to global trade. In India delays due to customs and handling lead to 30 per cent higher working capital requirement. In addition, trans-shipment and poor turn arounds impose an additional cost of 1.5 per cent on Indian exports versus other low-cost locations. In an era of dynamic markets, these create a powerful customer-servicing barrier to sourcing from India.
- Cascading taxes at all levels add to the cost differential.

**India today has certain intrinsic advantages**:

- Our commitment to democracy, an established judicial system,
- A large domestic market, and
- Third largest pool of science and technology trained people in the world.

However, customers today do not view India as a sourcing centre of choice, in terms of quality, reliability and customer service. It is critical to change this perception by creating visible examples of India's potential leadership in two or three sectors. Japan used its leadership in the electronics and auto industries to establish itself at the cutting edge of quality and innovation. Korea has done this with consumer electronics.

Can India also build up its image? Yes it can if we can learn a lesson or two from HLL's experience. HLL in its report says that there increased investment in safety and health lead to greater productivity. Similarly, environment friendly processes have resulted in lower costs. In the last five years, HLL's water consumption has come down by 65 per cent and specific energy consumption by half.

## Process Competitiveness

Despite the ongoing reform process, India ranks as one of the most restrictive and opaque economies to do business with.

In the Country Business Ranking done by the Economist Intelligence Unit, India was ranked 46 among 60 countries on several business enabling factors, while Korea, Mexico, Thailand and China ranked higher. Both industry and government score poorly on process efficiency. Even getting an approval to convert an operating unit to a 100 per cent EOU takes over three months, with several departments being involved in the process. These factors make an enormous difference to the attractiveness of an outsourcing location. Thus there is a urgent need to reduce complexity and delay in our processes.

**How to make India Competitive**

It is important to acknowledge that a number of major Governmental initiatives in the recent past are all in the right direction.

The creation of Special Economic Zones (SEZs) to facilitate global trade, the beginning of privatization of Mumbai port and the Golden Quadrilateral Project adding 1500 km. every year to our National Highway network will all add significantly to our international competitiveness.

But still a lot could be done to improve India's competitiveness.

*Instead of trying to do all at a time if we could create visible success in few sectors, which could help, build our image.*

Within our country's portfolio, Pharmaceuticals, FMCG and Processed Marine Products are three industries which could make the difference's'.

In Pharmaceuticals, we have large pool of talented chemists and good entrepreneurial ability. A sizeable export business of US $ 350 million has already been built in Active Ingredients for generic drugs and formulations. However, the global generics market is about US$ 30 to 35 billion in size, and there is tremendous headroom for up scaling exports by making pharma a 'Star' sourcing sector.

In the US$ 60 billion Processed Marine Products market too, India has the potential to become a big player. We have considerable unexploited natural marine wealth and are also well below the 'maximum sustainable yield' levels in fishing. An emerging cost advantage vis-à-vis economies like Korea and Thailand which dominated global sourcing in the past, also gives us important leverage.

Similarly, our experience in FMCG also indicates that it too can be a 'Star' sector.

NASSCOM played a crucial role in positioning India as a global IT services sourcing base. In a similar manner an APEX Sourcing Body could help build the image of Indian Inc brand.

The success of this depends a lot on government backing through funding and proper linkages to Commerce and Finance Ministries independently managed by professionals deputed from industry.

The Government is committed to removing fiscal incentives for exports over a period of time-this would save government a lot of money. Some of this could be used to support the Apex Sourcing Body as well as other initiatives to build the 'Made in India' brand.

**Create 'Virtual SEZs'**

The current Special Economic Zone (SEZ) legislation aims to create world-class infrastructure within a specified region. While this is a welcome initiative but a lot still needs to be done.

First, to enjoy the benefits of this legislation, a company needs to be physically located within the SEZ. This would require an existing exporter to spend valuable resources in relocating manufacturing facilities (and potentially suppliers) to an SEZ. An added complexity is that many industries need to be located near the source of raw materials or skilled labour pools and it does not make economic or business sense to move such industries.

Another issue is speed. Even if we start building an SEZ today, it will take two to three years to begin functioning with the full infrastructure in place. There is clearly a need for some interim action.

The solution lies in creating a network of what I call 'Virtual SEZs' (VSEZs). A VSEZ is similar in concept to the current EOUs. Any unit that exports more than 50 per cent of its production in a block of three years, wherever it is located, will be a deemed VSEZ. Consequently, these VSEZs would enjoy all the benefits available to an SEZ, including fiscal advantages, freedom from administrative procedures, labour management, and so on. The only advantage they would miss out on, of course, would be the infrastructure and shared service benefits that an SEZ offers. The administration of these VSEZs could be similar to that of EOUs—through EOU/SEZ Commissioners—to preserve the autonomous operating system.

This approach would enable companies to quickly pilot outsourcing for global companies from their existing domestic units without making major investments. Once these pilots are successful, they could establish larger capacities in SEZs.

### *Privatize 2 Major Ports to Create World-class Infrastructure*

The experience in privatizing three terminals in Chennai and Mumbai ports has been very encouraging. In Chennai, P&O data shows that within three weeks of privatization, berthing delays came down from 200 hours to virtually zero and the number of containers handled went up 4.5 times—and all this was achieved through merely adopting better port management practices and greater process discipline. This privatization has also brought in investment of Rs. 1400 crore.

Government needs to take advantage of the current momentum around divestment and fully privatize two ports. This will not only enhance efficiencies and bring down costs, but also earn in addition to the annual revenue streams. This will establish world-class processes and systems in atleast two ports in India and serve as a model to rapidly privatize other ports as well.

### *Drive Industry Productivity and Process Excellence through TPM*

Indian industry must develop an obsessive commitment to productivity. Traditional methods of activity analysis and process up-gradation will certainly bring some gains. But a step change in productivity will come from introducing and entrenching process excellence in every shop floor.

### *Moving to an Enabling Fiscal and Regulatory Regime*

Our approach to the regulatory regime for exports in the past has been one of control, stemming from the need to conserve foreign exchange, rather than to actively enable exports as a growth driver. There are two areas where the regime puts us at a distinct disadvantage, which we need to urgently address:

- *Comprehensive VAT for Exports*: Outside of EOU/SEZs, there are no schemes for zero-rating of all indirect taxes for exports. Consequently, they add to the cost burden of the Indian exporter and make him uncompetitive. The proposed introduction of State VAT will be a good step, but we will need to move rapidly to a Comprehensive VAT covering all indirect taxes on both goods and services, to be globally competitive. 140 out of 147 countries in the WTO already have Comprehensive VAT.

- Government needs to introduce Comprehensive VAT for the exports sector immediately. This would also provide usefull llearning's for implementation subsequently in the domestic sector.
- *Simplify Transfer Pricing Rules*: The current transfer pricing rules are restrictive rather than enabling for exports. We must recognize that price fixation in international markets is subject to many variables, all of which may not be common across firms, industries or, indeed, across time. In view of this, we must make our transfer pricing rules less straitjacketed and formulaic. A simple solution is to increase the margin for variance from 5 to 15 per cent, and simplify the administrative and documentation procedures.

## Building India's Competitive Advantage through Promotion of Agriculture

Every country must adopt a growth strategy tailored to its country advantages, population needs and resource availability. We would benefit by looking at how another large, diverse and developing economy has leveraged agriculture for overall growth. A lot has been written about the success of China in attracting FDI and making infrastructural investments. However, not much mention is made of its major strides in agriculture, making this a true growth driver for the rest of the economy.

Agriculture is a major force in China's economy just like in India. 70 per cent of China's population lives in rural areas and is economically active in agriculture. In the 90's, China's agriculture grew at 5.1 per cent p.a., increasing incomes across a very broad population base. The number of rural poor declined to 50 million, bringing a large number of new consumers into the economy and driving demand for industrial goods and services. Agriculture thus also played a major role in driving industrial growth and overall GDP.

Today, China's agricultural sector accounts for only 17 per cent of GDP (as compared to 24 per cent for India). Despite that, it has been accorded the top priority in the National Economic Development agenda in their new millennium blueprint up to 2010. While many of the specific measures that China took to achieve high agricultural growth are not relevant in the Indian context, one aspect of their strategy is very compelling. They have used the twin planks of productivity improvement in agriculture and the creation of a thriving food-processing sector to build a vibrant rural economy. This has helped contain urban migration, in addition to accelerating agricultural growth and therefore driving overall GDP growth.

***The task for us in India lies in achieving a similar end result through appropriate strategies designed to suit our condition.***

### *Importance of Agriculture in building Competitive Advantage for India*

The recent growth in Information Technology is the result of Indian technological excellence and cost-competitiveness, well supported by the necessary policy and legal framework. However, impressive as it is, the IT boom has directly impacted less than 500,000 people—a very small proportion of our total population.

A high rate of economic growth is sustainable in the long-term only if it is broad-based and benefits a majority of our people, thereby creating a virtuous demand-led growth cycle. While agriculture contributes less than a quarter of India's GDP, over 70 per cent of India's billion-strong population is dependent on it. This is why it is an important potential demand-base for industry and services, in addition to being the supply base for food and raw material. Already, almost half the demand for PMCG goods, and black and white television sets, pressure cookers, table fans, sewing machines, watches and other consumer durables comes from rural consumers. Agricultural growth has a strong multiplier effect across the economy.

The recently announced National Agriculture Policy is timely. It is now essential for both Government and industry to take some bold initiatives to ensure its implementation and bring about another structural change—a Food Revolution.

### Pit falls in Indian Agriculture

1. We have godowns overflowing with grain but on the other, large sections of our population still have one of the lowest

per capita calorie consumption. This is because these consumers cannot afford to buy food at the current prices.

2. Further on it will be difficult to increase agricultural incomes by increasing the minimum support price or subsidies. Because even at the current prices, food is not affordable to a large section of people. In fact, high food stocks have led to farmers often realizing significantly lower prices.

If prices cannot be increased any further, the only option to protect and increase farm incomes is to impact the Volume or Consumption. The focus should be on increasing consumption to increase agricultural income.

The 1997 NSS statistics shows that 42 per cent of our rural population and 49 per cent of urban population are shown to receive less than the accepted daily calorie intake norm—and these proportions have virtually remained the same in the last decade. Thus the economic modeling shows that consumption of wheat amongst the lower income groups will increase by over 25 per cent, if the price was to be reduced by Rs. 2/kg reflecting the level of unfulfilled demand. This increase of 25 per cent is equivalent to an incremental demand of 41 mln. Tons of cereals.

The key question therefore is—how do we increase food consumption?

A short-term imperative is to liquidate the excess stock of food-grain that we are currently carrying through appropriate schemes like "Food for Work" and increasing the amount of food released through the PDS for the "Below Poverty Line (BPL)" segment.

In long-term it is important to bring about structural changes to increase productivity and manage cost.

*What are the limitations of Indian farmers? Some other contributory factors are:*

*Low incomes and limited capacity to invest in inputs*:

- *Absence of Support*: In today's unpredictable agricultural situation, the farmer, already burdened by expensive credit, has no crop insurance to fall back on. Nor does he have other support facilities like demand projections for crop planning, soil testing and weather forecasting to guide planting, inputs and harvesting.

- *Inefficient Supply Chain:* The supply chain from the farmer's field to the consumer is also quite inefficient. Instead, if the food processor was allowed to buy wheat directly from the farmer, he could save at least Rs. 500/ton of wheat through reducing commissions and transit/storage losses.

*Solutions to the above problems*:

- *Precision Farming* whereby a farmer adjusts farm practices to match the variation of soil and terrain across time and the area of his plot, rather than following the current practice of a "one size fits all" approach, which manages crops at the lowest common denominator.
- Small farmer needs access to best practice in Precision Farming, affordable credit, crop insurance, farm inputs, and modern farm equipment in order to increase productivity. He also would benefit from direct access to the market.
- Partnership web between the farmer and agri-input companies, banks, insurance companies, grain handling and storage companies, and food processors. This will help get over the problem of expensive village credit, inefficient supply chain structure resulting to increased costs.

Such a model will certainly drive down the cost helping farmers to increase the revenue by increasing the consumption of foodgrains as planned earlier. This will be a win-win for farmer and consumer.

## Steps Required to be take to build up Agricultural Sector

### *Redirection of Government Effort*

We have made great strides through the Green Revolution so now the government policies should be in promoting efficiencies and value addition rather than managing shortages. Government should move from being regulatory to supportive.

Case of emerging sectors like processed fruits and vegetables, seed production, organic farming, floriculture—all sectors which play to our country advantages—the Government should take on a proactive role in encouraging investment in R&D, manufacturing, market and infrastructure development.

### *Amendments in the Legal Framework*

The Market Committee legislation of various States currently limit produce from an area to be sold through the mandi in that area only. These will need to be dropped to facilitate free movement across the country as well as direct purchase by a food processor from the farmer.

Forward contracts should be permitted, enabling the food processor to contract for a crop even before it is sown.

Could bring our food laws in line with the international Codex prescribed for food trade and widely followed in the world. This would greatly enhance innovation, while continuing to protect adequately the Indian consumer.

## Methods Required to Encourage Food Processing Units

At present what is happening is Agriculture processed food is taxed at various stages at primary level at raw material level which has a cascading effect on the prices. Further, packaged goods attract higher rates of Sales Tax while the same food products sold loose or unpackaged are either exempt or subject to very low rate of taxes. This encourages sale of loose commodities, which are often sub-standard and/or adulterated.

One solution to the above problem is to bring some fiscal reforms to encourage packaged processed food firstly it could do away with cascading taxes and preferably have a single excise duty to encourage free and easy movement of goods within the country, as has been done with tobacco and textiles.

This would truly revolutionize agriculture in India, by improving its productivity and creating a vibrant food processing industry, leading to sustainable benefits for both the farmer and the consumer.

*As a conclusion all that we can say is we need to create a model which would increase the overall functioning of the economy by increasing the overall quality of life by increasing the income of people depended on agriculture. This would in turn drive demand for the rest of the industry and services sector, leading to a sustainable growth cycle. Equally, increased consumption of food will improve the quality of life and productivity of our population. The creation of a vibrant food processing industry would add further value, generating employment and prosperity.*

**Conclusion**

The era of nationalism may be over, but national images are still powerful influences on our imaginations.

Every nation has an image, favourable or unfavourable, positive or negative. Some nations are viewed as benevolent and progressive, others as contemptible and repressive. Some are noted for engineering prowess, others for design skills. Whatever these views, they color both investors' and consumers' perceptions of a country's 'brand'.

As consumers are the targets of all marketing efforts, their perception of a nation can be an important determinant of there purchasing decision. These perceptions partly determine the brand's marketability, whether in the form of exports or as a place to establish a subsidiary. While a nation's 'brand' or image is certainly of concern to its leaders, it is equally important to private and public organizations that are trying to stimulate both incoming investment and tourism and encourage cooperative alliances between business companies.

Today, countries such as Scotland, Great Britain, New Zealand, Germany and Taiwan have developed national image campaigns with the advice of image consultants.

Japan's national image as a first class manufacturer of consumer durable goods has given it a competitive advantage world-wide. Additional examples include Italy's image as a leader in design and style; Germany's advantage lies in workmanship, Switzerland is known for precision, while Israel is known for its high-tech engineering. On the other hand, countries possessing real manufacturing prowess but with poor country images lack competitive advantage. Cases include some of the former Communist bloc countries such as the Czech Republic, Poland and Hungary.

Thus it has to be kept in mind is that India to create Sustainable Competitive Advantage cannot happen only bringing reforms and development in the sectors mentioned above but the effort has to be matched to meet the global standards which would help build its brand image. Like brand images, country images dynamically change over time. Rather than leaving it for chance, governments, trade organizations and companies should join forces in forging promoting and maintaining country images that yield competitive advantage.

All this is possible only if there is a sincere and focused effort on the part of the government with full support of the public in general. Thus it is important for government to make policies taking public in confidence. Public needs to understand that the whole effort is made to improve their quality of life, which is directly related to the development of the country.

## REFERENCES

Aaditya, Mattoo, Robert M. Stern. *India and WTO*, Rawat Publications, Jaipur and New Delhi.

Cherunilam, Francis (2005). *Industrial Trade Export Management*, Himalaya Publishing House.

http.faculty.insead.edu

www.direttextbook.com

www.ebay.com

15

# Recent Developments in the Farmer–Market Linkages of Agri-Business in Gujarat

ANITA ARYA

*Gujarat agricultural landscape is going through an unprecedented change. Value-added crops such as lemongrass, super cash crops like herbal plantations, cashew nuts and organic vegetables and fruits are replacing conventional crops like wheat, bajara, cotton and groundnut. Farmers of 16 districts in Gujarat including Porbandar, Bhavnagar, Paramours, Dangs, Kutch, Surendranagar and Gandhinagar are changing hats to transform into new age farmers. In Saurashtra, the heartland of groundnut farming, farmers is switching over to grow cashew nut. The unique feature of cashew nut farming is that the plants total life is nearly 40 years. Once it is planted, farmers can reap fruits for four decades without bothering too much about fertilizers, insecticides, pesticides or even water (as it requires less water). In some areas, cotton farmers too have started growing cashew nut. Similarly, herbal plantation like safed musali, kuarpata (alovera), lemongrass (used in the preparation of cosmetics), pamaroja, pancholi, Japanese mint have become popular among farmers in the districts of Anand, Porbandar, Bhavnagar, Kheda, Navsari, Amreli, Rajkot, Narmada, Ahmedabad and Gandhinagar. There is a growing demand for dry fruits such as raisins and figs. Hence farmers in Rajpipla and Kutch are shifting from conventional crops. There is a new initiative in Bharuch and Narmada districts to grow plants such as Yam, Japanese mint, turmeric, yellow water melon, papaya and rajma. The farmers in this tribal belt are finding more remuneration from these cultivations. The Gujarat Government is now busy finding ways and means of marketing of these new products being produced in Gujarat for the first time. In Gujarat a total of 85 lakhs hectares of land remains under various crops during kharif season while in rabi season, it is nearly 25 lakhs hectares. To begin with safed musali has occupied 100 hectares, cashew nut 40 hectares, grapes 9 hectares papaya 60 hectares, ginger 15 hectares, rajma 25 hectares, Japanese mint 2 hectares, tissue culture banana 5 hectares. Of the total 37 lakhs farmers (account holders) so far 12 lakhs have been issued soil health cards. To total agricultural land spread through 18000 villages in Gujarat will be covered under soil testing programme by the end of 2007. Krushi Mahotsav is just of its kind in the country where the primary processors are made the hub of the economic wheel and made aware of the benefits of liberalization and globalization. The development of Dholera Port will aid the development of agro-industries around Ahmedabad city and north of Gujarat. The current Mahotsav focused on value addition and market linkages. More than 8000 farmers would be sensitized to value addition techniques and setting up of small agro-processing units in Jyotigarm villages would be looked into. Apart from this, the Phase II will have entrepreneurial development programme for farmers turned entrepreneurs also. The draft policy has looked into backward and forward linkages of the farm produces, supporting industries and special instrument vehicles for development of infrastructure relating to this industry. Ahmedabad is planning to be developed as a hub where all modern infrastructure and ancillary support relating to agro-industry is set up. The state government is following up with the centre for setting up a perishable food cargo complex. The industrial sector of Gujarat had grown at a rapid rate and agro-industries have 8.5 per cent share of total production of the state. Only true and effective participation in genuine producers' institutions will give our farmers their rightful and deserved place in our agricultural economy.*

There is a need to encourage food processing and agricultural marketing with a view to reduce post harvest loss. We need scaling up of our food processing sector to add shelf life to agricultural produce. More and better warehouses for storing our buffer stocks and better transportation facilities (less broken trucks that leak the grain as transported) can go a long way in reducing the post harvest losses. According to the latest World Bank Report—*Gujarat Agricultural Development for Growth and Poverty Reductions,* the share of agriculture in total output has fallen over time to 13.6 per cent of GSDP. The report says that the government has been actively supporting water saving irrigation technology (trickle, drip and other micro-emitters) but this is not enough. Raising rural incomes and conserving water through diversification into higher value products will require market reforms, it emphasizes state sponsored agricultural marketing yards monopolize on the sale of all farm produce, acting as a deterrent on contract farming which alone can raise farm income.

The good monsoon last year has changed the face of the state as total agriculture yield has crossed 25000 crores mark this year as against Rs. 19,000 crores last year. The good crops have attracted many entrepreneurs to set up their agro-based industries in rural areas. About 200 rice mills in Bavla and rural areas of Ahmedabad district which were facing closure some time back have reopened. The farm land is now more fruitful as they can get any crop of their choice because of Narmada water. Besides helping *Kharif* crops, the monsoon will equally benefit the *Rabi* crops including wheat, chana and cumin and variyali (fennel seed) in the state. Over 2.50 lakh wells have been recharged by more than 75000 check dams in the state were overflowing which provide an ample opportunity for agriculture in non-irrigated zones.

Gujarat agricultural landscape is going through an unprecedented change. Value added crop such as lemongrass, super cash crops like herbal plantations, cashew nuts and organic vegetables and fruits are replacing conventional crops like wheat, bajara, cotton and groundnut. Farmers of 16 districts in Gujarat including Porbandar, Bhavnagar, Palanpur, Dangs, Kutch, Surendranagar and Gandhinagar are changing hats to transform into new age farmers. In Saurashtra, the heartland of groundnut farming, farmers is switching over to grow cashew nut. The unique feature of cashew nut farming is that the plants total life is nearly 40 years. Once it is planted, farmers can reap fruits for four decades without bothering too much about fertilizers, insecticides, pesticides or even water (as it requires less water). In some areas, cotton farmers too have started growing cashew nut. Similarly, herbal plantation like safed musali, kuarpata (alovera), lemongrass (used in the preparation of cosmetics), pamaroja, pancholi, Japanese mint have become popular among farmers in the districts of Anand, Porbandar, Bhavnagar, Kheda, Navsari, Amreli, Rajkot, Narmada, Ahmedabad and Gandhinagar. There is a growing demand for dry fruits such as raisins and figs. Hence farmers in Rajpipla and Kutch are shifting from conventional crops. There is a new initiative in Bharuch and Narmada districts to grow plants such as Yam, Japanese mint, turmeric, yellow water melon, papaya and rajmah. The farmers in this tribal belt are finding more remuneration from these cultivations. The Gujarat Government is now busy finding ways and means of marketing of these new products being produced in Gujarat for the first time. In Gujarat a total of 85 lakh hectares of land remains under various crops during *Kharif* season while in *Rabi* season, it is nearly 25 lakh hectares. To begin with safed musali has occupied 100 hectares, cashew nut 40 hectares, grapes 9 hectares, papaya 60 hectares, ginger 15 hectares, rajmah 25 hectares, Japanese mint 2 hectares, tissue culture banana 5 hectares. Of the total 37 lakh farmers (account holders) so far 12 lakhs have been issued soil health cards. All the 18000 villages in Gujarat will be covered under soil testing programme by the end of 2009.

Garlic the most important bulk crop after onions can be developed into an export oriented cottage industry. It offers tremendous scope for processing into dehydrated flakes, powder, granules, paste, oils, juice, garlic salts. Some of the major garlic powder growing States like Madhya Pradesh, Gujarat and Maharashtra process garlic powder by drying flaked garlic. Odourless garlic oil and oleoresin are also produced for exports. There should be a common forum for contract farming of garlic for fresh export and value addition.

The centre has allocated 27.39 crores to Gujarat for development of horticultural activities under its National Horticulture Mission (NHM) during 2005-06. The government has come out with a total financial outlay of Rs. 252 crores under the National Horticulture Mission for the development of horticultural activities in the country during the next three years. According to official sources, the centre has allotted 68.44 crores during 2005-06, Rs. 88 crores for 2006-07 and Rs. 96 crores in 2007-08. Rabo India was appointed by the Ministry of Agriculture to review action plan submitted by Gujarat.

The Ministry of Agriculture had circulated operational guidelines to the states mentioning mission objectives, structure, procedures for approval and implementation, ongoing schemes, mission intervention and management and overall targets under NHM. Rabo discussed the initial plan with State Horticulture Department. It was followed by collection of data for mapping market linkages (food parks, AEZs, processing facilities, pack houses, cold storages and mandies). Further, it held discussions with other stakeholders including processors with facilities in the state and traders in mandies. Rabo also used its existing databases and international network. In fact horticulture sector has contributed significantly, to the GDP in agriculture (28.5 per cent from 8.5 per cent area). The objective of NHM is to double the horticulture production i.e. to achieve a production of 300 million tones by 2011-12. The districts and area expansion suggested by Rabo for each crop include Valsad, Navsari, Surat, Junagadh, Baroda, Anand have been recommended for papaya. Similarly for cumin the districts include Bhavnagar, Baroda, Junagadh, Amreli, Mehsana and Sabarkantha.

*Krushi Mahotsav* is just of its kind in the country where the primary processors are made the hub of the economic wheel and made aware of the benefits of liberalization and globalization. The development of Dholera Port will aid the development of agro-industries around Ahmedabad city and north of Gujarat. The current *Mahotsav* focused on value addition and market linkages. More than 8000 farmers would be sensitized to value addition techniques and setting up of small agro-processing units in Jyotigarm villages would be looked into. Apart from this, the Phase II will have entrepreneurial development programme for farmers turned entrepreneurs also. The draft policy has looked into backward and forward linkages of the farm produces, supporting industries and special instrument vehicles for development of infrastructure relating to this industry. Ahmedabad is planning to be developed as a hub where all modern infrastructure and ancillary support relating to agro-industry is set up. The state government is following up with the centre for setting up a perishable food cargo complex. The industrial sector of Gujarat had grown at a rapid rate and agro-industries have 8.5 per cent share of total production of the state.

Gujarat Agro Industries Corporation (GAIC) is set to develop the world class infrastructure near Ahmedabad airport. They have received Rs. 3 crores for developing central infrastructures. It is hoping to rise to around Rs. 17 to 18 crores. The investment is likely to be raised the way of 3P's. The Airport Authority has allotted land of 5000 sq. meters to GAIC as per the policy guidelines of central government laid down for Agro Export Zone. Larger firms like Mittal group and Reliance which are foraying into food processing business may set up their AEZ units. There are already 3 AEZs operational in the state. Gujarat is currently developing AEZs for commodities like mangoes, onion, sesame, and castor to be exported in larger volumes. The major thrust would be to make cargo accessible for convenient transportation, through facilities such as handling centers for perishables.

Recent growth in horticulture, patterns in Gujarat has attracted many private firms and cooperative sectors to this potentially lucrative sector. The state government has taken up the initiative to focus more on processing units and cold storage houses. In order to spread awareness about this, the government is planning to cover every single farmer in remote areas by way of seminar presentation to 160 villages. The objective of this would be to promote awareness about the marketing methods with which farmers would enhance their income. The basic idea is to increase the number of processing units and cold storage houses for the commodities. Few domestic firms and cooperative sectors have shown interests in setting up such processing units and cold storage houses for their new units. The firms have approached the state experts for soil preservation, scientific techniques and the available benefits before entering into such units.

Moreover, the official maintained that few cooperatives from Gujarat are talking with the agriculture department, to enhance their production by combining with value added products. Processing units and cold storage houses help in keeping the perishable units alive. The central government has set up horticulture mission board in Ahmedabad to promote the present capacity of the processing units. The board has already identified 10 districts where it will increase the number of processing units and would increase the number of districts in future. The state has geographic capacity of 196 lakh hectares of land of which 96 lakh hectares is purely cash profit land and rest of the areas has been engaged in cultivating other related commodities. In the last few years the production in horticulture has immensely increased due to techniques like cold storage and processing units.

Gujarat could do to Chiku what New Zealand did to Kiwi. Despite hundreds tonnes of production of Chiku (Sapota) and banana in

Gujarat, farmers in state are unable to get remunerative returns on these fruits due to lack of pre and post-harvest technology. According to market sources, both chiku and banana are seasonal products. Gujarat produces about 500 to 700 tonnes of chiku per day during peak season which lasts about six months of a total season of nine months in a year. However, chiku remains in demand from the northern region states and also gets same response from other states. But the export is very negligible and that too confined to Middle East and Gulf said Ajit Desai of Navsari based Desai Cold Storage. The marketing of these fruits could not be expanded on account of non-availability of technology for bye-products and value-added product like conversion into powder form or making wafers. Though an entrepreneur made efforts to convert chiku into powder form, he could not get order for the product. Even pickles made of chiku would not get any response from the market. Therefore, research and development laboratories associated with agriculture universities and institutes should devise ways and means for the bye-products and also value-added products from these two important fruits resulting in getting farmers more remunerative prices for their products. Mr. S.C. Srivastava MD of Gujarat Agro Industries Corporation (GAIC) feels that in order to encourage farmers and exporters of fruits, the Gujarat Government had introduced a special subsidy of 25 per cent on air freight. Meanwhile, the Gujarat Government as part of its Gujarat Agro-Vision 2010 programme has identified groundnut, banana, castor, cotton, sesame, mango, rapeseed, mustard, onion, cumin, potato, fennel, chiku, isabgul, guava, garlic, tobacco and papaya on the basis of their production and productivity so that adequate attention could be focused on them. Accordingly government has announced to set up four Agricultural Export Zone (AEZ). While the AEZ in Central and South Gujarat regions will take care of mangoes and vegetables, the North Gujarat AEZ will be meant for castor, the Saurashtra AEZ for onion and Saurashtra and Kutch SEZ for groundnut and sesame seeds. While necessary government resolutions have been passed for mangoes and vegetables, castor and onion, GR for groundnut and sesame seeds is yet to be issued. The AEZ is aimed at taking a comprehensive look at a particular produce located in a contiguous area for the purpose of developing and sourcing the raw materials, their processing and packaging, leading to final exports. Thus the entire effort is centered on the cluster approach of identifying the potential products, the geographical region in which these products are grown and adopting an end to end approach of integrating the entire process right from the stage of production till it reaches the market.

Big corporate such as, Welspun and Godrej Agrovat, are exploring possibilities of contract farming in Gujarat. Welspun which is setting up textile SEZ in Kutch wants to grow cotton in the region. Welspun is the latest company interested in contract farming. The company has approached the Government of Gujarat for 2000 hectares of land for growing cotton. The company expects the state government to provide us with land that is spread over two to three locations in the state. The current quality of crop is not up to the mark and the supplies are not consistent and hence they have decided to go into contract farming. The company requires less contaminated cotton which is regularly available. The company is talking with a few Israel based companies for technical support in drip irrigation. Kutch is dry and arid zone. The company intends to grow cotton on a vast expanse of over 300 acres of land. Drip irrigation systems would be very effective. The 2000 crores diversified Welspun Group plans to set up SEZ—the first of its kind in this sector in Gujarat—which will be spread over 700 acres. The government rules suggest that whoever wishes to buy present or future agricultural produce directly from the farmers, may enter into an agreement—a tripartite agreement between farmer, contract sponsor and the APMC which will play the role of a facilitator. The contract may be seasonal, annual or long term (3-5 years). The scheme of contract farming is here from 31st March 2005.

Godrej has already approached the government to start necessary procedure for growing palm for oil. Godrej Agrovat Ltd., a group company of FMCG giant is planning to grow oil palms in Gujarat in a big way. The company at present is looking at Southern Gujarat for oil palm plantation. In addition, the company will also set up a processing mill. The company is planning to bring close to 10000 hectares of land under oil palm cultivation and currently a team of experts from the company is in the process of identifying land in South Gujarat. The company has already got approval from the state government for growing oil palm in Gujarat under contract farming system. The company has identified 3 districts in South Gujarat, namely, Valsad, Navsari and Surat where there is a vast land having potential for the plantations. Disclosing the company is already engaged in cultivation of oil plants in Andhra Pradesh and Karnataka.

Godrej Agrovat now is all set to foray in Mizoram where it will bring 5000 hectares of land under cultivation. Further, to make processing of oil palms easier, the company is also in the process of setting up oil palm processing mill in the state for which the company plans to invest close to 10 crore. Keeping the longes-term view in mind, the company will invest 80 to 100 crores over ten years. The company imports 4 to 5 million ton palm oil every year from Malaysia while the domestic demand for edible oil is 12 to 13 million tons. The company sources oil palm saplings from Malaysia and develop them in the nursery. After that it is supplied to the farmers for cultivation.

In this context, Dhari Krushak Vikas Producers Company Limited (Amreli District in Gujarat) is the first of its kind to get registered in Gujarat. Initially farmers of 10 villages in and around Dhari that had implemented watershed programme with Development Support Centre supporting as Project Implementing Agency (PIA) collected a share of rupees one lakh. Each of the ten watershed association's contributed Rs. 100,000 (Rs. One lacs) as share capital and started the process of registration of Farmer Producer Company Limited on 23rd June 2005 from the Registrar of Companies, Gujarat.

In a net shell only true and effective participation in genuine producers' institutions will give our farmers their rightful and deserved place in our agricultural economy. There is a need to encourage food processing and agricultural marketing with a view to reduce post harvest losses. We need scaling up of our food processing sector to add shelf life to agricultural produce. More and better warehouses for storing our buffer stocks and better transportation facilities (less broken trucks that leak the grain as transported) is the need of hour.

# Index